the rise of the image the fall of the word

Mitchell Stephens

Oxford University Press
New York Oxford
1998

Oxford University Press

Oxford   New York
Athens   Auckland   Bangkok   Bogotá Buenos Aires   Calcutta
Cape Town   Chennai   Dar es Salaam   Delhi Florence   Hong Kong   Istanbul
Karachi Kuala Lumpur   Madrid   Melbourne Mexico City   Mumbai   Nairobi
Paris   São Paulo   Singapore Taipei   Tokyo   Toronto   Warsaw

and associated companies in
Berlin   Ibadan

Published by Oxford University Press, Inc.
198 Madison Avenue, New York, New York 10016

Oxford is a registered trademark of Oxford University Press

Library of Congress Cataloging-in-Publication Data
Stephens, Mitchell.
The rise of the image, the fall of the word/by Mitchell Stephens
p.   cm.
Includes bibliographical references and index.
ISBN 0-19-509829-3
1. Television broadcasting—Social aspects.
2. Television—Philosophy.   3. Motion pictures—Philosophy.
4. Visual communication.   I. Title
PN1992.6.S73   1998
302.23'45—dc21   98-13281

9   8   7   6   5   4
Printed in the United States of America
on acid-free paper

For Lauren, Seth and Noah

In the thought of tomorrow there is a power to upheave all thy creed, all the creeds, all the literatures of the nations.

—*Ralph Waldo Emerson*

contents

preface: "A Transitional Period"

Many things
indicate that
we are going
through a
transitional
period when
it seems that
something is
on the way
out and
something
else is
painfully
being born.
—Václav
Havel, 1994

In much of the developed world the last third of the twentieth century has been characterized by relative peace and prosperity, yet it has been filled with a kind of despair. There is a sense of exhaustion in philosophy, politics and the arts. We worry that vanity, materialism and cynicism reign unchecked; that our civic life has eroded; that we have lost touch with basic values, with what is real. This book will argue that these phenomena can be explained in part by the transition from a culture dominated by the printed word to one dominated by moving images.

However it is also the thesis of this book, a more controversial thesis, that the moving image has the potential to help resolve this crisis of the spirit. No, we will not be transported back to neighborhoods filled with good conversation, bustling libraries and old-fashioned sincerity. That world (if it ever really existed) is disappearing; it will not return. But this new form of communication should provide us with the tools—intellectual and artistic tools—needed to construct new, more resilient ways of looking at our lives.

This will take time. Television has been stuck at an early stage of development, condemned mostly to imitating older forms of communication. Film has not advanced much further. We are just beginning to develop the original techniques that will exploit the full potential of moving images, of video. But that potential is large.

Moving images use our senses more effectively than do black lines of type stacked on white pages. In a video there is so much more to see, not to mention hear. Moving images can cut in, cut away, dance around, superimpose, switch tone or otherwise change perspective, without losing their audience's attention; they can encompass computerized graphics, even words. Seeing, consequently, can become a more complex activity; we might see from more perspectives. For when video is cut fast, it allows the interchanging and juxtaposition not just of actions within a scene, not just of angles upon a scene, but of entire scenes themselves—dozens of them. Printed words risk their believability and entertainment value when they attempt such maneuvers.

Video, I will argue, is the medium of which the twentieth century's avant-garde has dreamed: It can follow the meanderings of a skittish consciousness and grow surreal, even abstract, yet all the while still engage. It moves easily, ineluctably to an ironic distance and might therefore lead us to whatever truths lie beyond ironic distance. It has the potential to present us with new mental vistas, to take us new philosophic places, as writing once did, as printing once did.

This book, I should make clear, is the work of an inveterate reader and writer—someone who is unable to enter a bookstore or library without a sense of excitement but who contemplates racks of videos with nary a smile. The book uses the established, wonderfully proficient medium of printed words to proclaim the potential of video, an immature and still awkward medium. The book attempts, in other words, to look without prejudice beyond its author's inclinations, beyond its own form.

In the sixteenth century the French writer Rabelais exclaimed, "Printing...is now in use, so elegant and so correct, that better cannot be imagined."[1] Almost half a millennium has passed. My contention, simply stated, is that we are finally ready to imagine better, that once again we have come upon a form of communication powerful enough to help us fashion new understandings, stronger understandings.

This argument on behalf of video may discomfit my fellow print lovers. I have tried, however, to write with an appreciation for the grand accomplishments of the written and printed word and, therefore, for what it means to state that the moving image will surpass those accomplishments.

$$\frac{\text{image}}{\text{word}}$$

ABOVE: Television took only eight years to penetrate half of America's homes.

BELOW: President John F. Kennedy being interviewed by CBS News in 1963. His televised smile helped images begin to gain the upper hand over words.

INTRO

chapter one

ABOVE LEFT AND BELOW: Three images from the introduction to the 1995 ABC News documentary *Peter Jennings Reporting: In the Name of God:* a remarkable amount of information and impressions in a short period of time.

ABOVE RIGHT: A time when reading was not missing from pictures—here of a New York subway.

DUCTION

"the next room"

Y ou are about to begin reading," wrote the novelist Italo Calvino.

Best to close the door; the TV is always on in the next room. Tell the others right away, "No, I don't want to watch TV!" Raise your voice—they won't hear you otherwise—"I'm reading! I don't want to be disturbed!" Maybe they haven't heard you, with all that racket; speak louder, yell: "I'm beginning to read...!"[1]

In this case, however, you are beginning to read a book that looks forward to the eclipse of reading by the offspring of TV.

It is only the opening to a longer program—the first ninety-six seconds of a one-hour 1995 ABC documentary about changes in American churches.* In those ninety-six seconds fewer than two hundred words are spoken—some by the reporter, Peter Jennings, some by ministers and church members. A book or newspaper reader could probably digest twice as many words in that period of time.

Yet those ninety-six seconds, the work of a young producer named Roberta Goldberg, also feature fifty-one different images, most showing separate scenes: churchgoers praying, laughing, weeping and collapsing; a Christian stage show; a congregation joining in aerobics; ministers preaching; ministers using show-business techniques; ministers defending their use of show-business techniques. Intercut are pictures of religious icons, bending and blurring. Three candles are shown blowing out. Additional images are sometimes superimposed. Words from the Bible flash on the screen. Ethereal yet insistent music plays. Cameras dart here and there.

This piece uses techniques that have begun appearing with greater and greater frequency in some of the less prestigious corners of television and film—in promotional announcements, commercials, music videos, title sequences, sports highlights and trailers, and occasionally in news stories or on public TV. The piece has an almost balletlike beauty, but it is not particularly profound. It is, after all, only the introduction to an otherwise traditional documentary; it lasts less than two minutes. (I will describe other, more ambitious examples later in the book.)

However, this segment of videotape, like its young cousins elsewhere on our screens, does manage to impart a remarkable amount of information and impressions in that short period of time—to the point where the more conventionally edited one-hour documentary that follows begins to seem superfluous. This brief introduction, therefore, suggests that images—fast-cut moving images mixed with some words and music—have the potential to communicate at least as efficiently and effectively as printed words.

Although moving images are gaining responsibility for more and more of our communication, this is a suggestion most of us have great difficulty accepting.

Perhaps it was John F. Kennedy's handsome face or the opportunity most Americans had to watch his funeral. Maybe the turning point came with the burning huts of Vietnam, the flags and balloons of the Reagan presidency or Madonna's writhings on MTV. But at some point in the second half of the twentieth century—for perhaps the first time in human history—it began to seem as if images would gain the upper hand over words.

We know this. Evidence of the growing popularity of images has been difficult to ignore. It has been available in most of our bedrooms and living rooms, where the machine most responsible for the image's rise has long dominated the decor. Evidence has been available in the shift in home design from bookshelves to "entertainment centers," from libraries to "family rooms" or, more accurately, "TV rooms." Evidence has been available in our children's facility with remote controls and joysticks, and their lack of facility with language. Evidence has been available almost any evening in almost any town in the world, where a stroller will observe a blue light in most of the windows and a notable absence of porch sitters, gossip mongers and other strollers.

We are—old and young—hooked. While he was vice president of the United States, Dan Quayle embarked upon a minor crusade against television. It took him to an elementary school in Georgia. "Are you going to study hard?" the vice president asked a roomful of third-graders. "Yeah!" they shouted back. "And are you going to work hard and mind the teacher?" "Yeah!" And are you going to turn off the TV during school nights?" "No!" the students yelled.[2] When children between the ages of four and six were asked whether they like television or their fathers better, 54 percent of those sampled chose TV.[3]

Evidence of the image's growing dominance, particularly among the young, can be found too in my house, a word lover's house, where increasingly the TV *is* always on in the next room. (I am not immune to worries about this; nothing in the argument to come is meant to imply that my attempt to guide my children or myself through this transitional period has been easy.)

Television began its invasion about fifty years ago. The extent to which it has taken over—familiar as the statistics may be—remains dazzling. No medium or technology, before or after, "penetrated," as the researchers put it, our homes more quickly. It took seventy years before half of all American homes had a telephone. Apple sold its first all-in-one personal computer in 1977; IBM, which began selling computers to businesses in 1952, sold its first personal computer in 1981. It is true that processing chips are now imbedded in our cars and coffee makers; nevertheless, as this is written, personal computers themselves have still not found their way into half of America's homes, and a percentage of those that have made it there sit mostly unused. Yet it took only eight years, after the arrival of full-scale commercial television in 1947, before half of all American homes had a black-and-white television set.* And disuse is not a fate likely to befall a TV.[4]

A television set is now on in the average American home up to, depending on the time of year, eight hours a day—which means, subtracting time for work or school and sleep, basically all the time.† We each sit in front of a TV an average of anywhere from two and a half to almost five hours a day, depending on which estimate or survey you believe.[5] The average fifth-grader *reports* (they likely are underestimating) spending almost seven times as much time each day watching television as reading.[6] We are as attached, as addicted to television as we, as a society, have been to any other invention, communications medium, art form or drug.

Recently, it is true, television has begun to seem like yesterday's invention. Digital communications have mesmerized the technologically advanced and have won most of the press. Tens of millions of people have already begun using computers and the Internet to work, send written messages, shop, do research, and explore new corners of our culture—all with unprecedented speed and efficiency. This is certainly impressive. But television, which is less than a generation older than the computer, has already won over humankind.**[7]

Reliable global statistics are hard to come by, but the evidence indicates that almost three billion people are already watching televi-

* Some limited commercial television operations had flickered to life, using sets that "would soon be museum pieces," before the United States entered World War II.

† According to a Nielsen study in January 1997; summer viewing would be somewhat lower.

** Electronic television was first demonstrated in 1927; ☞

sion regularly, for an average of more than two and a half hours a day, according to one international survey.[8] That means most of the world's inhabitants are now devoting about half their leisure time to an activity that did not exist two generations ago. Most of the rest are held back only by the lack of electricity or the money to buy a set.

Why? Television's unprecedented appeal rests in large part on the easily accessible, seemingly inexhaustible diversions it supplies. But it goes beyond that. We have not sufficiently recognized the power of moving images. There is a magic in their ability to appear on command in our homes, and there is a magic in them, a magic that may come to dwarf that of other forms of communication.

"The [World Wide] Web is going to be very important," computer pioneer Steve Jobs, cofounder of Apple Computer, was quoted as saying in 1996. But then he added, "It's certainly not going to be like the first time somebody saw a television.... It's not going to be *that* profound."[9] It would be a mistake to underestimate the impact of our new digital communications systems, particularly their likely role in distributing moving images, but video remains the communications revolution of our time.

This does not mean we will continue to have what computer mavens dismiss as "dumb metal boxes" facing our couches—boxes to which we can do little more than change the channel and adjust the volume. Moving images undoubtedly will find new, more flexible, more clever means of presenting themselves. Silicon chips will be increasingly involved in their distribution. Perhaps we will soon locate our video at sites on the World Wide Web or some similarly interactive, global, cross-referenced, content-rich successor. Stations, networks, schedules and sets may all go the way of rabbit-ear antennas. However, if humankind's preferences over the past half century are any guide, whatever new screens and services do find their way into our homes in coming decades are going to be filled not so much with words or still graphics but with moving images.

The word *television* appears often in these pages. This is the form of moving images at which we have directed most of our attention and most of our criticism, the form that has conquered the world. However, this book views television as only one stage in a larger movement. Photography and film provided the initial thrust for the image's rise. And new kinds of moving images viewed in new ways are likely to lead to its triumph. A term is needed that encompasses the stages to come, that recognizes the increasing interchangeability of television and film, the coming "convergence," as the business pages put it, of television and the computer. The best alternative seems *video*—a com-

mechanical television is a few years older (although Boris Rosing in Russia had reported some "crude" and short-lived success in transmitting the image of "four luminous bands" in 1911). The first functional electronic computer was demonstrated in 1946.

pact word with a suitably broad meaning, derived from the Latin verb *vidēre* "to see."

When I talk of the video revolution, I mean video as content, not any particular size screen or variety of box. I mean that, by whatever improved means, we are going to continue staring at those magical moving images and obtaining more and more of our entertainment, information, art and ideas from them. "When I began here, I thought the writing was all that mattered," recalled the producer of that introduction to ABC's documentary on churches, Roberta Goldberg.* "Now not only do I think the visuals matter, but I think they matter more than the writing."[10] That too is what I mean.

* This remains a surprisingly common belief. See the comments of Don Hewitt in chapter 12.

What's missing from these pictures?

- Three people sit in a doctor's waiting room. One stares at the television that rests on an end table. The head of the second is wrapped in earphones. The third fiddles with a handheld video game.
- A couple of kids, waiting for bedtime, lie on the floor of a brightly painted room, squabbling over who gets to hold the remote control.
- Two hundred people sit in an airplane. Some have brought their own tapes, some doze; most stare up at small screens.

What is missing, of course, is the venerable activity you are engaged in right now. And such pictures are not difficult to supply. Reading is now missing from countless scenes it once dominated: at kitchen tables, on buses and trains, in beds at night, on couches, even in some classrooms.

When "the TV is always on in the next room," eventually large numbers of us stop yelling, put down what we were reading, and go into that room. The result—the opposite and (more or less) equal reaction to the arrival of the moving image—has been a significant lessening in the importance of the printed word.

The anecdotal evidence that print is in decline is copious and compelling. "When I go out socially in Washington," confided Daniel Boorstin, the historian and former librarian of Congress, "I'm careful not to embarrass my dinner companions by asking what they have read lately. Instead I say, 'I suppose you don't have much time to read books nowadays?'"[11] Novelists perceive the same situation, with perhaps even more dismay: "There's been a drastic decline, even a disappearance of a serious readership," moaned Philip Roth.[12]

This much-remarked-upon decline, nevertheless, is not easy to capture with statistics. Books seem to be doing reasonably well. According to the Book Industry Study Group, sales of adult trade books did drop in the mid-1990s, but this was after many years of steady increases. *Books in Print* now lists more than eighteen times as many titles as did its first edition, printed in 1948. And for a time the number of bookstores in the United States was growing at a rate second only to that of fast-food restaurants. Reports of the death of the book have been exaggerated.

Ah, but are those books actually being read? Not, in many cases, from cover to cover. The Gallup Poll found many more people in 1990 than in 1957 who said they are currently reading a book or novel, but many fewer than in 1975 who said they have completed a book in the past week. In a society where professional success now requires acquaintance with masses of esoteric information, books now are often purchased to be consulted, not read. Almost one quarter of the money spent on books in 1994 went for business, legal, medical, technical or religious books. Another large chunk was spent by or for the captive audiences in schools.[13]

Fiction and general-interest nonfiction for adults represented only about $4.3 billion of the $18.8 billion book industry in 1994.[14] Such trade books have also been filling a function other than their ostensible one. Instead of being read, they have been replacing the bottle of scotch and the tie as gifts—with about the same chance of being opened as those ties had of being worn.

In 1985 Michael Kinsley, then with the *New Republic,* conducted an experiment. He hid little notes, offering a five-dollar reward to anyone who saw them, about three quarters of the way through seventy copies of certain select nonfiction books in Washington, D.C., bookstores. These were the books all of Washington seemed to be talking about. "Washington" was apparently basing its comments on the reviews and maybe a quick skim. No one called. "Fortunately for booksellers," Kinsley wrote, "their prosperity depends on people buying books, not on people actually reading the bulky things."[15]

Here is perhaps the most frightening of the statistics on books: According to the Gallup Poll, the number of Americans who admitted to having read *no* books of any kind during the past year—and this is not an easy thing to admit to a pollster—doubled from 1978 to 1990, from 8 to 16 percent.* "I cannot live without books,"[16] Thomas Jefferson, certainly among the most dedicated readers of his era, once confessed to John Adams. More and more of us, apparently, can.

Magazines would appear better suited to life with television, if for no other reasons than that they require a smaller time commitment

* Public library circulation in the United States has grown from 4.7 "units" per capita per year

in 1980 to 6.4 in 1990, according to the Library Research Center at the University of Illinois. However, "units" now include cassettes, CDs, CD-ROMs and videotapes.

* Here's one attempt: According to *Folio Magazine,* of the five highest-grossing magazines in the United States in 1995 (not a particularly bad year), one (*Reader's Digest*) reported no change in circulation; the other four (*TV Guide, People, Time, Sports Illustrated*) lost circulation.

than books and that they themselves contain plenty of pictures. However, because magazines come in so many different varieties, gathering evidence to confirm or deny this surmise is not easy.* The best indicator of whether we are spending more or less time with magazines may be time-use studies like those compiled by John Robinson at the University of Maryland. These show that the proportion of the population that reads a magazine on a typical day dropped from 38 percent in 1946 to 28 percent in 1985. Magazine publishers, however, can take some encouragement from the fact that most of that drop occurred with the first onslaught of television in the 1950s.[17]

The statistics on newspaper readership are much less ambiguous and much grimmer. According to those time-use studies published in *American Demographics*, the share of the adult population that "read a newspaper yesterday" declined from 85 percent in 1946 to 73 percent in 1965 to 55 percent in 1985. The numbers on per capita newspaper circulation and the percentage of American homes that receive a daily newspaper form similar graphs—graphs you could ski down.

"I'm not sure how much people read anymore," H. Ross Perot commented shortly before announcing his candidacy for the presidency in 1992. "What happens on TV is what really impacts on people."[18] During the 1996 presidential campaign, only 18 percent of a sample of voters in the United States said they received "most" of their information about the campaign from newspapers.[19]

Those time-use studies actually discovered an increase of about thirteen minutes a week from 1965 to 1985 in the amount of time people say they spend reading books and magazines. But if you throw in newspapers, the total time people spent with reading as their primary activity has dropped more than 30 percent in those years—to less than three hours a week.

And this drop has occurred at the same time that the amount of formal education Americans obtain has been rising dramatically. The percentage of Americans over the age of twenty-four who have completed four years of high school has more than tripled since 1940, according to the Census Bureau's Current Population Survey. It increased from 69 percent to 82 percent just from 1980 to 1995. And since 1940 the percentage of Americans completing four years of college has increased by a factor of five. If education still stimulated the desire to read, all the statistics on reading would be expected to be shooting up. That they are not may say something about the quality of our educational system and about the interests of the students it now attracts. It certainly says something about the word and its future.

Reading's troubles are not difficult to explain. A hundred years ago, on days when no circus was in town, people looking for entertainment had few alternatives: eating, drinking, strolling, procreating, singing, talking, reading. Those looking for information were restricted to the latter two. Many of our ancestors, to be sure, were unable to read, but many of those who could relied upon it, as Thomas Jefferson did, with a desperation that is difficult for us to imagine.

The printed word, in those days, had a unique power to transport. "There is no frigate like a book," wrote Emily Dickinson, "To take us lands away."[20] Now, of course, that journey can be undertaken by a different route, one that allows us to *see* that which is beyond our direct experience. Another way of summarizing what has been happening to reading, and to our lives, is that the image is replacing the word as the predominant means of mental transport.*[21]

The image's ascent has certainly occupied its share of spoken and written words. Most of those words, however, are tinged with anxiety, annoyance, even anguish. We fret; we bemoan; we hope against hope; we indulge in righteous indignation. The revolution we are undergoing may be acknowledged, but only with chagrin. The photographer Richard Avedon recently dared state—on television—that "images are fast replacing words as our primary language." He did not display the requisite gloom. He was assaulted. "That, precisely, is the problem," thundered *New York Times* television critic John J. O'Connor, "as Amerian culture drifts ever more distressingly into superficiality."[22]

This is no easy subject. We are talking not only of the present, which is hard enough to see, but of the future. In which direction are we currently drifting? In which direction are we likely to drift? Formidable questions. Still, on issues of this importance, we should not have to settle for fretting, bemoaning, wishful thinking and indignation. The discussion does not have to be so windy and predictable.

I recently came upon a calender decorated with this quote from Patrick Henry: "I know of no way of judging the future but by the past." When pondering the image's rise, we have no difficulty working up nostalgia for the past, but we tend not to put much stock in the lessons of the past. Contemporary society—with its mastery of circuits and bits—chooses to think of its problems as unique. However, the video revolution is, by my reckoning, humankind's third major communications revolution, and the disruptions occasioned by the first two—writing and print—are surprisingly similar to those we are experiencing now. The stages in which the new technologies were adopted seem comparable, as does the profundity of the transformations they cause. Even the anxieties and anger sound familiar.

The first part of this book, consequently, spends much of its time with subjects that do not often find their way into discussions of tele-

* Writing is "more resistant than has been thought," protests the French historian of reading Roger Chartier. Perhaps so. But oral discouse also demonstrated tremendous resistance and still surrendered much of its cultural importance to writing and then print.

vision: one-hundred- to five-thousand-year-old episodes in the history of the word. The book begins by looking to the early development of writing, print and a few other communications technologies for perspective on what we have seen from television and are likely to see from video.

The book's second part mines a different history. The rise of the image begins not with CNN or even *See It Now* but with photography and film. Many of the issues raised by video productions such as Roberta Goldberg's introduction to that ABC documentary can be traced to disputes over early photographs and over the work of such filmmakers as D.W. Griffith, Sergei Eisenstein and Jean Renoir. I revisit these disputes in an effort to rethink these issues.

The history of television itself and of the creation of a new kind of video weave in and out of these first parts. But only in its third and final part does the book restrict its attempts to understand the future and the consequences of video to an examination of what has been appearing on screen in our time. Otherwise this book employs Patrick Henry's method.

Part I

Suspicion of the New

A sense of fear of the unknown moved in the heart of his weariness, a fear...of Thoth, the god of writers, writing with a reed upon a tablet and bearing on his narrow ibis head the cusped moon.

—James Joyce, A Portrait of the Artist as a Young Man

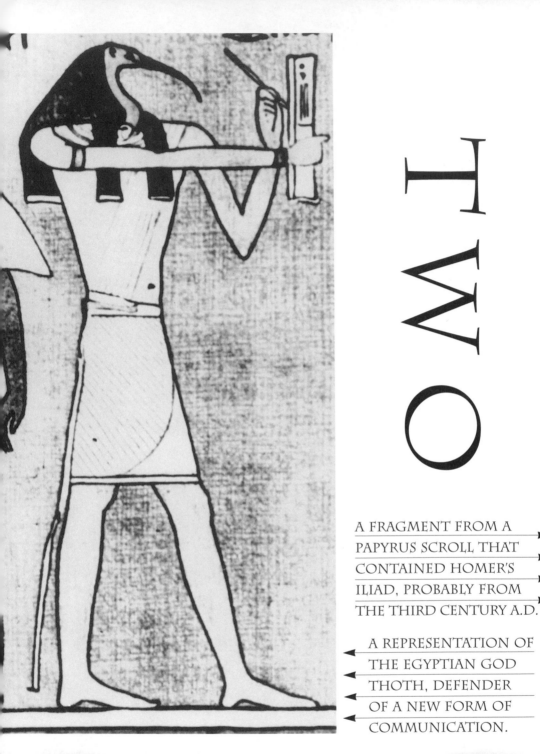

TWO

A FRAGMENT FROM A
PAPYRUS SCROLL THAT
CONTAINED HOMER'S
ILIAD, PROBABLY FROM
THE THIRD CENTURY A.D.

A REPRESENTATION OF
THE EGYPTIAN GOD
THOTH, DEFENDER
OF A NEW FORM OF
COMMUNICATION.

"In the far north, where there is snow, all bears are white. Novaya
Zemlya is in the far north and there is always snow there. What color
are the bears there?"
Answers to this question provide evidence of how forms of communication can influence thought.

"These TRADITIONAL SPLENDORS OF LETTERS"

Writing and the Power of New Media

Early forms of writing: Babylonian clay tablets in various shapes with cuneiform writing, dating back as far as 2600 B.C.

For the word
was the glory
of mankind…
—Thomas
Mann, *The
Magic
Mountain*

i n the beginning," Genesis informs us, "God created the heavens and the earth." But the notion of a beginning—as well as notions of God and the heavens and probably even the earth—would be impossible without language. Words enable us to acknowledge that to which we cannot point—a realm that includes not only those parts of the earth and the heavens that are beyond our sight but the past, the future, the possible, the impossible, the analogous and the non-material.

Words were born with humankind—perhaps a hundred thousand or even as long as a million years ago.* To be human, for those unencumbered by disability, is to use and understand words. Most of what we can sense, feel or imagine we can express through language.[1] Can we think without language? This question has perplexed many generations of undergraduates, but certainly it can be agreed that without language most of us could not think about much. Perhaps that is some of what the Gospel according to John has in mind when it reports, "In the beginning was the Word."

This is the first reason that talk of the fall of the word causes so much anxiety. At stake is not simply one form of communication; at stake is the way we think, where we begin.

What about images?† Our ancestors undoubtedly did have a well-developed visual sense before they could speak; all healthy primates do.[2] We saw (with what understandings is not clear) before we could describe what we saw. However, *images*—by which I mean not just sights but created or reproduced sights—came later.[3]

The archaeological evidence is that humans first began experimenting with markings, carvings, colorings and decorations as early as seventy-five thousand years ago. Attempts at figurative art—including depictions of animal heads and of what experts decorously label "female reproductive organs"—apparently date from between 35,000 and 25,000 B.C. The cave paintings discovered in Lascaux, France—among the earliest known—were probably created about 15,000 B.C.[4]

* Even this
seemingly
broad range
does not cover
all current theo-
ries; older and
more recent
dates have also
been
suggested.

† The Dogon of
Africa have a
creation legend
that begins
with the image.

So all these scratchings and drawings—the oldest ancestors of video— likely arrived tens or hundreds of thousands of years *after* language. Indeed, they would probably have been impossible if humans were not already speaking: Achieving such art requires a level of thought that seems dependent upon language—colors must be prepared, animals must be denoted.

In exalting the word, the Bible is also exalting writing. The ability to record language in inscribed symbols is not, like speech, a part of our genetic inheritance. Writing is a technology, a human invention.*[5] The written word arrived relatively late in human history—in Sumeria and then Egypt a little more than five thousand years ago. It was the offspring of both words and images.

The earliest writing systems used icons that represented things—a plow, a fish, the head of an ox. But they also referred directly to sounds: The name of the Egyptian king Narmer, who reigned around 3150 B.C., was indicated, for example, by the character for a catfish, pronounced with the consonents *nr*, and that for a sculptor's chisel, *mr*.[6] Writing, in other words, was always tied to language. As it developed in the Middle East the connection between characters and images weakened, while the connection between characters and phonetic sounds strengthened.[7]

"Writing," stated Voltaire, "is the painting of the voice; the closer the resemblance, the better it is."[8] Such "paintings" do not, however, need to resemble actual objects in the world. Indeed, the less use writing systems made of images of things, the more efficient they became.

In about 1500 B.C. the world's first alphabet appeared among the Semites in Canaan. It featured a limited number of abstract symbols (at one point thirty-two, later reduced to twenty-two) out of which most of the sounds of speech could be represented. The Old Testament was written in a version of this alphabet. All the world's alphabets descend from it. After the Phoenicians (or earlier Canaanites) brought the Semitic alphabet to Greece, an addition was made that allowed the sounds of speech to be represented less ambiguously: vowels. The oldest surviving example of the Greek alphabet dates from about 750 B.C. This is, via Latin and give or take a few letters or accents, the alphabet in which this book is written.[9] It has never been improved upon.

By "painting" the voice, writing was able to borrow the voice's great expressive range. Because just about anything that was spoken could be written, just about anything that was thought could be written.

But there's a larger point here. Writing would also significantly add to the power of the word, and in so doing it would change the nature of what could be thought. This was the first great communica-

* Sven Birkerts, a member of the swelling legion of defenders of the book, proclaims that "language and not technology is the true evolutionary miracle." But his beloved print is the product not only of Gutenberg's technological advance but of one of the most powerful of technologies: writing itself.

tions revolution—a revolution that had begun in Sumeria and Egypt, gained force among the Semites, and scored some of its greatest triumphs in Greece.

Not that many centuries after the invention of the Greek alphabet, the world saw something new: widespread literacy. In Greece in the fifth century B.C., aided by the ease and efficiency of that alphabet, large numbers of people—not just scribes—were trained in school to read and write.[10] The written word freed the citizens of the Greek city-states from the need to memorize their culture's store of accumulated wisdom. It also began to transform and expand that wisdom.

Plato, who lived through this crucial phase of the writing revolution, told a story in one of his dialogues about the Egyptian god Theuth, or Thoth. This was a god of varied and considerable talents: He appeared sometimes in the form of a long-beaked bird, the ibis, and sometimes in the form of a baboon. (He is depicted as a baboon in King Tutankhamun's tomb.) Thoth also could be found coursing through the heavens as the moon. His responsibilities included science, language and even wisdom itself.[11] But Plato was interested in Thoth in yet another role: "It was he who first invented numbers and arithmetic, geometry and astronomy, dicing, too, and the game of draughts and, most particularly and especially, writing."[12]

In the *Phaedrus* Plato had Socrates describe a remarkable scene: Thoth came before the Egyptian king Thamus, "exhibited his arts and declared that they ought to be imparted to the other Egyptians." In other words, this god, like an exhibitor at an electronics show, is trying to win acceptance for his inventions. Socrates quotes Thoth's argument for only one of his "arts," the one of concern to Plato, writing: "'This discipline, my King, will make the Egyptians wiser and will improve their memories: my invention is a recipe for both memory and wisdom'"[13]—a cogent statement of the power of writing, from the mouth of a god.

Although I can't claim to be an inventor, let alone a god, I feel some affinity with Thoth. I too presume to defend not just some new electronic gizmo but an entire, relatively new form of communication. He made the case for writing in spoken words. I want to make the case for video in written or, more precisely, printed words.

I will argue that once we move beyond simply aiming cameras at stage plays, conversations or sporting events and perfect original uses of moving images, video can help us gain new slants on the world, new ways of seeing. It can capture more of the tumult and confusions of contemporary life than tend to fit in lines of type. Through its ability to step back from scenes and jump easily between scenes, video can also facilitate new, or at least previously underused, ways of thinking. It promises, I will argue, to help us escape the artistic, political and philosophic doldrums in which the printed word, after centuries of filling our sails, seems to have left us. I believe video too will prove "a recipe" for new kinds of "wisdom."

This is an argument that will, if I am correct, be much easier to make tens or perhaps thousands of years from now. After all, the full impact of writing and the communications revolution it unleashed did not become apparent for more than five thousand years after Thoth or some mortal brought writing to Egypt; it did not become apparent for more than two thousand years after Plato wrote. We grasped the scope of this first great communications revolution in the twentieth century.

This book is concerned primarily with two epochs: today and tomorrow. Yet in its search for perspective on them it will not only ask the reader to go back in time but to leap with some frequency between disparate times. It will make use, in other words, of some fast cutting of its own (fast for a book, at least). Here's one such cut: It requires temporarily taking leave of both video's future and writing's early history for a quick visit to Uzbekistan and Kirghizia in the early 1930s. A young psychologist, Alexander Luria, conducted interviews at that time with people who lived in these remote areas of the Soviet Union. What he found provided some of the most compelling evidence we have of the power of forms of communication to work the sort of transformations in thought I am predicting for video. In this case the form of communication in question was Thoth's invention.

Most of the peasants Luria interviewed were illiterate or, more accurately, preliterate: They lived, as generation after generation of their ancestors had lived, in small villages where they had almost no exposure to writing.[14] Information was exchanged by word of mouth. The Soviets, however, were in the process of introducing collectivization and formal education. Luria's goal was to record the *before*: how these people, in what he considered an early stage of social and cognitive development, thought.

To do that he asked them questions: "In the far north, where there is snow, all bears are white. Novaya Zemlya is in the far north and there is always snow there. What color are the bears there?" A typical response: "I don't know. I've seen a black bear. I've never seen any others.... Each locality has its own animals." These preliterate Soviet peasants, Luria concluded, did not analyze such problems the way we would; their thinking instead was "situational."[15]

One of the great intellectual accomplishments of the twentieth century has been an understanding of the extent to which people in

* In the work of
Lucien Lévy-
Bruhl and
Claude Lévi-
Strauss, for
example.

† Soviet author-
ities were not
persuaded;
Luria was
unable to pub-
lish his work for
forty years.

different cultures can think differently.* Communications theory has
made a major contribution to this understanding. Marshall McLuhan
speculated, famously, on the way media such as print or television
have left us more or less detached, aggressive, individualistic, tribal or
"cool." Other theorists, such as McLuhan's student Walter Ong,
approached the same problems less speculatively. McLuhan was fond
of quoting *King Lear* and *Finnegans Wake*. Father Ong, a Jesuit priest,
cited Luria.

No insult to peasants should be read into Luria's study, both he
and Ong insisted.†[16] Oral cultures have produced glorious poems, tales
and religious testaments. But a certain kind of abstract thinking is,
Ong argued, primarily a product of literacy, of writing. The absence of
familiarity with a system of writing goes a long way toward explaining
the inability of Luria's subjects to solve what seems to us a fairly simple syllogism about bears.

The key is writing's ability to transform words into objects. Words
that are written down, not just enunciated, are freed from the individual situations and experiences ("I've seen a black bear") in which they
were embedded. Written words—arrayed on pages, stacked in lists—
can be played with, examined, rearranged and organized into new categories (black bears, white bears, places where there is always snow).[17]

When the preliterate Soviet peasants Luria interviewed were
shown a round geometric figure and asked to describe it, they said they
saw a plate, a bucket or the moon—not a circle. Instead of a square
they said they saw a door, a house or a board for drying apricots.[18]
They perceived, in other words, concrete things where those exposed
to writing perceive more abstract categories.

Evidence that peoples without writing tend to look at the world
this way has also been found in studies of, for example, the Pulawat
Islanders in the South Pacific or the LoDagaa of northern Ghana.
Preliterates certainly divide their surroundings, as all humans do, into
categories: edible, inedible; sacred, profane; houses, doors. However,
these categories do not often escape the (presumed) practical; they do
not often escape specific situations. The LoDagaa, an anthropogist
who studied them observes, appear to have no word, for instance, for
"word."[19]

After being shown drawings of four objects—hammer, saw, log
and hatchet—and being asked to group them, Luria's preliterate subjects were stumped. "They're all alike," one responded. "The saw will
saw the log and the hatchet will chop it into small pieces. If one of
these things has to go, I'd throw out the hatchet. It doesn't do as good
a job as a saw." The emergence of an abstract category like "tool" owes
much to literacy. When a twenty-year-old from the same area who had

some exposure to writing was asked this question, he had no difficulty excluding the log.[20]

These differences can be exaggerated. Preliterate societies, as anthropologist Jack Goody noted, are certainly not devoid of "reflective thinking." Some of these societies made great advances. The wheel, the first use of metal and the development of agriculture all appear to predate the invention of writing.[21] Still, the claim that can be made for writing is a large one.

Our system of logic decrees that if the statement "All bears in the far north are white" is true and the statement "Novaya Zemlya is in the far north" is true, then the statement "Some bears in Novaya Zemlya are black" *must* be false. This is the law of contradiction. "It is certainly easier to perceive contradictions in writing than it is in speech," writes Goody, another early proponent of the connection between media and mentalities.[22] When statements are written down, we gain the habit of pulling them out of the flow of experience and subjecting them to a narrow, rigorous analysis—noting their correspondences, connections or contradictions. Ong, Goody and others have come to believe that our system of logic—our ability to find abstract principles that apply independently of situations—is to some extent a product of literacy, of the written word.

In other words, the means we use to express our thoughts, as McLuhan and others began arguing in the 1960s and 1970s, change our thoughts. Teach people to read and you do more than improve their access to information; you remake their understanding of the world. And it does not much matter what they read, as long as they read. "The *medium*"—not its content—"is the message." Writing changes our minds. Political attitudes, social attitudes and even philosophies can shift, the argument goes, as the ways information is exchanged shift.

Overstated, this argument can become a blinding form of technological determinism; it can seem as if the influence of other factors—politics, economics and religion come to mind—is being denied.[23] Let us not overstate the argument, then. Nothing said here is meant to suggest that communications technologies are the *only* variable or to negate the importance of other variables. I certainly do not mean to say that lack of literacy is the *only* explanation for differences between the way those Soviet peasants thought and we think.

But this is not a book about the influence of politics, economics or religion. As we grapple with the effects of our own communications revolution, I want to insist that that the way people communicate can have *an* effect, a profound effect, upon the way they think. The main purpose of this cut to Uzbekistan and Kirghizia has been to open the possibility that the moving image has been working and will continue to work different but equally profound changes upon *our* ways of thinking. (These changes are discussed most thoroughly in this book's final chapter.)

The evidence of writing's effect on thought is not only to be found in anthropological studies such as Luria's. It also can be found in history—in Babylonia, Egypt and many other places, but perhaps most clearly in the intellectual and artistic explosion that followed the arrival of widespread literacy in Greece.[24]

The Homeric epics—likely composed before the Greeks began writing—provide another indication of the nature of preliterate thought.*[25] They are filled, twentieth-century scholars have noted, with formulas and larger-than-life characters. In the *Iliad* and the *Odyssey* the name Odysseus, for example, is often mentioned with the adjective *clever,* and the sentence "There spoke up [or "out"] clever Odysseus" occurs seventy-two times. Formulas are easy to remember. Nestor, in these poems, is usually old or wise, Achilles frequently swift or brilliant. The monumental and the heroic also stick in the mind.[26] Writing would begin to release Greek thought from a reliance upon such repetitions, truisms, exaggerations and other aids to memory.

Oral cultures are also burdened with the need to repeat old thoughts and retell old tales; otherwise they will be lost. With writing it became possible to invent new ideas, embodied in new poems, dramas, dialogues and even prose accounts. The written word began to tear down the walls of tradition with which human culture had been protected and constrained.†

Because it enabled events and observations to be recorded, writing also eased the reliance upon legend and speculation. It deserves much of the credit for the development of science and history. The Greeks knew little of what had happened to them before the year 650 B.C. and not much of their history before 550 B.C. Events in Greece in the next century, however, were sufficiently well recorded so that the whole world has been able to learn about them.[27] Writing and reading helped clear the mists.

Thoth was correct: Writing was indeed a recipe for wisdom. The commmunications revolution it spawned helped make possible the intellectual accomplishments of the Egyptians, Babylonians, Hebrews, Christians and Moslems; of the Greeks and Romans; of the Chinese, Indians and Japanese. It helped make possible, in other words, most of our cultures.

Few benefited as much from the changes in mentalities encouraged by

* Earlier forms of writing had been in use on Crete and among the Minoans and perhaps the Mycenaeans before 1400 B.C., but these are not generally thought to have played a role in transcribing Homer.

† Jack Goody insists on the word *constrained* rather than *imprisoned* here.

writing as Plato himself. Writing freed him from the obligation to memorize and pass on legends and parrot proverbs; it freed him to create new "dialogues" filled with new thoughts—decidedly abstract thoughts. Those dialogues have survived for almost 2,400 years because they were written. Little of this, however, was apparent as Plato wrote in the early fourth century B.C. It certainly wasn't apparent in Thoth's time, thousands of years earlier.

As Socrates tells the story in Plato's *Phaedrus,* the final verdict on each of Thoth's inventions is left to King Thamus, who represents Thoth's progenitor and superior, Ra, the sun god.[28] And when it came to writing, Thamus was unpersuaded.

He had—says Socrates, wrote Plato—two critiques: "This invention will produce forgetfulness in the souls of those who have learned it," the king began by arguing. "They will not need to exercise their memories, being able to rely on what is written." Thamus's second complaint is that written words, since they come "without benefit of a teacher's instruction," will produce only "a semblance" of "wisdom," not "truth," not "real judgment."[29]

Socrates (and therefore Plato) tells this tale approvingly. He does not see the glory we see in the written word. He agrees with the king that writing is a step backward. As defender of a great communications revolution, in the early stages of that revolution, Thoth had failed.

Now we are in the early stages of another great communications revolution, surrendering what Emerson called "these traditional splendors of letters" in favor of the moving image, in favor of video.[30] This seems at first glance quite a powerful new tool, especially when compared to the little scrawlings Thoth was promoting. Indeed, were visitors from Plato's time (or Emerson's) to find their way into one of our homes, they might marvel at the machines we have invented for cooking, cleaning, calculating and sending mail electronically; but would not their gaze be transfixed by that box in front of the couch, with its constantly changing array of images, its miniaturized people, intense dramas and brilliantly colored scenes?

Our gaze has been transfixed by it. Yet our Platos too are glum.

A controversial

new from

of communication:

the pencil

with an

new from

Pages from the 1450s on printing press as a dangerous new machine.

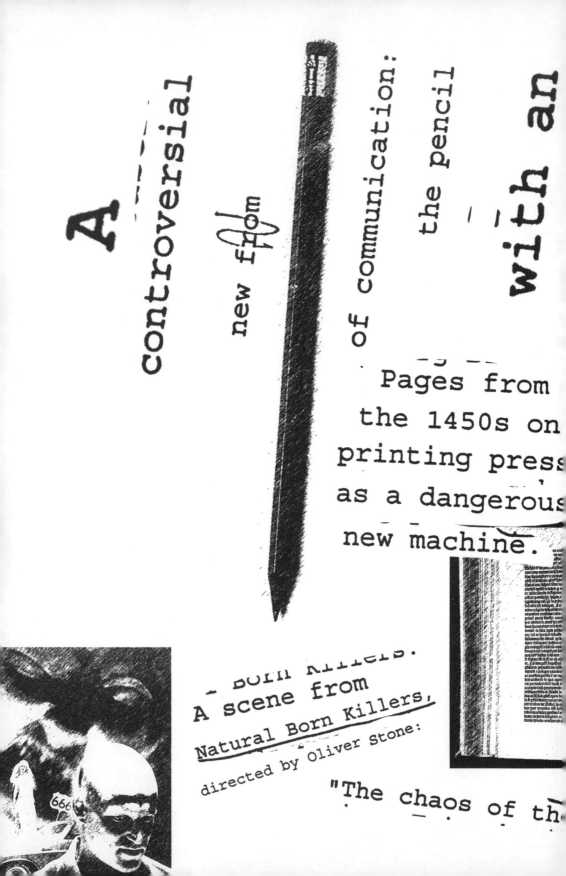

A scene from Natural Born Killers,
directed by Oliver Stone:

"The chaos of th

chapter three

"Ignorance's Weapons"

Print and the Threat of New Media

eraser.

the Bible printed in
Johann Gutenberg's
— soon seen by many
and destablizing

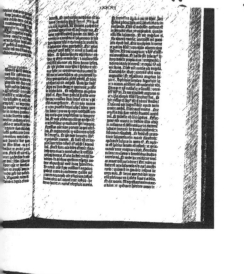

ilm was upsetting."

Humanists are such
natural Luddites. . . .
—Richard A. Lanham

most of those who have taken the time to worry about television's influence have been dismayed by that influence. "Chewing gum for the eyes," the architect Frank Lloyd Wright called it more than thirty years ago.[1] At about the same time, theorists of the Frankfurt School, such as T.W. Adorno, accused television programs of producing "the very smugness, intellectual passivity and gullibility that seem to fit in with totalitarian creeds," while the historian Theodore Roszak was attributing to those programs a "narcotic disintegration of the sensibilities." "There is something about television," the *Economist* observed in 1962, "that prompts many eminent men to strike many illiberal attitudes."[2]

Countless other eminent personages have weighed in since; their attitudes do not appear any more liberal. The political theorist and former diplomat George F. Kennan complained that television is "essentially antisocial" and spoke of its "peculiarly druglike, almost narcotic, soporific power." Pope John Paul II is among those who have charged that television "glorifies sex and violence and recklessly spreads false values." The educator Neil Postman moaned that this medium has left us so busy "amusing ourselves" that we are losing the capacity for serious thought.*[3]

* In his life if not his work, even Marshall McLuhan took a conservative view: McLuhan's family was the last on its block to purchase a TV set, and he insisted that it be relegated to the basement.

Television is routinely treated as beyond salvation. "We would all be better off if television got worse, not better," wrote Postman, a champion of the off button.[4] "Just turn off the television and almost anything you do will be less sendentary," stated Dr. William Dietz, who has investigated the relationship between television and obesity.[5] "Turn off the TV," former vice president Quayle suggested. "Simply turn the set off," the pope advised parents. Similar suggestions pop up in hundreds of other writings and hundreds of thousands of conversations. They are ignored, of course; nevertheless, many of us still experience a twinge of guilt as we settle in on the couch. And optimism about the future of this form of communication remains exceedingly rare.

Recently *New York Times Book Review* editor Charles McGrath conceded that television "has become a medium you can consistently rely on not just for distraction but for enlightenment." However, he hastened to add that "TV will never be better than reading, thank goodness."[6] The fact that McGrath's realization was the cover story in the *New York Times Magazine* shows just how uncommon, and therefore newsworthy, is even so qualified an endorsement.

Our media barons have been driven into a frenzy by visions of the hundreds of channels that are about to or are already entering our houses via cable, satellite and computer modem. But who has any confidence in the programming that seems likely to appear on those channels? Most educated people, eminent or not, find themselves asking why video can't more closely resemble more respected forms of communication, such as books, theater, concerts or conversation. Why is it so superficial? Why, as in that ABC News introduction, does it move so fast? Why can't "sound-bites," the time given newsmakers for uninterrupted speech, run longer? Why does video rely so heavily on flat, glossy images? Video's millions of critics are prepared to jump on any sign that words have won a minor victory: exulting, for example, when it turns out that our current generation of computers has difficulty juggling bit-hogging moving images—although the limits in memory and processing power that have restricted use of such images are clearly temporary.

I was born just after the arrival of commercial television—at the end of the 1940s. A bulky, wood-paneled set with a round dial for changing channels arrived in my family's living room about when I became old enough to plop myself on a couch. It was not long before I was lost in *Howdy Doody, Leave It to Beaver* and reruns of *My Little Margie*. I recall sitting at the edge of my perplexed parents' bed as the Beatles first shook their bangs on *The Ed Sullivan Show*. Nevertheless, like many members of my outsized generation, I was suspicious of television, concerned that I was, if not subjecting myself to harm, at least squandering my time.

In a 1961 speech Newton Minow, then chairman of the Federal Communications Commission, made what has become the best-known of the attacks on TV. Minow described the medium he was in charge of regulating as "a vast wasteland." I was just old enough to be aware of this critique and, although at the time I was spending many after-school and prime-time hours planted in front of a TV, I could not disagree.

The members of my generation have gone on to live their lives with television. The history we experienced—from Dallas to Baghdad—most of us experienced most powerfully on television. Yet that suspicion remains. No matter how many channels have become available, even if we're fond, like McGrath, of a dramatic series or two, we feel there is something wrong with our attachment to the "idiot box." In our darker moments, we worry that our society has taken a step backward because its members spend so much time lost in that "wasteland."

We have sacrificed much to television; that is an additional cause of our unease. All this watching, after all, has come at the expense of talking, visiting, playing, strolling, fiddling and reading. Few laments about the "death" of the first five activities on this list have as yet been heard. However, television's culpability in the decline of reading has inspired a constant wail. The written word was the great teacher of Minow's generation and of mine. It has still not surrendered the lectern. The word's distress causes most educated people distress.

Which is to say that we have come around on writing. All of our philosophers and kings hear Thoth clearly now; it only took thousands of years. They bow down before Thoth's invention. They grieve over its decline. It is just this new invention that they have trouble with.

On the thirtieth anniversary of his famous speech, Newton Minow mentioned some pictures that would take advantage of the new television technologies and, presumably, make the medium less of a "wasteland." Not surprisingly, Minow chose the least threatening of images: pictures "of thinking human beings"—that is, pictures of people mouthing words.[7]

The second great communications revolution, like the first, involved words. It began in Europe in the middle of the fifteenth century. Its roots, however, were in China.

The initial Chinese contribution was a superior writing surface. The Egyptians, Hebrews and Greeks had written on papyrus. The Romans eventually switched to parchment—pieces of animal hide.[8] According to legend, paper, made from a pulp composed of mashed plant fibers, was invented by Ts'ai Lun, a Chinese eunuch working for the emperor, in A.D. 105.[9] It proved cheaper, more abundant, smoother and better able to take ink than parchment. Still, paper took a thousand years to find its way to Europe.[10]

Printing, as we know, also began in China. By the eighth century multiple copies of various works appear to have been produced from carved wood blocks.[11] By the tenth century, five centuries before Gutenberg, a Chinese artisan named Pi Sheng had even developed moveable type—individual characters that could be reused. However, Chinese writing, with its plethora of characters, required that a huge store of type be available for moving, and China's authoritarian, often monolithic political structures resisted the wide dissemination of knowledge. Moveable type was not a big success in China. The printing revolution began, instead, in fragmented, fractious Europe.[12]

In the middle years of the fifteenth century the elements that led to the European printing press were first brought together. Johannes Gutenberg, a debt-ridden German goldsmith working in Mainz, was definitely one of the first, probably the first, to accomplish this. Gutenberg's press (of which he soon lost control) printed its first books sometime in the 1450s. A book dated 1460 includes a note some have attributed to Gutenberg: "This noble book was made without reed stylus or pen but by a wondrous agreement...and harmony of punches and types."[13] A strong but meltable lead alloy, from which molds shaped by those punches might form type; a thick, black ink; a press, based on a wine press; and, of course, the Latin alphabet also joined in that "agreement and harmony."[14] The results were astonishing.

Printing spread across Europe at a rate that puts many twentieth-century inventions to shame: Strasbourg gained a print shop in 1458, Italy in 1465, France in 1470, the Low Countries in 1473, Poland in 1474 and England in 1476. In 1483 a scribe might have charged a florin to copy twenty pages. That year the owner of a printing press charged three florins to print twenty pages. The number of copies that money bought differed, however: 1 versus 1,025. And by 1489, only thirty or forty years after the first print shop, 110 European cities and towns had print shops.[15] The French historians Lucien Febvre and Henri-Jean Martin estimate that "about twenty million books were printed *before 1500*."[16] Here truly was an information explosion.

Francis Bacon, writing in 1620, credited "printing, gunpowder and the magnet" (or compass) with having "changed the whole face and state of things throughout the world."[17] The case may be more difficult to make for gunpowder and the magnet.

Printing, according to Bacon, worked its changes upon "literature." The extent to which that realm was transformed was remarkable indeed. Writings had attracted audiences before printing, but they had been tiny. Scholars had been able to consult wide selections of books before printing, but that had usually required considerable travel. Writers certainly had taken pride in their writings before printing, but with their work always subject to error or emendation by copyists, there had been less sense of authorship or ownership of words. Good copies had been available before printing, but no exact copies.[18]

Books certainly predated printing, but uniform spellings, standardized rules of punctuation and even standard ways of writing numbers had been rare or nonexistent. There was an alphabet before printing, of course, but alphabetical order was not widely known until printed reference works made it useful.

News had been energetically circulated before printing, occasionally even in periodicals, but widely distributed newspapers were the product of the press. Tales and stories, epics and legends predated printing as well, but not for the most part extended pieces of prose with original plots and commonplace details, not the novel.

And printing's effects were hardly limited to "literature," even broadly defined. As one of the first machines of mass production, the press brought ideas and information to new masses. It helped spread the Italian Renaissance throughout Europe. It rapidly circulated news of Columbus's first journey: Numerous different editions of a letter the explorer himself had written about his discoveries were printed in Europe the year he returned. The press circulated, too, exact copies of the maps that would aid and encourage further explorations. It placed editions of books by Copernicus, Galileo, Kepler and Newton under the gaze of individuals capable of expanding upon their discoveries. It was the means by which the first scientific journals were produced. It facilitated the scientific revolution.

"It is a mystery to me," Martin Luther wrote to the pope in 1518, "how my theses...were spread to so many places."[19] But, of course, those theses had the benefit of the printing press. By one estimate more than three hundred thousand copies of Luther's works were printed between 1517 and 1520. So the press spread the ideas of the Protestant Reformation, too. It would also spread the Enlightenment ideas that inspired the American and French Revolutions.

The siren song of technological determinism becomes particularly hard to resist here. "He who first shorted the labour of Copyists by device of *Moveable Types*," Thomas Carlyle wrote in 1831, "was disbanding hired Armies, and cashiering most Kings and Senates, and creating a whole new Democratic world."[20]

Some of this was apparent early on. Printing was "a divine art," more than one fifteenth- and sixteenth-century observer concluded. In 1515 Pope Leo X declared that printing "had come down from the heavens as a gift from God."[21]

However, Leo's statement came in a decree instituting censorship of that gift. The printing press and its products were often feared; that we remember. They were also—and this has mostly been forgotten—frequently reviled, and not only by religious and political leaders. A surprising number of writers in the sixteenth, seventeenth, eighteenth and even nineteenth centuries thought this new invention, despite all it did for their writings, was a setback for humankind. In other words, there was something about print too in its early centuries that prompted the eminent "to strike many illiberal attitudes." They came down, it might be said, not on Thoth's side but on King Thamus's.

In the history of communication that side has usually been crowded. The point is that television is far from the only young form of communication to have inspired dismay. Indeed, it is in good company.

The hostility that greeted new approaches to painting has been often noted, with impressionism the classic but far from only example. However, bursts of hostility have also been aimed at what seem today to have been more clearly useful and less overtly rebellious new arrivals: paper, for example. When Europeans finally encountered this improved writing surface, many responded by disparaging it as fake and fragile. In 1231 the Holy Roman emperor, Frederick II, prohibited the recording of public acts on paper rather than reliable old parchment.[22]

An even harsher and longer-lived hostility greeted Arabic numerals when they began to replace the traditional Roman numerals in Europe at about the same time. In some places our positional ten-digit system for writing numbers was banned. Its crime, in part, was introducing an alien and disturbing concept: the zero.[23]

Indeed, most of the inventions, techniques or art forms we now hold dear were once dismissed as useless or even evil. Opera? In eighteenth-century England many intellectuals reviled it as a senseless, mind-numbing spectacle of sight and sound—"chromatic tortures."[24] The theater? For the young Ralph Waldo Emerson it was "the sewer in which the rebellious vices exhaust themselves."[25]

Henry David Thoreau was one of the more vehement and consistent critics of the new. In 1854 he famously dismissed the telegraph lines that were just beginning to traverse the country by suggesting that "Maine and Texas...have nothing important to communicate." Thoreau professed having no use for any such "pretty toys": "Improved means to an unimproved end," he harrumphed.[26]

In 1877 the *New York Times* fulminated against the "atrocious nature" of Alexander Graham Bell's improved version of the telegraph: the telephone. Invasion of privacy was the charge. Twenty years later, the indictment stood: "We shall soon be nothing but transparent heaps of jelly to each other," one writer predicted. Another early complaint against the telephone was that it deprives us of the opportunity "to cut a man off by a look or a gesture."[27]

In 1893 the *Nation* lamented the increasing use of photographs, or "cuts," in newspapers: "The 'cuts' will in their turn have to be supplemented by something more infantile still. The reader will demand and have to get a rattle or a colored India-rubber balloon, or a bright ball of worsted, or a jack-in-the-box, with each year's subscription."* [28]

A new medium's strength, particularly its ability to divert the masses, is routinely turned against it. Radio, Will Irwin stated in 1936,

* Additional attacks on photography, and on film, are ☞

discussed later
in this book.

has access to "the magic inherent in the human voice." But this led him to conclude that it "has means of appealing to the lower nerve centers and of creating emotions which the hearer mistakes for thoughts."[29]

We rarely trust the imposition of a new magic on our lives, and we rarely fail to work up nostalgia for the older magic it replaces. Over time, in other words, one person's new "toy" becomes another's tried and true method. At the beginning of this century, pencils with erasers were attacked and occasionally even excluded from classrooms based on the following logic: "It might almost be laid down as a general law, that the easier errors may be corrected, the more errors will be made." Yet by 1938 the *New York Times* was honoring the pencil with an editorial, which noted that "living must have been more laborious before the pencil age." What had changed? The pencil itself was now threatened: "The universal typewriter," this editorial lamented, "may swallow all." Thoreau, the great scourge of technological improvements, maintained a soft spot for at least one technology, one his father crafted, one he himself tried to improve: an early incarnation of the pencil.[30]

It is clear where our soft spot lies in the age of the image: Even the least faithful lover of words these days can romanticize print. Most of us are rarely as satisfied with ourselves as when we crack a book. Television programs have ended with plugs for related novels or histories. Oprah Winfrey attempts to transform installments of her weepy TV talk show into a reading group. We try everything from bribes to punishments to induce our children to read half a chapter between *Friends* and bed. "If I came upon Junior engrossed in the Marquis de Sade's *120 Days of Sodom*," P.J. O'Rourke has written, "my reaction would probably be, 'He's *reading!*'"[31] According to the Gallup Poll, 61 percent of us proclaim reading "more rewarding" than watching television; 73 percent lament that we spend too little time reading books; and 92 percent of us attest that reading is a "good use" of our time.

While he was working for President Reagan, the late Lee Atwater, according to a *New York Times* story, assigned an aide to read and summarize books for him. Atwater would then brag that he read three books a week.[32] Who today brags, legitimately or not, of having watched television?

But reading and writing—as Plato's tale demonstrates—once took their share of abuse. Plato's soft spot instead is for "discourse which is inscribed with genuine knowledge in the soul of the learner."*[33] Discourse—spoken language—still seemed more attractive to Thomas Aquinas more than sixteen hundred years later: "It was fitting that

* The use of the word *inscribed*, sometimes translated as
☞

Christ did not commit His doctrine to writing," he concluded, "for the more excellent the teacher, the more excellent should be his manner of teaching."[34]

When printing began to replace handwritten manuscripts in the fifteenth century, producing books the slow, old-fashioned way occasionally took on that familiar, romantic glow. "Printed books will never be the equivalent of handwritten codices," asserted the abbot and bibliographer Trithemius of Sponheim in 1492. He gave a "simple reason": Scribes displayed "more diligence and industry" than printers.[35]

The Florentine book merchant Vespasiano da Bisticci's paean to the duke of Urbino's library, written late in the fifteenth century, noted that "all the books are superlatively good, and written with the pen, and had there been one printed volume it would have been ashamed in such company."* (Vespasiano was not an unbiased source, as he sold only handwritten manuscripts.[36] However, most of those who publish criticism of television today are likewise vulnerable to charges of conflict of interest.)

A few decades after the printing press arrived in Venice there was a call for it to be banished.[37]And the press was severely restricted in most of the countries of the world at one time or another over the following five centuries. The object, we now conclude, was to limit the flow of ideas. But at the time many of those who did the restricting saw themselves as grappling with a dangerous and destabilizing new machine.

On Europe's southern flanks, Moslem societies had been using paper and block printing much earlier than their Christian neighbors, but they resisted the letter press. "According to their view," a traveler reported after a visit to Istanbul in 1560, "the scriptures, their holy letters, once printed would cease to be scriptures." A press with Arabic type was not established in Istanbul until the eighteenth century, and even then it was not allowed to print the Koran or other religious books.[38]

In 1671 Virginia's longtime governor, Sir William Berkeley, thanked God for the absence of printing presses in his colony.†[39] Men of letters at the time were hardly petitioning God for their spread. In 1680 the philosopher and mathematician Gottfried Wilhelm von Leibniz suggested that a "fall back into barbarism" might result from "that horrible mass of books which keeps on growing."[40]

And then there is the case of Alexander Pope. Pope was the sort of cultured, clever intellectual who today would be expected to have little patience for television, except for the occasional PBS show. But Pope

written, undercuts Plato's formulation in interesting ways, as Jacques Derrida has noted.

* More recent scholarship has shown that the duke's library did in fact contain printed books.

† Berkeley was similarly grateful for the absence of free schools.

came of age in the early eighteenth century; the medium he had little patience for was print.

In 1728 Pope published a satirical epic, the *Dunciad,* in which he took swipes at many of the published writers of his time, whom he dismissed as "dunces." (The term, deriving from the name of the medieval scholastic philosopher John Duns Scotus, originally meant "hair splitter" or "pedant" more than "dullard.") Riots broke out as Pope's poem was sold: "A Crowd of Authors besieg'd the shop," a contemporary reported; "Entreaties, Advices, threats of Law, and Battery, nay Cries of Treason were all employ'd, to hinder the coming out of the *Dunciad.*"[41] The battles over this poem gained a name: the "War of the Dunces."

In the preface to a later edition of his epic, Pope (referring to himself in the third person) explained "the occasion and the cause which moved our poet to this particular work":

> He lived in those days, when (after Providence had permitted the invention of Printing as a scourge for the sins of the learned) Paper also became so cheap, and printers so numerous, that a deluge of Authors covered the land: Whereby not only the peace of the honest unwriting subject was daily molested, but unmerciful demands were made of his applause, yea of his money, by such as would neither earn the one, nor deserve the other.[42]

Pope's sortie against the products of the press was, typically, mounted in defense of the products of an older medium. Along with many of his fellow Augustans, he was outraged by those of his contemporaries who failed to realize they were unworthy of sharing bookshelves with such classical writers as Homer, Plato, Aristotle, Demosthenes, Virgil, Horace and Cicero.*[43] These works from the great age a millennium and a half or more before Gutenberg were, as one of Pope's fellow supporters of the "Ancients" protested, being "dispossessed of their Place and Room" by the deluge of awful printed works by "Moderns."[44]

Understanding why Pope was so desperate to repulse this particular threat is no easy task for us more than two and a half centuries later. Although some of the works his contemporaries published were indeed mediocre or worse, they were *books.* Nevertheless, Pope and the other Augustans saw great danger in them. "It is a melancholy thing," Joseph Addison wrote in the *Spectator* in 1714, "to consider that the Art of Printing, which might be the greatest Blessing to Mankind, should prove detrimental to us, and that it should be made use of to scatter Prejudice and Ignorance through a People."[45]

Before their descendants lined up against television, many gener-

* The *Dunciad* reserved much of its scorn for those pedants who presumed to correct the established texts of these classical authors.

ations of intellectuals joined this crusade against the press and its degradations. For example, as Leo Tolstoy was letting loose his philosophy on page 1441 of *War and Peace,* he maintained that the "most powerful of ignorance's weapons" is "the dissemination of printed matter."

Even in those days before the "couch potato," print's eminent critics did not lack a name for the new medium's victims: "Instead of Man Thinking, we have," Emerson muttered, "the bookworm"—"meek young men [who] grow up in libraries." Emerson feared that "original talent" was being "oppressed under the load of books."[46] The young Abraham Lincoln's neighbors reportedly thought he was lazy because he spent so many hours buried in his books. When Lincoln arrived in Congress his fellow congressmen, by one account, dismissed him as a "bookworm."[47] (Ah, to be labeled a bookworm today!)

As many of the perpetrators of contemporary television have demonstrated, those who work in an upstart medium are perfectly capable of expressing antipathy toward that medium. Plato's *Phaedrus* was written; Pope's *Dunciad* was printed; and Cervantes, the first great practitioner of what for us is among the most sublime of forms, was also the first great satiric critic of that form. The cause of Don Quixote's having "lost his wits" was his having "passed the nights in reading from sunset to sunrise." Cervantes describes his hero's reading matter as "books of knight-errantry"—in other words, chivalric fiction, early precursors of the novel.[48]

Novels have a secure place on the long list of amusements to which right-thinking folk have considered it unwise to have too much exposure. They offended by focusing on the particular, when the classical ideal had been to aim for the general and universal; they offended by inventing mundane plots and circumstances, instead of borrowing tested, distinguished plots and circumstances.[49] In 1778 the Reverend Vicessimus Knox, master of Tonbridge School in England, concluded: "If it be true, that the present age is more corrupt than the preceding, the great multiplication of Novels has probably contributed to its degeneracy.... The reserved graces of the chaste matron Truth pass unobserved amidst the gaudy and painted decorations of fiction."[50]

This last charge, beneath the flowery imagery, is similar to Neil Postman's major objection to television. The fact is that few of the criticisms directed against television are original. Is the "boob tube" overrun with "junk," with "pablum"? In the 1790s a book reviewer characterized contemporary fiction as "a horrible mass of hurtful insignificance." Has television, as occasional Democrats and many Republicans charge, contributed to a kind of moral decay? That was a widespread complaint against printed fiction in eighteenth-century England: "'Tis NOVEL most beguiles the Female Heart," George Colman declared in the prologue to his play *Polly Honeycombe* in 1760. "Miss reads—She melts—She sighs—Love steals upon her—And then— Alas, poor Girl!—good night, poor Honour!"[51]

Has television turned politics into show business? In the late eighteenth century, when newspaper reporters in England first began covering Parliament, one of its members fumed that politicians were being treated like "actors."[52] Has television chopped information into segments that are too short to allow "education or entertainment" to be "absorbed"? That was the accusation one newspaper leveled against "the present style in radio programs" in 1925, though the segments in question then were considerably longer: five minutes.[53] Indeed, a similar critique of "the constant diffusion of statements in snippets" was made against newspapers in 1889—the age of the telegraph.[54]

What about television's role in the reported explosion of youth violence in the 1960s, 1970s and 1980s? In 1948, when commercial television was just leaving the womb in the United States, a study in *Collier's* magazine warned that "juvenile crime is on the increase in almost every locality in this country" and pinned the blame squarely on the comic book. Its effect, the study concluded, "is definitely and completely harmful."[55]

My personal grievances against television turn out to be equally unoriginal. I find it, to begin with, devilishly addictive. When not doing research on television, I turn one on less often than the average American. In part this is because when I do turn on a television set, I have a great deal of difficulty turning it off: If I decide to take a peek at the evening news, for instance, too often I'll end up, six hours later, watching *Late Night with Conan O'Brien*. But didn't Don Quixote have a similar, though somewhat larger, problem with "books of knight-errantry"? They would keep him in their grip until dawn.

At the end of such long evenings with the tube I often find myself—and this is my major complaint—feeling empty and dull. Television seems to deplete, rather than replenish, my store of creative energy. But a similar charge was leveled against newspapers more than one hundred years ago: "The mental powers grow stagnant," complained an 1886 edition of *Lippincott's Monthly Magazine*. I do sometimes wonder if, after a few of these sessions, my brain hasn't turned into "a pulpy, spongy mass"—exactly the result that magazine attributed to reading newspapers.[56]

Even the language in which such attacks are phrased is sometimes the same. In nineteenth-century America, a critic stated that cheap novels, "offering neither savor nor nutriment," are "the chewing gum of literature."[57]

        &   &   &

Of course, the critiques collected here had many and varied inspirations: some intellectual, some political, some moral. Sometimes the irritant was the technology; sometimes it was the form, the style or the content. I don't mean to negate the distinctions among these critiques. I do mean to suggest that a larger nervous, nostalgic suspicion of the new may have been lurking behind the bulk of them.

It is also true that some, often many, celebrated each of the new arrivals mentioned here, just as some, not many, have welcomed television.* Not all new inventions are attacked quite so vehemently or pervasively as television has been, but just about all new inventions are attacked. In the nineteenth century, Harvard anatomy professor Oliver Wendell Holmes even took a satiric poke at the new stethoscope. It had, he worried, the potential for misleading doctors into inaccurate diagnoses.[58]

> * Celebratory statements will receive their due in subsequent chapters.

Usually those on the attack have a point. Maine and Texas probably did not burn up the telegraph wires with great ideas; pencils with erasers do make us a bit less careful; writing does reduce the exercise our memories receive; printing did unloose a barrage of mostly undistinguished literature.

There is truth, too, in most of our indictments of television. We have paid a price for our moving images, a steep price. Print is now in decline. The great culture it authored is fading. But every new invention, technique or art form exacts a price in old ways and old patterns of thought. In time, we are usually repaid.

Printing's payoff—like writing's—has been large indeed, but Cervantes, Leibnitz, Addison, Pope and Tolstoy—like King Thamus and Plato—could not see it. These great communications revolutions are never easy to comprehend, especially in their early stages. The evidence is too thin, our fears too great. By the time Bacon, in the forward ranks of the Moderns, noted that the printing press had changed "the whole face and state of things throughout the world," it had been around for more than a century and a half. Another century and a half passed before the press spread the ideas of the Enlightenment and helped make revolutions in America and France.

The size of the word's gifts may indeed be a measure of what we are losing with the rise of moving images. But if we get beyond our suspicions, we should also be able to view the size of the word's gifts as a measure of what this new way of communicating might bring.

Director Oliver Stone was a controversial figure as *Natural Born Killers*—a particularly intriguing collection of moving images—was released in 1994. Many still resented his reworkings of history in *JFK*, a film he had made a few years earlier. And this new movie was earning Stone new enemies. In its attempt to satirize tabloid culture, *Natural Born Killers* splattered a formidable amount of violence and other outrages on the screen; the film consequently offended many of those who shared Stone's professed revulsion with tabloid culture. The style of this film was an additional source of controversy: It jumped in and out of scenes, dreams, time frames, dramatic genres, musical styles, film speeds and even film stocks with disconcerting abruptness and speed. Many found *Natural Born Killers* too fast, too fidgety, too wild. "The chaos of the film was upsetting," Stone himself noted.[59]

This book will include no defense of *JFK*, no disquisition on the merits of screen violence (satiric or otherwise), but it will delve deeply into that apparent chaos. Indeed, it will find there many of video's potential gifts. In *Natural Born Killers* scenes sometimes bump up against each other: galloping horse, huge newspaper headline, demons, Las Vegas lights, homicidal couple in a convertible. In so doing, might scenes find new ways of commenting upon each other, as words—bumping up against each other on pages, in lists—once did? Might we learn to think more analytically about the relationships among scenes? In this film Stone allowed himself to cut suddenly to black and white or slow motion, to mix in a few frames of bloody premonition, a situation-comedy laugh track or a glimpse of animation. Might these constant variations in approach increase the range of variation in perspective? Might we become as efficient at stepping back from perspectives as we now are at stepping back from situations? In a song used on the sound track of *Natural Born Killers*, Leonard Cohen's low, hoarse voice announces that "the blizzard of the world has crossed the threshold." Might a film like this, with its gusts and swirls, provide us with new ways not only of conveying but of understanding that "blizzard"?

Under the heading of what I am calling video, others are beginning to hurl images at us at an even more rapid, more explosive rate. This book sees in that kinetic mass of images not the horror Leibniz saw in his era's "mass of books" but a new way to communicate, a new tool.

"Man is a tool-using Animal," wrote Thomas Carlyle in what might serve as an answer to the chorus of concern that greets each of our new inventions.

> Weak in himself, and of small stature, he stands on a basis, at most for the flattest-soled, of some half-square foot, insecurely enough; has to straddle out his legs, lest the very wind supplant him. Feeblest of bipeds! Three quintals are a crushing load for him; the steer of the meadow tosses him aloft, like a

waste rag. Nevertheless he can use Tools, can devise Tools: with these the granite mountain melts into light dust before him; he kneads glowing iron, as if it were soft paste; seas are his smooth highway, winds and fire his unwearying steeds. Nowhere do you find him without tools; without Tools he is nothing, with Tools he is all.[60]

Carlyle, writing almost four centuries after Gutenberg, understood the printing press as a tool, an extremely powerful tool. Now humankind is back in its workshop, fashioning—in its usual distracted, desultory, self-critical manner—a new tool. Stone and others are beginning to experiment with techniques that make it possible to objectify and rearrange scenes, as writing and print objectified and rearranged words. With the help of these techniques, video might enable this feeble biped to remake "the whole face and state of things throughout the world" yet again.

Imitation: a page from a handwritten book (with notes by a student), and a page from a 1497 printed book by Thomas Aquinas. Note the similarity between the handwriting and the typeface.

Imitation: Alexander Pope as a Roman (bust by Louis-François Roubiliac, 1741).

4

"Shrouded in the Traditional Form"

When Media Are Young

They are ill discoverers that think there is no land, when they can see nothing but sea.
—FRANCIS BACON, *1605*

Imitation: televised theater—the first installment of the live-drama anthology series *Studio One* on CBS, "The Storm," starring Margaret Sullivan and Dean Jagger (right).

electronic television was first demonstrated by Philo Farnsworth in San Francisco on September 7, 1927.* The first image he transmitted on his new system was a simple line. When this line on a slide in front of the camera was turned ninety degrees, the image on the screen also turned. "The damned thing works!" the twenty-one-year-old inventor and one of his partners telegraphed a third partner. A dollar sign was among the first two-dimensional images Farnsworth transmitted. "When are we going to see some dollars in this thing, Farnsworth?" an investor had asked. Another early moving image was equally uninspiring if not quite as perspicacious: the cloud of smoke billowing from a cigarette.[1]

Of course, television's inventors knew there would be much more to the medium than that. In 1925 C. Francis Jenkins, who was working on the earlier but less successful mechanical version of television, had predicted that "folks in California and in Maine, and all the way between, will be able to see the inauguration ceremonies of their President, in Washington; the Army and Navy football games; ...baseball; ...photoplays, the opera, and a direct vision of world activities."[2] Jenkins predicted, in other words, much of the content of what would be the first era of video.

That era can be said to have started when Farnsworth began transmitting a loop from a Mary Pickford/Douglas Fairbanks silent movie. In its first era video was used mostly to broadcast events or entertainments that existed before television: political events, sporting events, conversations, concerts, "photoplays"—all borrowed forms of programming. Indeed, that film loop, which Farnsworth transmitted over and over while he tried to improve picture quality, was a borrowing of a borrowing: a film of Shakespeare's play *The Taming of the Shrew*.[3]

The first era of video—the era of Philo Farnsworth and C. Francis Jenkins, of Tim Allen and Ted Koppel—is just now beginning to end.

One of the characteristics of the first era of any new form of commu-

* Different accounts of Farnsworth's experiments have been published with widely different dates. I have gone with David E. Fisher and Marshall Jon Fisher's recent version, which is based on new interviews, Farnsworth's lab notes and Elma Farnsworth's memoir.

nication is that those who live through it usually have no idea that that's what they are in. What little they're getting tends to be all they believe the medium capable of giving. During its first era, writing was used in Mesopotamia and Egypt to preserve records of business dealings, administrative transactions, prayers and the flooding of the Nile. Except for some manuals for training new scribes, that is all that would be written for five hundred years.* No creation myths, no legends, no epics were etched out on clay tablets during this period.[4]

Why not? Perhaps those with an investment in older forms of communication resisted, consciously or not, full use of the new one.†[5] Visionaries and reactionaries may have tussled some. However, the main explanation for the lengthy delay in exploring the religious and literary potential of the written word is probably both simpler and more powerful: The thought—a large, unfamiliar thought—did not occur to anyone, just as the thought did not occur to most of the early experimenters in radio that the transmitters and receivers they were experimenting with were anything but a means for one-to-one communication.

When he was beaming messages over hills in Italy in 1895, young Guglielmo Marconi thought he had perfected "wireless telegraphy." When, on Christmas Eve 1906, Reginald Fessenden succeeded in replacing dots and dashes with a voice reading from the Gospel of St. Luke, it was assumed that "wireless telephony" had arrived. Not until 1920 did it begin to become clear that radio's great potential was not, like the telegraph and telephone, in communication between individuals but in communication to masses—in *broad*casting.[6]

"One can invent and perfect discoveries that still have to... justify their existence," Bertolt Brecht noted, writing about radio. "Then this stripling who needed no certificate of competence to be born will have to start looking retrospectively for an object in life." With hindsight, it is usually easy to see the "object in life" of some new invention. At the time it is nearly impossible. As late as 1932, Brecht was convinced that radio's proper purpose was "two-sided," telegraph- and telephonelike communication.[7]

Sometimes people are aware that their inventions have yet to "justify their existence." This nagging feeling seems to have stayed with the makers of personal computers from the start, as they have attempted to determine what—beyond processing words, managing data, manipulating spreadsheets and sending electronic mail—might be done with the undeniable power of microprocessors. However, when a new invention performs an important function well, it is not easy to conceive of it doing something more important even better. Writing was a great success as a record keeper. Why worry about literature?

* In *A History of Reading,* Alberto Manguel declared that much of the magic of writing sprang to life "with a single act—the incision of a figure on a clay tablet." It was not that simple.

† Brian Winston, in his study of more recent technologies, made much of this explanation. He dubbed it "the law of the suppression of radical potential."

Television is great at showing us football games, dramas and people chatting. Few, at present, expect it to contribute much that is original to art or thought.

New forms of communication, in other words, do not arrive with user's manuals. Instead, generations stumble and struggle—usually against conventional wisdom—to divine how best to exploit the strength of that new form. And it is when a medium is young and its users are stumbling that that medium is most vulnerable to attack.

The Egyptian god Thoth's own written *oeuvre,* the myths tell us, consisted of records of the seasons and the stars, letters written on behalf of the gods, records of judgments on the dead, perhaps the entire Book of the Dead (charms for use in the afterworld) and something entitled the Book of Thoth, which, according to one papyrus account, consisted of two pages of magic spells kept in a golden box, surrounded by snakes and scorpions, beneath the Nile.*[8] Thoth was clearly no Thucydides, no Cicero. No one in ancient Egypt was. This god could argue that writing was a "recipe for...wisdom," but what examples (assuming, as Plato assumes, he had in mind something beyond magic) could he point to? They did not yet exist. The point is, Thoth had a hard sell not only because his invention was new and therefore suspect but also because it was still undeveloped.

The role of critic of a new invention—King Thamus's role, Plato's role—appears easier. Critics score points by comparing the new arrival with the already perfected methods it threatens. It would, for example, be some years before doctors became as adept with the stethoscope as they were with their hands and naked ears.

"The best of the past," the historian Elizabeth Eisenstein has stated, "is set against the worst of the present."[9] But it is more than that: Mature techniques developed in the past are set against an immature technique under development in the present. The prose history written by Herodotus—among the world's first—is not the coherent achievement that the *Iliad* and *Odyssey* are. But as the classicist William Chase Greene suggested, "His work comes still rather early in the growing and experimental movement of historical writing, while the Homeric poems come at the climax and virtually at the end of the period of epic poetry."[10] This is, more or less, what Plato saw: experiments in writing attempting to compete with mature products of the oral tradition.

And the time required for a new technique to mature is always much longer than its critics or users imagine. All forms of communication start out slowly—usually very slowly. Consider the mechanics of writing: Classical Greece produced awkward papyrus scrolls, not

* Another version of the myth claims a longer, more ambitious version of the Book of Thoth; still we are not talking analytic prose.

easy-to-open, easy-to-peruse books. Imperial Rome eventually collected its thoughts in parchment books, but most still did not have chapters, lower-case letters, punctuation or even spaces between words.
They were intended, like a musical score, to be read out loud, syllable
by syllable. Silent reading, and the textual conveniences that helped
make it possible, did not begin to appear in Europe until the Middle
Ages.[11] Writing, therefore, meant something very different to Plato
than it does to us—in form as well as content. Might this help explain
why he found it wanting?

Print did not arrive fully grown on the scene, either. Early printed
books were still rather difficult to read. Their content, too, took a long
time to develop. The press had been around for more than two centuries when Leibniz denounced it in 1680. It hardly seemed a new
invention. Nevertheless, most of the great intellectual achievements to
which printing would contribute still had not appeared. Two printed
works that would later stir Leibniz himself, Isaac Newton's *Principia
Mathematica* and John Locke's *Essay Concerning Human Understanding,*
had not yet been published in 1680; they had not yet had a chance to
distinguish with their presence what Leibniz was then dismissing as
"that horrible mass of books."

When the Reverend Knox attacked the novel in 1778, more than
170 years after *Don Quixote,* few novels of lasting value had yet been
written. Knox agonized that a student would not study Homer, Livy or
Virgil "while he can read *Pamela* and *Tom Jones,* and a thousand infe-
rior and more dangerous novels."[12] That students would one day have
the opportunity to read and study *Emma, Madame Bovary, Crime and
Punishment, War and Peace* and *Remembrance of Things Past* was, of
course, well beyond Knox's imagining.

It is similarly difficult for us to see beyond this first era of video.

But hasn't everything speeded up? Shouldn't the development of
moving images be much further along now than writing and print
were at comparable points in their history? I'm not so sure.*[13] Yes,
technology races on. Nevertheless, despite our crowds of pundits and
scholars, new ideas don't seem to arrive that much faster now than
they did in Plato's Greece. Paradigms don't seem to shift that much
more quickly than they did during the Renaissance or the
Enlightenment. I don't think it is so easy to dismiss the lessons of history. I see no signs that the art of television, which is half a century old
now, has been maturing all that quickly. To the contrary.

As the commercial begins, a mustached, gentle-voiced man wearing an
apron and a bow tie is fondling an artichoke and discoursing on its
nature. Five seconds pass. The camera stays with him. The viewer's

* Sven Birkerts
had fewer
doubts. For the
transition
between print
and "electron-
ic" culture, he
wrote, "fifty
years, I'm sure,
will suffice."

remote-control finger begins to itch. "This is a fresh one, of course." Seven seconds, eight seconds. "They also come frozen, frozen artichoke hearts...."

But then, just when viewers are about to zap this fellow, the screen explodes with frantic, often fuzzy images of tumbling, dancing, screaming young people—thirteen different shots, none longer than a second. Flitting in and out between them are the words "Be Young. Have Fun. Drink Pepsi."

This commercial, completed in 1993 by the BBDO agency, is ostensibly about the virtues of youth versus age: Pepsi was fawning over the members of yet another new generation in an attempt to get its flavored corn syrup into their digestive systems. But the commercial has another meaning. The cascade of images with which it concludes makes use (to no great end, alas) of some of the newest, freshest techniques in video—techniques also found in sections of *Natural Born Killers* and that ABC News introduction. The static image of the cooking show with which the commercial begins, on the other hand, is a caricature of the first era of video, a caricature of television.

The word *television* combines a prefix of Greek origin, meaning "far off," with another form of the Latin verb for "seeing." The word may be linguistically illegitimate, but semantically it is perfect, for the great miracle of television has been its "far seeing." "It extends man's range of vision," a book aptly stated in 1942.[14]

Various television systems were demonstrated in Britain and the United States in the decades leading up to the World War II. In 1925 some officials in Washington could actually make out a film of a windmill slowing down and then turning backward on C. Francis Jenkins's mechanical "radio vision." Two months earlier John Logie Baird had showed off a similar mechanical system at a London department store. By 1930 Baird and the BBC were televising a play. In 1939 the opening of the New York World's Fair was televised by NBC to fewer than a thousand sets, using the more effective electronic system on which Philo Farnsworth had been working. A baseball game was televised later that year.[15] "Already," a book on this infant medium enthused in 1940, "television is fully equipped to present news events, games, athletic contests, drama, in a word anything that can be presented to the eye."[16]

The development of television was slowed by World War II, then began to race forward. Six television stations remained on the air through the war, broadcasting sporadically to about seven thousand receivers by war's end. By 1950 the United States had 104 television stations broadcasting regularly to more than ten million receivers. Viewers tuned in to watch comedian Milton Berle perform, to see

Lucille Ball's baby debut on *I Love Lucy* and, on the opening program of Edward R. Murrow's *See It Now,* to view concurrent shots of the Brooklyn Bridge and the Golden Gate Bridge. They were invited by early NBC newscaster John Cameron Swayze to go "hopscotching the world."

This huge audience, which quickly grew larger than that gathered for any other form of communication, soon saw the goings-on at party conventions; it saw accused assassin Lee Harvey Oswald being shot; it watched a man setting foot on the moon, a space shuttle exploding and Germans dancing atop the Berlin Wall. This audience has seen the world's top actors, musicians, comedians, conversationalists, athletes. It has seen the prettiest sights, the prettiest people.

Just about everything eventually appears on TV: a president resigning, American bombs landing, the police beating a black suspect, one of the century's most sensational murder trials. New cable networks and videotaped pornography have removed what shreds of clothing remained as an obstacle to the television audience's all-seeing eyes. Every evening this audience sees further than most of those who lived before television saw in a lifetime. Sports fans have seen what they always wanted to see: the game from up close, the coach's press conference, the champagne celebration. Citizens have seen their leaders debating, joking, answering charges of corruption, sweating, lying. Even food lovers have been treated to the precious sight of the cleverest (if not always the best) chefs in the process of preparing food—an artichoke, perhaps.

There is only one sight this audience has not seen much of during this first era of video: original uses of moving images.

When they are young, stumbling and struggling through their first stages, all media imitate, slavishly. Their inventors need a model, so their inventors borrow a model.* Photographers, for instance, tried to make their work look like paintings, even going so far in the early days as to soften their focus, use textured paper or dab on something that might give the appearance of a brush stroke.[17] "The art of the photographer, as now explained, is to make his photographs look as much like something they are not as he can," the artist Joseph Pennell stated in 1897. "The man who sells margarine for butter, and chalk and water for milk, does much the same."[18] Imitation doubtless can be helpful: Painting at least gave the early photographers somewhere to start.[19] In a more recent example of mimicry, the personal computer seems to have benefited from use of the "desktop metaphor," from the pretense, in other words, that the screen is covered with files, scissors and other familiar office objects.†

* Marshall McLuhan noted that the content of any new medium is the medium that came before.

† E-mail, too,
☞

makes use of an
obvious
metaphor;
Windows is a
less predictable
borrowing.

However, such "metaphors" or models inevitably end up imposing limitations upon a developing form of communication. The personal computer had to begin to escape what has never been called the "typewriter metaphor" before it could become more "user-friendly." It may soon have to escape the desktop metaphor as well. Writing had to stop trying to look like little images. Photography had to find artistic purposes of its own.

The home video camera—or camcorder—is the latest example of a technology lost in imitation. Much boring videotape of silent, waving children has been produced by parents unable to see beyond what might be called the "still-camera metaphor." "Men discover new instruments," the painter and photographer László Moholy-Nagy wrote in the 1920s. "Often, however, it is a long time before the innovation is properly utilised; it is hampered by the old; the new function is shrouded in the traditional form."[20]

The early history of printing in Europe provides the best example of the limitations imposed by imitation. It is, therefore, an instructive history for anyone who anticipates the lifting of the shroud that has covered video.

The earliest printed books look so much like handwritten manuscripts that laymen often have difficulty telling them apart.[21] Scribes had left room in the books they copied for large initial letters to be added by a "rubricator." Artists often illuminated the pages of these handwritten manuscripts with elaborate, colorful designs. Not to be outdone, the early printers also hired rubricators to add initial letters to their books and artists to illuminate them—even though those designs might have to be painted by hand on hundreds of copies.[22]

Handwritten manuscripts featured dense, complex, swirling lettering, with different styles used in different regions and for different categories of books. The early print shops went out of their way to reproduce in type these idiosyncratic, difficult-to-decipher "black letters." Handwritten letters were often joined together, and early printers duplicated these ligatures as well. Scribes had reduced their burden by using numerous abbreviations: an *a* with a line on top, for example, might mean *an*. Early printers increased their burden by cutting extra type to reproduce each of these abbreviations.

Was this an attempt to deceive readers, to "pass off" printed books as manuscripts? Lucien Febvre and Henri-Jean Martin, the authors of the foremost history of the book, scoffed at that suggestion. It would have been both difficult to fool fifteenth-century eyes and pointless to try. Early printers imitated scribes primarily because they had no choice. "How could they have imagined a printed book other than in the form of the manuscripts on which they were in fact modelled?"

Febvre and Martin asked.

A new book eventually did debut, a book designed to be read more than appreciated for its beauty, a book that was reader-friendly, not scribe-friendly. But it took time. It was well into the sixteenth century before Europeans could expect to see a book with illustrations printed by woodcuts, without ligatures and abbreviations, with a legible type-face (Roman),* with Arabic numerals on each page and with indexes and tables of contents.[23] Even more time passed before the content of these books stopped imitating that of the old handwritten manu-scripts.

The presses began by putting into print the accumulated store of handwritten manuscripts. Of the books printed in Europe by 1500, Febvre and Martin calculated that 77 percent were in Latin, and of the rest many, probably most, were translations from Latin. Cicero's works appeared in 316 printed editions before 1500.

Renaissance Europe, of course, was inspired and transformed by the rediscovery of classical authors such as Cicero. But it is also true that during and after the Renaissance, Europe had great difficulty see-ing beyond those classical authors. Battles over the canon at the University of Paris in 1503, for example, centered on whether students were spending too little time reading Cato (dead for 1,652 years) because they were spending so much time reading Aristotle (dead for 1,825 years). And in the sixteenth century, Febvre and Martin explained, the proportion of reprinted works by classical authors actu-ally grew.[24] In 1583 Oxford University had a statute decreeing "that Bachelors and Masters who did not follow Aristotle faithfully were liable to a fine of five shillings for every point of divergence."[25]

Five generations had had an opportunity to work with the print-ing press by the year 1600 and perhaps two hundred million books had been printed, yet still there was little in the content of these books that would have surprised a medieval monk. The two forms that would do the most for printing—the novel and the newspaper—were still in gestation. (*Don Quixote* appeared in 1605;† the oldest surviving print-ed weekly news pamphlets are from 1609, in Strasbourg and Wolfenbüttel.[26])

"Hee knowes most who knows as much as the ancients taught us," concluded Sir William Temple, a seventeenth-century English diplo-mat and man of letters.[27] Ancient forms and authors maintained their grip on European printing well into the eighteenth century. There is no better way to demonstrate that than to pay another visit to Alexander Pope. Pope's *Dunciad,* typically, was modeled after Virgil's *Aeneid.* Pope also frequently applied himself to "imitation" (his word) of Horace.[28] The great crisis of their age, concluded Pope and other dis-

* The develop-ment of Roman type is also instructive: It was copied from a script that itself attempted to imitate the handwriting used in classical manuscripts.

† Some would count earlier prose romances in Europe and elsewhere as novels; some would not count *Don Quixote.* My point is not much affected by this dispute. Perhaps the novel had an even longer infancy; per-haps it was

☞

even longer in
the womb.
Either way it
was quite slow
in developing.

tinguished acolytes of the Ancients, remained an insufficient respect for and fidelity to such models. The Moderns, with their interest in such relatively new pursuits as analytic science, textual analysis or the novel, "wrote and floundered on," Pope sneered:

> *But, high above, more solid Learning shone,*
> *The Classics of an Age that heard of none.*[29]

In about 1740 the sculptor L.-F. Roubiliac produced a marble bust of Pope with an inscription in Latin from Horace. Pope is portrayed as having short curls, which he seems not to have worn, and a strong chin, which he seems not to have possessed.[30] He is draped in a toga. This sickly English poet looks almost as Roman as a Caesar. Such impersonations undoubtedly were useful for many eighteenth-century intellectuals. The model was powerful, the alternatives still unimpressive. That is why imitation dies so hard, why the first era of print lasted so long.* The road to the future, however, lay elsewhere.

* Baudelaire
was still bat-
tling neoclassi-
cism in the
nineteenth
century.

Television, it is often said, imitated radio. It is true that TV, which was launched in the United States and many other countries by radio companies, initially borrowed most of its programs from radio: situation comedies, variety shows, dramas. But these forms of programming had themselves been borrowed, just a couple of decades earlier, from theater, the music hall, burlesque. Even the term *program* represents such a borrowing.[31] And television hardly limited its appropriations to the radio: It filled its screen with conversations, sporting events and concerts. It took from literature, from newspapers and magazines, even from board games and, always, from film. "A televised drama today," wrote the film and stage designer Robert Edmond Jones in 1940, "looks rather remarkably like a talking picture seen in little."[32] It still does. No medium has cribbed as shamelessly, impersonated as freely, as television.

Indeed, serious-minded people have respected television most when it is imitating most vigorously, just as Alexander Pope and friends respected the press most when it was reprinting Cicero. In the first days of commercial television, Moss Hart tried to excite a group of his fellow writers with the potential of this new medium. "Think of it," he said, "with one twist of the dial, you can bring great drama, music, ballet, education, poetry, everything in the arts, right into everybody's living room!"[33] This is how we have continued to look at television: as a bringer of old arts, not as a creator of its own.† In 1996 when the writer Reynolds Price took a turn chastising television in a commentary on National Public Radio, his complaint was that it does not dramatize enough great American novels.[34]

† In 1942 Lee
De Forest, best
known as an
inventor of
radio, suggest-
ed that there

☞

The era that is universally praised as television's "Golden Age" was the era, significantly, when the imitation was purest. In 1952 an NBC script editor wrote of the need for "the television artist-playwrights to appear."[35] They did. Paddy Chayefsky, Rod Serling, Reginald Rose, Gore Vidal and many others wrote dramas for TV that were performed live on such shows as the *Kraft Television Theatre* and *Studio One*. Fourteen such live drama anthology series were on the air during the 1955-56 television season.[36] Critics raved. Television, the master mime, had transformed itself into a Broadway theater on opening night.

As a feat of mimicry, this ranked with the illuminated, black-letter printed book, and in the end these shows represented an equally ineffective use of a new medium. By 1960 only one of these anthology series remained.[37] Television would continue to imitate plays, but viewers preferred dramas or comedies that, while perhaps less tony, at least had the virtue of sustaining a familiar set of characters week after week.

Even this variation from the established model—a drama that returned for months or years—threw critics for a loop. "After the first show, I don't know what to say," moaned TV critic John Crosby in 1958, "and I don't know anybody else who does either."[38] Critics respect originality—within limits. The safest, surest place to look for quality is always in the familiar, the accepted. Fill a printed book with sentences from old handwritten manuscripts; if you want to please contemporary critics, fill a television screen with a serious concert, conversation or drama.

That is why many continue to pine after television's lost Golden Age, as Pope pined after the days when all honored the "solid Learning [that] shone" in the classics. "NBC Opera...is long gone," lamented Lawrence Grossman, a former president of both PBS and NBC News. "The fine arts and serious public affairs have all but disappeared from commercial television, and the ideal of a 'best seat in the house' for all is dead."[39]

That is why, when television's harsher critics admit that there might occasionally be something worth watching, their example is usually a show that makes the least possible use of the medium. Neil Postman, for example, named three television shows that proved themselves as a "carrier of coherent language or thought": *Firing Line, Meet the Press* and *Open Mind*—all, essentially, televised conversations.[40] Our critics, in other words, call for more imitation and then worry because the medium seems able to produce only that, only margarine.

Printing was known as the art that *preserved* all the other arts.[41] It

could be no "more fitting theme for a weekly half-hour of television than a quiet parade through some famous art gallery, pausing a moment before each masterpiece."

did this well; that is true. But printing turned out to be much more than a preserver, a more reliable version of writing. It also circulated, popularized, accumulated, regularized, systematized and exorcised many of humankind's demons; printing eventually helped invent new forms of art. Now we have accepted a view of video as the art that *presents* all the other arts. It is equally limiting.

Ours has been a century, of course, in which artists have celebrated the new, even made a fetish out of it.[42] Upon occasion the artistically minded have found themselves surprised and delighted by varieties of moving images. Their insights have been important. (Many are quoted in this book.) But lovers of the new are always ready to drop it in favor of the apparently newer. In the end they may have as much difficulty focusing on larger, slower changes—such as a communications revolution—as do traditionalists. The art world has discovered video (in a mostly minimalist, painting- or sculpturelike form). But not even the art world is currently celebrating the potential of video as a new means of communication. Confidence in our time in the original contributions that might be made by the communications medium of our time remains remarkably rare.

"People are thinking less than they used to," no less a technology buff than Apple cofounder Steve Jobs has asserted. "It's primarily because of television." Confronted with the vast potential of moving images, Jobs and most of the rest of us past MTV age are doing exactly what most of our ancestors, confronted with the printing press, did: We are looking back with an aching nostalgia to, in Pope's words, "happier days."[43] We are looking forward fearfully, with visions of decline and decay. In this first era of video, most of us over the age of thirty-five—avant-garde or not, technologically inclined or not—are on the side of the Ancients. "[Things] are getting worse!" Jobs exclaimed. "Everybody knows they're getting worse!"[44]

The Moderns have not even recognized themselves yet. The computer and the Internet (their screens still filled mostly with words) have their fanciers. Television certainly has enough users and even some fans, but there is still no school of thought that celebrates video, no ideology of hope for the moving image. Instead, even as they grasp the remote control, most thumbs continue to turn down. The moment, the era—as usual—belongs to King Thamus.

It is true that television's gifts to date have been small. Even film, for all its power and beauty, has produced little that ranks with the grander products of writing or print. It is difficult to come up with any television show or film that might be studied for the strength of its original ideas in the same way as might a book by Plato or Darwin. Nor are there that many collections of moving images that—like a play by Shakespeare, a book by Flaubert or Tolstoy—might be said to form a challenging, original and triumphant work, a transcendent work. Orson Welles's *Citizen Kane* would certainly be on the list of possible candidates. But Welles himself once said, "I really can't make a comparison between a moviemaker and Shakespeare. No movie that will ever be made is worthy of being discussed in the same breath."[45]

I suspect some readers have been frustrated by the absence in these early chapters of a clear example of the wondrous new form of communication I have been heralding—just one trailblazing, mind-altering, astoundingly brilliant fast-cut film or television show. I fear those readers may be frustrated by the absence of such an example in chapters to come, too. I will have much to say (mostly in the book's third part) about new, original video techniques and their potential contributions to art and thought, and I will present numerous examples, some quite impressive, of those techniques in action. But I have no example of their being fully utilized, of that potential being fully realized.

Welles, whether or not he is right about his fellow moviemakers, seems too eager to dismiss the work of their successors. I am hopeful that we might have future Shakespeares, future Flauberts working in these new forms of video. (In the book's final chapters I will sketch out a vision of the new art, the new philosophies with which they might present us.) But it hasn't happened yet. It may not happen for a while. The *Madame Bovary* of video—which will most decidedly *not* imitate the techniques or ideas of *Madame Bovary*—has yet to be produced.

With such an example locked away in the future, the case for video's ability to open new vistas must rest on the less definitive, harder-to-read evidence available in the present and the past. The historical analogies I have relied upon in these first chapters have their limitations. The fact that writing did, as Thoth predicted, turn out to be "a recipe...for wisdom" does not guarantee that similar predictions for video will also come true. The fact that other new inventions, techniques and art forms were attacked yet proved themselves does not guarantee that video will prove itself. The fact that other new forms of communication were lost in imitation during their long youths does not guarantee that video can or should stop imitating. The fact that the first two great communications revolutions took centuries to produce great work does not guarantee that video will eventually produce great work—that video will ever produce a *Madame Bovary* that is not like *Madame Bovary*.

Still, these historical comparisons should alert us to the possibility, even the likelihood, that we have judged video too soon and by the wrong standards. They should encourage us to take another look at the moving image and to do our best, based on the evidence that is available to us, to look beyond our suspicion. All this, plus a little imagination, will be necessary if we are to accomplish the difficult trick, Thoth's trick, of envisioning the potential of a form of communication before that potential has been realized.

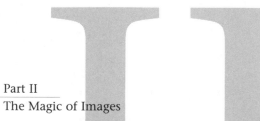

Part II
The Magic of Images

She quivered as she blew back the tissue paper from each engraving...those pictures of every corner of the world.
—Gustave Flaubert, *Madame Bovary*

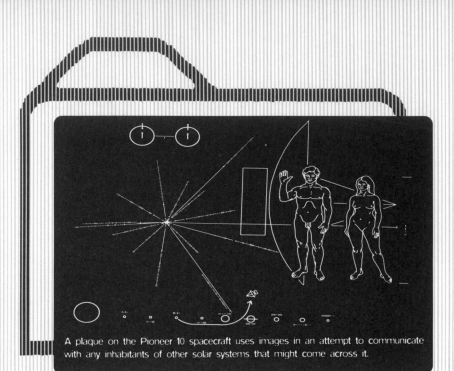

A plaque on the Pioneer 10 spacecraft uses images in an attempt to communicate with any inhabitants of other solar systems that might come across it.

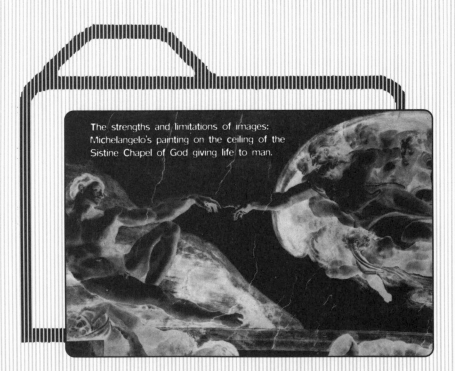

The strengths and limitations of images: Michelangelo's painting on the ceiling of the Sistine Chapel of God giving life to man.

An image intended to take the place of words: the danger symbol from the discussion of the "Star Wars" defense system in MTV's *Decade*.

CHAPTER FIVE

"by means of the visible"
a picture's worth

Pictures worth a whole sentence? Apple Computer's file-folder icons.

ask the creators of the wilder, more interesting-looking new television commercials, promotional announcements, news videos and even feature films where they found their inspiration, and their answer, more often than not, will contain the same three letters. Director Oliver Stone, when citing the antecedents of the jangled, fast-cut style he used in the movie *Natural Born Killers,* mentioned "commercials and MTV."[1] Don Schneider is senior creative director of the BBDO advertising agency, which has produced some groundbreaking Pepsi commercials, including that attack on the artichoke chef and the old TV. He made a more sweeping confession: "Ninety percent of this has to do with MTV."[2] ABC News took more than ideas from MTV: It hired one of the youth network's talented young producers, David Berrent.

MTV's influence begins, of course, with the music videos themselves—which "might be the only new popular art form in American life," Norman Mailer has suggested.[3] But many of the network's innovations appeared as more substantive supplements to those dizzying collages of guitar strummers and visual metaphors for lust. ABC wooed Berrent after executives saw his documentary *Decade,* a historical look, MTV-style, at the 1980s.

Decade includes a thirty-three-second segment on former President Ronald Reagan's planned "Star Wars" defense system. I make no claims for it journalistically, but in technique and style it is intriguing. An excerpt from a Reagan speech on national security is shown, along with an attack on Star Wars by the late rock musician Frank Zappa. These are sound-bites—the same (except for the use of Zappa as an expert) as might be seen in a traditional news story. But in between, Berrent placed a kind of rock video: While the phrase "guns in the sky" is sung over and over, and Zappa begins to talk, computer simulations of lasers attacking rockets are shown on screen. Those scenes, in turn, are interrupted by flashing, static images: a dollar sign, the symbol warning of possible nuclear contamination, the skull-and-crossbones symbol for danger.

Neither the word *danger* nor its synonyms is vocalized. Berrent clearly is relying on these flashing images not just to illustrate what is being said but to communicate their own meanings. In the introduction to that ABC documentary on churches, Roberta Goldberg, who learned from Berrent, does the same with the shot of three candles being extinguished. These images, the point is, are intended to take the place of words.

Many of the images that decorate our world have similar aspirations. Among the most interesting are the icons that increasingly crowd the edges of computer screens. Small drawings—of a file folder, for instance—first began to replace lines of text on computer displays at a research center run by the Xerox Corporation in the 1970s. The driving force behind this work was Alan Kay, a Ph.D. in computer science, whose dreams for the future of the computer, inspired in part by Marshall McLuhan, included a major role for images. Each icon used on the screen, Kay suspected, was worth not just a word but a whole sentence.[4]

A group of Apple Computer executives and engineers made an expedition to the Xerox center in 1979. They returned with many ideas and then added some of their own. In 1983 Apple released a slow, expensive, unsuccessful, "graphics-oriented" computer named Lisa and then, the next year, a faster, relatively inexpensive, hugely successful computer, using a similar operating system, named Macintosh. The indomitable Microsoft Corporation noticed the idea (Apple suggested, in court, a different verb), and with the success of the Windows operating system in 1990, sets of icons began to appear on most computer screens.[5]

Similar images currently express meanings on traffic signs, rest room doors, Olympic venues and biceps. Armies continue to march under images; the devout of many faiths continue to pray to them. The Pioneer 10 spacecraft, now embarked on a long journey toward the star Aldebaran, is equipped with a plaque designed to satisfy the curiosity of any aliens encountered along the way—a plaque covered not with words but with images (sketches of a naked man and woman, our solar system, the position of our sun, the hydrogen atom).[6]

Some meanings clearly are better communicated pictorially than verbally, as David Berrent, Alan Kay and most of the world's painters and sculptors have recognized. We live, however, in a culture that, despite the proliferation of images, not only has little faith in their ability but has at times been actively antagonistic toward them.

The Old Testament, characteristically, does not mince words: "Thou shalt not make unto thee any graven image, or any likeness of any thing that is in heaven above, or that is in the earth beneath"—a commandment second only to the demand that no other gods be worshiped before the source of these commandments. An antagonism toward images first appeared here at the beginning of Western culture. It appeared, too, after the development of the alphabet in Greece: Among Plato's targets in the *Republic* is the painter, whom he dismissed as "a magician and imitator." A similar scorn surfaced among Muslims: Muhammed is said to have proclaimed that "the angels will not enter a temple where there are images."[7]

This fury was unleashed, always, by partisans of the word—written or (for Plato) spoken. Behind it was a multifaceted fear: fear, to begin with, *for* the word. Images—easy to understand, fun to look at—inevitably threatened to turn the populace away from the deeper, more cerebral rewards of sacred writings or philosophic discourse.

There was fear too of the magic that seems to lurk in images. They steal likenesses. They do what only gods should be able to do: They recreate the living and preserve the dead. It is hard not to see this as black magic. Images allow us actually to look in on (not just hear about) the familiar from another perspective, an external perspective, often a disorienting perspective—to see ourselves, for example. They are, in this way, inherently unnatural—further evidence of magic.

Then there is the persistent "reality" issue. Images look real but are fake. They pretend to be what they are not. They lie. The portrait is a mute, lifeless substitute for the person; the idol, a primitive and superficial knockoff of the god. But that idol is also attractive and easy to see. It can distract from the more profound but more amorphous glories of the god. A painter, Plato warned, can deceive "children and fools" with mere "imitation of appearance," instead of "truth" or "real things."[8] Images can entrance.

Worse, in imitating "real things," images tend to devalue them. This is what the French theorist Jean Baudrillard called "the murderous capacity of images." Once we begin to lose ourselves in this world of illusions, it can begin to seem as if "truth" and "reality" are just further illusions (deserving of quotation marks). Images, on this level, are, as Baudrillard put it, "murderers of the real, murderers of their own model."[9] The person is now seen as if posing for a portrait. The god is perceived as if just another idol.

"Cursed be the man who makes a graven or molten image," the Old Testament proclaims. We have reconciled ourselves to painting and sculpture by now; nevertheless, echoes of that curse can still be heard in many of the jeremiads launched by television's critics—most of whom retain an almost biblical allegiance to the word. The fear behind that curse undoubtedly was also present in some of the admonitions I heard from my parents: "You've had that thing on all evening!" "You look like you're in some kind of trance!" I'm sure it is present too in some my children have heard from me.

For television also has been judged too easy to watch: not sufficiently challenging, cerebral or deep. It displays a similarly suspect magic: It too captures appearances. Television too is accused of being "unreal," of duping children and fools. And television too has seemed to make the world it portrays—the social and political world—less "real." It has helped fill it with "pseudo-events," to use Daniel Boorstin's often-repeated term. "The shadow has become the substance," Boorstin, with deference to Plato, warned.[10]

Here is a prejudice even Thoth did not face. Video is not only suspiciously new and immature; it is tainted by its reliance upon facile, shallow, unreal, cursed images.*[11]

* As James Reston put it, "All cameras tend to corrupt and television cameras corrupt absolutely."

Oddly, it was a group of thinkers not only steeped in biblical values but influenced by Platonic (or, more precisely, neo-Platonic) values who began to question this fear and scorn.[12] "We do no harm," Pope Gregory I wrote in a letter in 599, "in wishing to show the invisible by means of the visible." In the thirteenth century, Thomas Aquinas outlined an argument in support of "the institution of images in the Church."[13]

The power of the visible has been disparaged and then rediscovered many times since: with the development of painting in the Renaissance (including the use of perspective),[14] with the woodcut and the mechanical reproduction of illustrations, with the arrival of photography.†[15] Over the centuries, those prepared to defend images have produced various calculations of the comparative "worth" of pictures and words. They often seem silly. However, an investigation of the potential of video must begin by confronting the lingering prejudice against images and acknowledging that there *are* some things images do better than words.

† Wordsworth, one of the disparagers, labeled the use of photographs in newspapers and books "a dumb Art," "a backward movement... from manhood,—back to childhood," a "vile abuse!"

Images, to begin with, are marvelously (though never perfectly) accessible. Aquinas explained that the "unlettered" might learn from pictures "as if from books."[16] (Christians were not prepared to ignore the needs of the uneducated, of children or of fools.) We take advantage of the accessibility of images to aid those who may not understand a particular language—visitors to the Olympics, perhaps, or any space aliens who happen upon Pioneer 10.

Another strength of images is their concision—a significant advantage for drivers speeding by or on a crowded computer screen. A native American rock drawing found near a precipitous trail in New

Mexico, for example, shows a goat who is climbing but a man on a horse who has fallen.[17] It is difficult to imagine a sign made for the "lettered" that could communicate this warning more efficiently. David Berrent and the others who have begun flashing images on our screens are attempting to exploit this efficiency in their efforts to say a lot in a short time.

Images also can wield great power—religious, tribal, romantic, pedagogic. One of David Berrent's productions for ABC was a public-service announcement on behalf, of all things, of PLUS: Project Literacy U.S. In its thirty seconds, five or six fathers are shown reading to or reading with their children, with scenes from children's books and newspapers gently superimposed on top of them. The fathers explain why this activity is important, but the public-service announcement's power comes not from their words but from the images Berrent has placed before us—images of togetherness, of caring, of warmth.

Aquinas suggested that images can be used to "excite the emotions, which are more effectively aroused by things seen than by things heard."[18] That is why we find images in houses of worship, in military emblems and in tattoos, as well as in public-service announcements. "If the poet can kindle love in man, more so...the painter, as he can place the true image of the beloved before the lover," observed Leonardo da Vinci.[19]

There are also understandings, sometimes deep understandings, that can be put into images—accessibly, concisely, powerfully—but are difficult to put into words. The study of botany, zoology, anatomy, geography and astronomy were all advanced during or after the Renaissance by more precise depictions, models, representations and diagrams.[20] "Primates are visual animals," Stephen Jay Gould, the scientist and science writer, has asserted, "and we think best in pictorial or geometric terms. Words are an evolutionary afterthought."[21]

Bill McKibben was appearing on TV. This was an event akin to the Unabomber going on-line or Ralph Nader driving a Porsche. For McKibben, a distinguished environmental writer, had just published an ardent attack on television: a book, *The Age of Missing Information*, based on his experience in watching every program that had appeared on a ninety-three-channel Virginia cable television system during one twenty-four-hour period. McKibben wrote of his concern not only with what TV offers but with what it does not offer: highs, lows, perspective, consciousness of the body, an awareness of death, of the seasons, of nature and of what happens "behind a face." "We use TV as we use tranquilizers," he concluded.[22] But now here McKibben was on the *Charlie Rose Show,* himself part of the dose.

Among those savoring the irony was the *New Republic*'s Robert Wright, who admitted that McKibben looked more "earnest and thoughtful" than he had expected from reading reviews of his book. "TV has won for his cause one small battle that his book alone couldn't have won," Wright observed, "both because I don't have time to read it and because it is missing some kinds of information. (Some very 'natural' kinds of information, like how a person looks when saying what he believes. The written word, we sometimes forget, was invented as a crude if useful substitute for the real thing.)"[23]

That last thought is worth freeing from parentheses. No one, as Wright noted, has been earnest enough to read through, say, all the publications to be found one day on one newsstand (an exercise likely as dispiriting as McKibben's). But we can still come to some conclusions about what the printed word lacks.

Writing's great limitation grows out of its great strength: its abstractness. It is a system of representation, or code, that represents another system of representation, another code: spoken language.[24] The written word *face*—to oversimplify a bit—calls to mind the sound "fās." It is, therefore, two steps removed from that expressive skin sculpture itself.* These steps back needed to be taken and have been hugely productive. Still, it is important to keep in mind the price paid for that abstraction. Printed words may take us, metaphorically at least, "behind a face"; they can help us see what we might not ordinarily see in a face; but they must work hard to tell us what a glance could about the expression on that face. In interpreting the code we make little use of our natural ability to observe: letters don't smile warmly or look intently.

This code, writing, also ignores our ability to find spatial and temporal connections between objects in the world. When we speak with each other, we can point: "That belongs over there." We can demonstrate: "Then she did this with her hair." We can indicate: "You want to give them control over this?" And we can gesture—with a look, a shrug, a grimace. All this information could alternatively be put into words; it could be written down. But in reading it, rather than seeing it, we sacrifice our ability to quickly and intuitively spot relationships—between here and there, this and that, words and gestures, ideas and expressions. We sacrifice our ability to judge earnestness and thoughtfulness, say, by observing people's faces as they speak.

Comparing what he saw on those ninety-three channels to what his senses can pick up in nature or at a circus, McKibben moaned that we are "starved on television's visual Pritikin regimen."[25] This is a point I am anxious to debate. But for the moment it is sufficient to

* I am aware of the philosophical critiques that have been launched against such attempts to measure distance from "reality"; however, I don't think they threaten the rather simple point I am making here.

note that, if the measure is *direct* stimulation to our senses, a page of print makes a few moments of television look like a five-course French meal.

Printed prose is "an act of extraordinary stylization, of remarkable, expressive self-denial," stated Richard A. Lanham, who writes on Renaissance rhetoric and contemporary computers.[26] Our eyes were selected over millions of years of primate evolution for their ability to notice, search, compare, connect and evaluate. Increasingly, in the five thousand years since the development of writing, they have been reduced to staring at letters of identical size and color, arranged in lines of identical length, on pages of identical size and color. Readers, in a sense, are no longer asked to *see;* they are simply asked to interpret the code.

Written words, as Aquinas realized but we tend to forget, are hardly a perfect form of communication. No such thing exists. I don't want to overstate the case for images—at least still images—either. Certainly, as the Bible seems to suggest, but for centuries most Europeans tended to forget, nonmoving images have great difficulty conveying certain kinds of meanings. There are limits to what the Dutch humanist Erasmus called their eloquence.[27]

Alan Kay ended up dissatisfied with his experiments in the use of images on computer screens. He had understood, from having read educational theory, that icons were good at helping people "recognize, compare, configure." The success of the Macintosh and Windows operating systems has proven that his understanding was correct. But Kay had a grander ambition: He dreamed of using images to express abstract thought. Kay envisioned a kind of language of images.[28]

That is an old dream. It was long surmised that the mysterious hieroglyphs that could be seen on the Egyptian obelisks that had been dragged to Rome represented such a language of images. "The wise of Egypt...left aside...words and sentences," wrote Plotinus, the third-century neo-Platonist, "and drew pictures instead."[29] As late as the eighteenth century, the historian Vico assumed that "all the first nations spoke in hieroglyphs."[30]

Behind this notion was the belief, still held by many today, that nature is a "book" with a divine author.[31] If each tree, each ox, has a spiritual message for us, then that message might also be "read" in paintings or even iconic representations of trees or oxen. An image language would be closer to that original divine language. Over the centuries many Europeans attempted to craft such a language.* They produced various occult codes, systems of gestures, systems of concepts, guides to memory and tools for international understanding.[32]

* The seventeenth-century Jesuit scholar Athanasius Kircher is an example.

These various image languages all had something in common: To the extent that they tried to communicate meaning effectively without depending on words, they failed. The conviction that the Egyptians had succeeded in this also crumbled. In 1799 one of Napoleon's soldiers in Egypt happened upon an old stone that included an inscription written both in Egyptian hieroglyphic and in Greek. With the "Rosetta stone" Europe finally was able to piece together accurate translations of those mysterious Egyptian writings, and it became clear that not even hieroglyphic had escaped the dominance of language. Instead, like all other successful writing systems, these icons were directly connected to words: For example, they made heavy use, as in King Narmer's name, of phonetic indicators, of homonyms.[33]

Alan Kay's efforts to produce abstract thought from systems of icons on the computer screen failed, too. "All I can say," Kay wrote, "is that we and others came up with many interesting approaches over the years but none have successfully crossed the threshold to the end user." The problem: "In most iconic languages it is much easier to write the patterns than it is to read them," Kay explained.[34]

Here, for example, is the series of hand signals one Renaissance experimenter, the Abbé de l'Epée, used in his language of gestures to indicate the concept "I believe":

> I begin by making the sign of the first person singular, pointing the index finger of my right hand towards my chest. I then put my finger on my forehead, on the concave part in which is supposed to reside my spirit, that is to say, my capacity for thought, and I make the sign for *yes*. I then make the same sign on that part of the body which, usually, is considered as the seat of what is called the heart in its spiritual sense.... I then make the same sign *yes* on my mouth while moving my lips.... Finally, I place my hand on my eyes, and, making the sign for *no,* show that I do not see.

All that is quite clever, even poetic. It must have been great fun to devise but almost impossible for "end users"—those who were watching the abbé's energetic performance—to decipher. That undoubtedly explains why at the conclusion of his elaborate pantomime de l'Epée felt called upon to add one more action: "All I need to do," he stated, "is...to write *I believe.*"[35]

If images cannot form languages without a reliance upon words, it is in part because they have a great deal of difficulty escaping the affirmative, the past or present indicative.[36] De l'Epée was able at least to shake his head to put something in the negative; in some traffic signs we use a red diagonal line to say the same thing; but most still pictures must strain to say something as simple as "no" or to ask "why?" or to wonder what might be. They state much more effectively than they negate or interrogate or speculate. Pictures are better, similarly, with the concrete than the abstract, better with the particular than the general. These are significant handicaps.[37]

The other great obstacle to images forming a language of their own stems not from their muteness but from the fact that they tend to say too much. For example, Michelangelo's awe-inspiring depiction at the summit of the Sistine Chapel of God giving life to man through the touch of his finger also can be seen as showing a father-son relationship and perhaps a lover-beloved relationship; it can be seen as showing caring, effort, joy, and undoubtedly numerous other emotions. This richness of meaning is testament to the artist's genius. But if we did not receive some verbal explanation, how could we be expected to "read" this scene as we might read a piece of writing?

Knowing the genre helps. The location of this great fresco tells us that we should search for a religious interpretation in it.[38] But which one? The older man could be saving the younger man; he could be calling him to heaven; he could be giving or taking his soul. To know for sure, we must be directed to a story, to Genesis. Were this scene asked to serve as part of a language without the aid of such a story, how could we pinpoint specific meanings in it?[39] "The image is freedom, words are prison," wrote the film director Jean-Luc Godard, never one to shy from controversy, in 1980. "How are laws decreed today? They are written. When your passport is stamped 'entry to Russia forbidden,' it is not done with an image."*[40] True, but neither the Bill of Rights nor the Declaration of the Rights of Man was composed in images either. The freedom images provide comes at a price.

"The ability of a visual language to express more than one meaning at once," contended Umberto Eco, "is also...its limitation." Eco, whose academic speciality is semiotics, the study of systems of signs, called this excess of meaning "the fatal polysemy of...images."[41] Aquinas recognized the problem: "One thing may have similitude to many," he wrote. "For instance the lion may mean the Lord because of one similitude and the Devil because of another."[42] How can we develop a lexicon of images if we have no way of determining which of the many possible interpretations of an image is correct? (The perplexing graphics that are supposed to explain to speakers of different languages how to operate European appliances provide another example of this problem.)

To use images more precisely without captions, explanations or instructions—without words—it is necessary to rely on the most obvious of images, on clichés: a skull and crossbones, for instance, or a father snuggled up with a book and a child. France's expert on semiotics, Roland Barthes, gave the example of the use of a bookcase in the background of a photograph to show that a person is an intellectual.[43] As a result, as images that try to convey meaning without the use of words become less ambiguous, they also become less interesting, less challenging, and vice versa.

"I don't want there to be three or four thousand possiblities of interpreting my canvas," Pablo Picasso once insisted. "I want there to be only one."[44] However, the artist in his more thoughtful moments undoubtedly realized what anyone who has stood before one of his canvases has likely realized: That is impossible.

Words also can say too much, of course. *Man, woman* or *god,* for example, have no shortage of potential meanings. Dictionaries contain lists of them; occasionally we concoct our own. Writers can never be sure that their words have only one possible interpretation. As our literary theorists have spent a third of a century pointing out, readers bring different experiences and interests to the sentences they read and therefore take different meanings from them.

While working on this book, I reread *Madame Bovary* and, wouldn't you know, began to uncover in Flaubert's novel a series of lessons about images and words. Did he intend for me to read his book this way? Probably not. Nonetheless, Flaubert's problem with me and probably most of his other readers is much less acute than that faced by the authors of potential image languages. With the help (alas) of a translator I was able to get the gist of Flaubert's words. I followed his narrative. I was not so preoccupied with my own concerns that I missed the fact that he had many things to say that are not communications-related.*

Our strategies for reading words are fairly well understood. We can, at least, make use of those dictionaries, with their limited lists of meanings. And the problem of comprehending words is further eased, if never entirely eliminated, by syntax. Using a grammar, the basic structure of which seems built into our genes, we modify the form of our words to signify their relation to their fellows in sentences. And then we narrow their potential meanings further by surrounding them not only with various qualifiers but with prepositions and articles. There are few equivalents for such parts of speech in the realm of the image.

In spoken and written languages, word builds upon word, sentence upon sentence, idea upon idea. The ambiguity of images, on the other hand, is increased by what Alan Kay called their "unsortedness." Painters may have mastered some tricks for guiding our eyes across

*Contemporary literary theorists might question in a number of interesting ways my attempt to elude the ambiguities of language here.

canvases. But we are not born with, nor have we created, any particularly sophisticated systems for organizing still images to specify or build meanings. "Unlike paragraphs and lists of words, images have no *a priori* order in which they should be understood," Kay noted. "This means that someone coming onto an image from the outside has no strategy for solving it."[45]

This chapter might be helped by a depiction of Thomas Aquinas, Bill McKibben or Alan Kay. It would be useful actually to see how the Abbé de l'Epée looked when he made "the sign of the first person singular." But such concepts as "efficiency," "abstract thought" or "by means of the visible" would be difficult to communicate through still images. And how might an argument composed of such images be organized? Left to right? Up and down? In a kind of circle? Unless, following de l'Epée's lead, such pictures were appended to a written version of the chapter itself, an observer would not know what "strategy" to employ in understanding them.

David Berrent and others of the most interesting workers in video— MTV alumni or MTV watchers—aim a barrage of images at us. Those images can do some things better than words; once we move beyond the scorn and the fears of word lovers, that becomes clear. Certain pictures can put most sentences to shame. But this is as far as I'm willing to go in making the case for still images.

The truth is that I am not one of those folks who spend an inordinate amount of time staring at dew-covered fields, wizened faces, cloud formations, or paintings thereof. It took some decades, and the guidance of a photographer friend, before I learned to notice light, not just the things upon which it shines. I'm good for a few hours in major museums, not a few days. Which is to say that while this is a book that gets rather excited about the potential of image communication, it is not based on a particularly romantic view of images or our visual sense in general.

Some continue to argue that pictures are more honest and profound than words, that they can claim some direct, mystical path to a higher reality. You won't find that argument here. In fact, I've tried to make clear in this chapter that still images operate under severe handicaps when attempting to embody ideas. For certain important purposes, a picture may actually be worth *less* than a single, relatively narrow, well-placed word. I agree with Umberto Eco that some of the most complex uses of images must "still depend (parasitically) on the semantic universe of the verbal language."[46] This, perhaps, is the true "curse" upon those who attempt to communicate through such images, graven or otherwise.

However, Eco did allow for one possible exception to his rule about the limitations of images—an exception even someone who won't pull the car over to gape at a sunset can accept: Eco suggested, with some reservations, that "the images of cinema and television" might escape those limitations.[47]

There is a sense in which David Berrent and his colleagues and successors in video seem better positioned than Michelangelo, Picasso and computer guru Alan Kay might have been to communicate abstract thought unambiguously through images—for motion, sound and computer editing have indeed begun to solve the image's intelligibility problems. And at MTV speeds, in ten or fifteen minutes it is now possible to present *a thousand pictures*.

An anarchic energy: two characters from the film *Trainspotting* (played by Ewan McGregor and Ewan Bremner) running away after committing a robbery.

"Hyperedited": a "cut-up" image from *Buzz*, directed by Mark Pellington and Jon Klein, 1988.

Two shots from Eadweard Muybridge's revelatory and disturbing attempts to photograph horses in motion.

6 "FAST SEEING"

Photographic Reality

> The man that invented the machine for taking likenesses might have known *that* would never succeed; it's a deal too honest.
>
> —Charles Dickens, *Oliver Twist*

nitially, the editing on MTV was not consistently fast. When it premiered in 1981, the music videos the cable network presented sometimes lingered almost as long over their microphone-fondling rock stars as TV news reports lingered over then President Ronald Reagan. Just how different MTV might be in style as well as subject matter took some years to discover.

Mark Pellington, one of the discoverers, now flies back and forth between New York and Hollywood, directing commercials, music videos and public-television programs. His first feature film, *Going All the Way,* was released in 1997. Pellington, the son of a star linebacker for the Baltimore Colts, had majored in rhetoric at the University of Virginia. In 1984 his love of rock music inspired him to wrangle an internship at MTV.

Pellington worked his way up to production assistant (main responsibility: lugging tapes) and began playing around in MTV's editing rooms: "Oh, what does this button do?"[1] In 1985 he made his first video: a promotional announcement for the network.

MTV promos at the time, as Pellington recalled, generally confined themselves to showing some rock star saying, "Hi. I'm so-and-so and you're watching MTV." Pellington's promo, however, was a rapid-fire collage of images.

TVs were on all day at work. He had been reading William Burroughs. He was in his early twenties and in New York. The downtown club and drug scene was flourishing. "The world I was living in was getting faster and faster," Pellington explained. "I was reflecting that. I started cutting fast." Then-MTV president Robert Pittman was put off by the tone and pace of Pellington's promo. Judy McGrath, who is now president of the MTV networks, understood. "This is what MTV is," Pellington remembered her explaining.

It is, at least, what MTV became. The network's promos stopped featuring rock stars. Music video directors took notice. (Fast cutting, of course, meshes smoothly with rock's fast beat.) Pellington directed some of the most interesting rock videos himself. Advertising agencies took notice. A new generation of MTV production assistants, including David Berrent, who would go on to spread the gospel at ABC News, took notice.

How fast was Pellington cutting? "As many as four shots in a second," he recalled. People volunteered that such short images could only be experienced "subliminally." Pellington disagreed: "I said I could read each shot." Another of Pellington's innovations was throwing words, with his trademark rapidity, up on screen, where they seemed to gain an odd, poetic resonance. This technique, too, began showing up on many of the rapidly growing number of television networks.

Pellington, like most experimenters in television, had never studied film or television. He called MTV his "graduate school." In that case his dissertation was a thirteen-part series directed with Jon Klein in 1988 called *Buzz*. It remains the MTV production most likely to be screened at exhibitions of video art and one of the most interesting experiments in the new kind of video anticipated in this book.

Buzz certainly does not shy away from difficult ideas. (The problem of how to communicate abstract thought through images may not have been entirely solved here, but progress clearly has been made.) Among the subjects of *Buzz*'s often quick, sometimes dreamy, usually ironic collages are racism, censorship, militarism, and the aesthetics of "sampling" or found art (as in rap music and some of Pellington's own videos).2

This last topic is covered—*probed* might be a more accurate verb—in a segment three and a third minutes long. It features, to the beat of a rap song, quotes from musicians and artists (sometimes echoed in words on screen), and a multitude of images—some abstract, many by or of artists (including William Burroughs). Sometimes these images are superimposed; sometimes they are chopped into strips so that one picture peeks through from behind another. They appear at a rate of up to five images a second.

To what extent Pellington and Klein succeeded in harnessing this new form in *Buzz* is open to debate: Is the Burroughs-like randomness to which they at times aspire in fact the most interesting use of these video "cutups"? Might the images and the length of their appearances on screen have been more effectively controlled? Might the idea-to-minute ratio have been higher? The form itself clearly tests a director's ability to juggle and a viewer's ability to concentrate.

However, one point must be made: With the exception of some early film experiments, which will be discussed in the following chapters, nothing in the history of human communication looks like *Buzz*

or its "hyperedited" cousins.[3] Pellington and his fellow explorers have
come upon something new—new as the novel was once new.

The oldest member of the family of nineteenth- and twentieth-century inventions that led to video is photography. This is where the rise
of the image—by which we mean predominately the photographic
image—began. The medium that video, particularly the type of video
seen in Pellington's *Buzz*, most resembles, aesthetically and philosophically, is also photography. Much of the aesthetic and philosophical turmoil that is being caused by video is presaged in the history of
photography, particularly its participation in and challenge to realism.
Therefore, an effort to get a handle on our superficial media, charac-
terless yuppies, shallow youth and unreal politics can begin with the
frozen photographic instant.

It had always been possible to view a fairly exact copy of a scene—
in a pool of water, in a nearby eye, in a mirror and, as early as the fifth
century B.C., with the camera obscura (a "dark room" or box with a
pinhole or lens that allows in the inverted image of a well-lit object
outside).[4] And then, of course, there was the work of painters.
Photography, however, was a new kind of magic: a method, seemingly independent of the hand of an artist, of *preserving* the image of a
scene. The physician, essayist and photography buff Oliver Wendell
Holmes characterized it as a "mirror with a memory."[5]

By the beginning of the nineteenth century, Thomas Wedgwood,
son of the famous British potter, was able to grab an image on a paper
sensitized with silver nitrate, but it quickly faded; he wasn't able to
"fix" the picture. By 1827 a Frenchman, Joseph Nicéphone Niépce,
managed to capture and preserve images on metal plates. Niépce called
the process heliography ("sun writing"). The sun wrote slowly and
unclearly for Niépce, however. The plate, covered with an uneven coat-
ing of the chemical bitumen, had to be exposed in a camera obscura
for many hours or days. In the meantime shadows moved.[6]

In 1829 Niépce gained a partner, the painter Louis-Jacques-Mandé
Daguerre. By 1837, four years after Niépce's death, a combination of
enterprise and happy accident led Daguerre to a clearer, quicker
method of fixing images on coated metal plates using silver iodide—
the renowned daguerreotype.[7]

This invention, typically, produced a philosophical as well as technological excitement. "The daguerreotype is not merely an instrument
which serves to draw nature," Daguerre proclaimed to potential
investors the next year. "[It] gives her the power to reproduce herself."[8]
The English scientist William Henry Fox Talbot, who first preserved such
images on paper, described them as having been "impressed by Nature's
hand." His book on the process is entitled *The Pencil of Nature*.[9]

The exact rendering of nature was the aim in these decades of more than just photography ("light writing" or "drawing"). The nineteenth century saw many such attempts to turn away from human artiface, hypocracy and delusion, such as the early realism, or naturalism, of Gustave Flaubert's *Madame Bovary,* published in 1857.*[10] However, among these attempts photography had a special place. For here, remarkably, were images that seemed incapable of getting things wrong.

* While he produced a kind of realism, Flaubert, a partisan of Art, was hardly ready to have his work summed up by his contemporaries' conception of realism.

Writers had been able to describe a landscape. But no writer, no matter how skilled and no matter how committed to realism, could produce a representation of a landscape—or a room or a face—as completely and exactly as a photograph. This was a major new development in the ancient competition between images and words. Nature, after all, has never been persuaded to pick up a pencil and "reproduce herself" in words.

Photography was, in part, an early form of "far seeing": "Now, for an absurdly small sum, we may become familiar not only with every famous locality in the world," a columnist gushed in an English weekly in 1861, "but also with almost every man of note in Europe....We have...sat at the councils of the mighty, grown familiar with kings, emperors and queens, prima donnas, pets of the ballet, and 'well graced actors.'"† But photography was not just a way to see farther; it was a way to see more *clearly*. It enabled people to stare, as that columnist put it, "through a three-inch lens at every single pomp and vanity of this wicked but beautiful world."[11] In other words, the "pencil of nature" also served as what an awed Holmes called in 1859 "a pencil of fire"[12]—capable of exposing, of burning away, unnatural things like "pomp and vanity."

† This view of photography was stated by Henry Luce in 1936 in the prospectus for *Life* magazine: "To see life; to see the world; to eyewitness great events; to see strange things...is now the will and new expectancy of half mankind."

Of course, not everyone was impressed with this rite of purification. The poet Charles Baudelaire, positioning himself on King Thamus's side, put forward this assessment in 1859:

> The present-day *Credo* of the sophisticated...is this: 'I believe in Nature, and I believe only in Nature.... I believe that Art is, and cannot be other than, the exact reproduction of Nature.'...A revengeful God has given ear to the prayers of this multitude. Daguerre was his Messiah.[13]

Many post-Romantics, in Baudelaire's century and the next, did indeed worship Daguerre's device and its successors: "You cannot claim to have really seen something until you have photographed it," declared Émile Zola, amateur photographer and paragon of naturalism, in 1901.[14] A few decades later the professional photographer and exponent of modernism Edward Weston saw the camera—"an honest medium"—igniting a great bonfire of dishonesties, pomposities and vanities: "False fronts to buildings, false standards in morals, sub-terfuge and mummery of all kinds, must be, will be scrapped."[15]

Madame Bovary represents, in part, an effort to look behind the "false fronts" of bourgeois French society. For example, while pointing out the volumes of the *Dictionary of the Medical Sciences* on inept medical man Charles Bovary's shelves, Flaubert made sure to inform the reader that their pages are uncut.[16] This novelist saw himself, in the words of a letter he wrote at the time, as an artist "who digs and burrows into the truth as deeply as he can."[17] He was continually looking behind, peeking inside, exposing pretenses. Profound hypocrisies, intractable boredom, combustive yearnings and repeated adulteries appear where a staid, respectable French town had seemed to be.

Flaubert also revealed other writings to be false: the novels whose accounts of love affairs infect Emma Bovary with the notion that "noblemen were all brave as lions, gentle as lambs [and] incredibly virtuous"; the newspaper article that described a fireworks exhibition as "a brilliant display" that "illuminated the heavens," when in fact, as Flaubert told us, "now and then some pathetic little Roman candle would go off." Emma and one of her future lovers agree that they prefer writing that features "noble characters and pure affections and happy scenes."[18] Flaubert, however, insisted on demonstrating that such characters, affections and scenes are dangerous romantic confections.

Photography is mentioned only one time in this novel: Charles Bovary contemplates presenting his wife, Emma, with a daguerreotype of himself. As usual, he entirely misreads her. Emma loves images. In this image-hungry age, she is capable of losing herself in a lampshade with pictures of tightrope dancers painted on it. But a keepsake of the husband she despises clearly would have no interest for her. A daguerreotype would be an inappropriate gift for an additional reason—and this is my point, presumably not Flaubert's: Emma "quivered" when perusing engravings of such subjects as "a young man in a short cloak clasp[ing] in his arms a girl in a white dress."[19] Some nine-teenth-century photographers certainly tried to arrange shots that might make romantics quiver. However, a weak chin or a cold eye would often intrude. Even if Charles donned a short cloak, a photograph of him, like the book *Madame Bovary* itself, would likely have been too "realistic" for Emma's tastes.

The camera's revelations initially were confined to less emotionally charged matters than those of Flaubert's novel—the way a horse moves, for example. A question had arisen: Was it possible that all four of a horse's feet are sometimes, somehow off the ground at the same time? This question fascinated California railroad magnate, politician and racehorse owner Leland Stanford. The eye was incapable of making such determinations at trotting, let alone galloping speed. Could the camera? In 1872 Stanford hired Eadweard Muybridge, a long-bearded San Francisco nature photographer, to find out.[20]

It was no simple task. The cameras in use at the time were too slow for Stanford's prize trotter to appear as anything but a blur. However, by inventing new shutter designs and positioning a series of cameras along a track, Muybridge was eventually able to solve the mystery: Yes, at one point in both a trot and a gallop all four of a horse's feet are off the ground.[21] And the position of those feet sure looked odd.

Flaubert was tried for obscenity and blasphemy after his novel was published. (The prosecutor made an analogy between his book and "realistic," "lascivious paintings.")[22] What was Muybridge's reward for maintaining that, as a critic put it, "a horse trots part of the time and 'flies' the rest"? He was sometimes grouped with what a Philadephia photography magazine in 1878 called those "photographic quacks vending their nostrums, deceiving the credulous, and defrauding the ignorant."[23] And one of his photos was analyzed for signs of fraud with an industriousness that would have suited a Kennedy-assassination buff: the jockey wasn't leaning far enough forward, his sleeve wasn't wrinkled, the horse's legs weren't the correct length.[24]

For Muybridge's photographs posed not only a challenge to common sense but to a way of looking at the world. Generations of painters had portrayed horses in midgallop with front legs reaching out and rear legs pushing off, together, in a simple, efficient, coordinated motion, like a hand opening and closing. It was a romantic image. Now Muybridge was demonstrating that it was no more accurate than a view of bourgeois French wives as docile, asexual and content. The horse's legs in a gallop and a trot instead formed an irregular and complex pattern. "The strange attitudes assumed by each animal excited much comment and surprise," noted the *San Francisco Chronicle* in an 1878 article on Muybridge's photos, "so different were they from those pictures representing our famous trotters at their full stride."[25]

"Strange" may be the most significant word here. Muybridge's photographs, with their scientific aspirations, were not typical of this art form, but I believe they point to something inherent in this art form. I believe they demonstrate that the camera's revelations would have implications at least as disturbing as Flaubert's, implications that would in fact disturb Flaubert.

"I've read everything there is to read," a preadulterous Madame Bovary moans to herself. As a result, "she sat," Flaubert explained, "holding the fire tongs in the fire till they glowed red, or watching the falling of the rain."[26] This is one of many circumstances described in this book that seem dated. While we certainly have not eradicated boredom, most of us have telephones to dial, automobiles to escape in, and televisions—not just books, fires and rain—to stare at. Our world, a century and a half later, is in numerous ways not Emma Bovary's world. The logic to which Flaubert's novel subscribes, however, seems considerably more current.

Madame Bovary presents its view of the real in a story. False feelings, "false standards in morals," are exposed over time. Actions follow each other as words follow each other on the page, one at a time: "They dismounted. Rodolphe tethered the horses. [Emma] walked ahead of him on the moss between the cart tracks."[27] Novels are certainly capable of switching point of view, digressing, flashing back, eliding or expanding time, but they never escape time. They have beginnings, middles and ends.

The narrative, of course, is hardly an invention of the novel. Humans likely have been telling each other stories just about as long as they have been telling each other anything. And spoken words, too, proceed in time—one word after another. However, when we speak, our words are usually surrounded by a three-dimensional swarm of expressions, gestures, inflections and sensory impressions. And when we tell each other stories, we are much less likely to stick to a straight narrative line; time often gets tangled. In oral epics, for example, ends hover over beginnings; plots present themselves more than unfold. As it developed in the nineteenth century, the line of type—expressionless, undemonstrative, unilluminated, colorless, silent, nontactile, odor-free—encouraged a particularly linear conception of narrative and time.*

* All of us who attempt to grapple with print's linearity owe a debt to Marshall McLuhan.

Flaubert repeatedly exposed the clumsiness with which his characters move through time: Their ceremonies are ruined by "dawdling," by "not knowing whether to begin the proceedings or wait a while longer." When they do finally act, it is often with a very unsystematic kind of "locomotive frenzy." None of them, save the moneylending merchant Lheureux and Emma's "brutal and shrewd" lover Rodolphe, can foresee what ends will follow from their beginnings.[28] Emma, Charles and the others don't see the lines that might be drawn from actions to results, from causes to effects. Their grand plans, therefore, repeatedly lead to disasters. *Madame Bovary* is, by this reading, a tragedy of individuals who violate not only the laws of society and of the gods, but the laws of the printed page.

Print enforces a certain kind of logic: one-thing-at-a-time, one-thing-leads-directly-to-another logic, if/then, cause/effect—the logic most of us have internalized. Emma Bovary reads romantic novels (novels that are themselves, Flaubert seemed to be saying, unworthy of print); *consequently* she is filled with unrealistic desires. Emma Bovary is a romantic in an unromantic world; *consequently* she is ruined. The reality we perceive—the reality realism and naturalism aimed to uncover—is to a large extent a product of such sequences of consequences, such stories.

Print's worldview long ago spread to other forms of communication. The last couple of hundred years of plays, conversations and even songs reflect, to a greater or lesser degree, the triumph of this logic, this line-of-type linearity, this novel-like sense of unfolding narrative. Things proceed that way most of the time on *Home Improvement* and *Nightline,* too.

However, it proved difficult to locate this reality in a photograph.

One of the liabilities of having come of age in the late 1960s is a weakness for quoting Bob Dylan. "Someone showed me a picture and I just laughed," the bard jeered in a relatively recent song. "Dignity's never been photographed." Many would disagree. Some people—usually people with lived-in, unlifted faces—do manage the trick of projecting dignity in photographs; some photographers manage the trick of capturing it. But Dylan may have been on to something. Certain long-rooted matters of character—decency, greed, altruism and malevolence may be better examples than dignity—do seem to give photographers trouble. Integrity and virtue, both of which seem less discussed now than they once were, also belong on that list. And a particular view of reality often seems to have escaped being photographed, too.

The camera, for all its claims to objectivity, sees some things better than others. An obscure French writer, Charles-François Tiphaigne de la Roche, produced the first account of what photography might subtract from our view of the world—about half a century *before* its invention. In his utopian novel *Giphantie,* written in 1760, Tiphaigne de la Roche imagined a machine through which "nature,...with a sure and never-erring hand, draws upon our canvases." De la Roche understood the magic, if not the chemistry: "The mirror shows the objects exactly; but keeps none; our canvases show them with the same exactness, and retain them all." He also understood that this might be a suspect magic: For those canvases, Tiphaigne de la Roche wrote, "deceive the eye and make reason to doubt, whether, what are called real objects, are not phantoms." These images, he seemed to sense, precisely because they are "painted with such truth," would cause us to question what is true.[29]

This is the great irony of photography: The realer images become, the less real reality seems. Photographic images are, in this sense (Baudrillard's sense), the most "murderous" of images. And this begins to explain why integrity and virtue, which depend on a fairly secure notion of what is real and true, are threatened by photography. Can a phantom have character (or dignity, for that matter)?

Oliver Wendell Holmes, who had the advantage of actually having seen photographs, suggested that they enable us to "hunt all curious, beautiful, grand objects...for their *skins,* and leave the carcasses as of little worth." "We have got the fruit of creation now," Holmes added, "and need not trouble ourselves with the core."[30] Integrity and virtue appear to reside nearer the "core" than the "skin." When someone proposed to Franz Kafka that a new machine that could take multiple photographs was "a mechanical *Know-Thyself,*" he responded, "You mean to say...*Mistake-Thyself....* Photography concentrates one's eyes on the superficial."[31] Character runs deep.

Another explanation for the relative scarcity of integrity and related qualities in photographs is that they are not needed there. Matters of character are crucial to print. Flaubert had to convince us that a living, breathing person has been created out of a collection of printed words. That is a formidable task. Anything capable of indicating that person's nature is useful. Qualities such as decency and altruism, or greed and malevolence, help sustain literary creations. Yes, we know Rodolphe's type—he's "brutal and shrewd."[32] And if Rodolphe doesn't stay recognizably brutal and shrewd, a convincing explanation for the change had better be presented. Characters in books must be reasonably consistent to be believable.

Photographs, however, have little need for such devices. The person in a photograph already seems lifelike. A face is before us in all its complexity. Characterizations of that person's "nature" begin to seem extraneous, forced, phony, banal. Once we escape the province of narrative, the idea that we must each possess a single, determinable, consistent character begins to seem foolish and restrictive.

Charles Dickens published *Oliver Twist* in 1837, the year of Daguerre's first successful experiments. This novel is chockablock with easily discerned character: decency (Mr. Brownlow), greed (Fagan), integrity and virtue (young Oliver himself is an outstanding example). Almost everyone displays a consistent character, in most cases either altruistic or malevolent. These qualities are revealed through the flow of events, demonstrated over time. Daguerre's invention rips moments out of time. We are virtuous for what we have done or not done. Integrity is an achievement, the result of struggle, in Oliver's case perhaps the result of *destiny.* Photographs—lacking beginnings, middles and ends—have difficulty embodying destiny, struggle or any other doings or not-doings.*

* There are

Many paintings have managed to illustrate or even tell stories. Photographs are more likely to subvert stories. The odd moments they represent—so often awkward, even goofy—seem to insist that our narratives and explanations have stopped. It is possible to look stylish or sexy in a photograph, easy to look silly. It is more difficult to show integrity.

In fact, it is hard, for all of us who have been trapped in a snapshot, not to look a little strange. Susan Sontag suggested that photographs are inherently "surreal."[33] If reality is assumed to be composed of cores, not skins, if it is seen as the subject of stories, if we identify it with the meanings found in lines of type, then this is true. Photographs, as a rule, do not show that reality.

An ominous sentence appears in the middle of *Madame Bovary*: "Quite apart, outside the arena, a hundred yards off, was a big black bull with a strap harness and an iron ring through its nose, motionless as a brazen image."[34] I'll suggest (without presuming that Flaubert would join me in the suggestion) that the photograph is that bull—standing apart, motionless, with all the terrifying power of the graven or brazen image, and then some.

For photos provided our initial glimpse of the instant—another first in human communication. It was a shock, a shock from which we have not yet recovered.

Eadweard Muybridge had a talent for scandal. His photographic investigations of the gait of horses had been interrupted in 1874 when he was jailed and tried for murder. Muybridge had shot his wife's lover. (The homicide was judged justifiable, and he was acquitted.) Horses were eventually replaced as subjects in his studies of motion by dogs, deer, lions and humans—with all the animals and most of the humans naked. His pictures of the latter were described by one angry patron in 1888 as "shocking to the moral sentiment, indecent and demoralizing."[35]

However, Muybridge's greatest outrage may have been his participation in the scandal of photography itself—particularly through those initial illusion-shattering shots of racehorses. "The result," concluded a publication called *Anthony's Bulletin* in September 1878, "is curious, if not elegant. All the grace and beauty of the animal's leaps...are eliminated, and the animal is seen in a series of grotesque positions."[36]

We are content to believe that the world is composed of a series of instants, but take those instants one by one, as photography was able to do, and a certain view of the world—a view of elegance, grace and beauty, of virtue, integrity and character—threatens to disappear. Yes, there are new beauties to be found in those instants, new realities. But

certainly exceptions to this rule: Joe Rosenthal's famous photo of marines raising the American flag on Iwo Jima comes to mind. But for every gripping news photo there are ten thousand desultory snapshots.

much must be surrendered on the way to them. "I detest photographs in proportion to my love of the originals," Flaubert wrote while working on *Madame Bovary*. "Never do I find them *true*."[37]

Virginia Woolf's novel *To the Lighthouse*, published in 1927, contains a scene—another dated scene—in which a woman simply sits in the same room with her distant husband and reads:

> And so reading she was ascending, she felt, on to the top, on to the summit. How satisfying! How restful! All the odds and ends of the day stuck to this magnet; her mind felt swept, felt clean. And then there it was, suddenly entire; she held it in her hands, beautiful and reasonable, clear and complete, the essence sucked out of life and held rounded here.[38]

It is precisely such "beautiful and reasonable" essences, such truths "held" by printed words, that are threatened by that brazenly "motionless" bull: the photograph.

Samuel Morse's telegraph was first successfully demonstrated in 1844. It is often credited with having introduced a new speed to human life. The telephone, radio and then television brought information and entertainment into our homes at variants of this speed.

However, there is another kind of quickness that is missing even from the dots and dashes of the telegraph but is inherent in the photograph. No matter how long we contemplate a photo, the instant that it encapsulates never lengthens. "Fast seeing," the modernist Alvin Langdon Coburn dubbed still photography in 1918.[39] Most film and television has lingered much longer over scenes; it allowed narrative back in. But videos like Mark Pellington's *Buzz* are composed of photolike instants. They have this revelatory, narrative-challenging, character-debunking, seemingly illogical, unvirtuous, graceless, surreal quickness.

The disruptions caused by the arrival of the photograph—all of them—will be felt once again with fast-cut, fast-seeing video.

Friends advised me that the brash, grimy British film *Trainspotting* might support my points about fast cutting and narrative. For a time after the film opened in New York in 1996 I resisted seeing it: As I've grown older, my interest in young junkies, even young Scottish junkies, has diminished, no matter how sharp and of-the-moment their alienation. But I saw the film, which was directed by Danny Boyle, and, as predicted, I saw something in the film.

Trainspotting is not *Buzz:* This movie, after all, is based upon a novel (by Irvine Welsh) that tells a story. In this case, alongside the disturbing depictions of squalid rooms and shared needles, the novel presents the not unfamilar tale of a "self-analytical" young man struggling to leave his "mates" behind and haul himself out of a dead-end life.[40] But while the book sticks to its narrative and is written in scenes, the film sometimes doesn't and isn't. In fact, like quite a few artistically ambitious, contemporary films, it manages to demonstrate many of the capabilities I ascribe to new forms of video.

In exploring characters' motivations and private thoughts, *Trainspotting* the film is much less enterprising than *Trainspotting* the novel. (The film's protagonist exhibits little that might pass for self-analysis.) But the film undertakes impressive inspections of the social worlds through which these characters stumble (in, for example, quick tours of their various sexual mishaps or of the many antidrug sermons they endure); it veers into the surreal in order to present their nightmares (a dead baby crawling across the ceiling, a trip into and through a filthy toilet bowl); and the film often fills the screen with an anarchic energy that the book, despite all its hip dialect and sordid details, struggles to convey.

Boyle's film accomplishes much of this by sometimes (not nearly as often or as vigorously as Mark Pellington does in *Buzz*) chopping situations into snapshotlike slices. Consider the film's opening minute and a half (always a good place to look for interesting technique): To the well-muscled but distracted beat of Iggy Pop's "Lust for Life," the main character's voice begins to harangue us, archly: "Choose life. Choose a job. Choose a career. Choose a family. Choose a fuckin' big television." What we see on-screen are a series of images—of that character and his buddies dashing from the scene of a robbery, chasing a soccer ball, experiencing a drug rush; a series of quick, sometimes frozen images; images dancing, brazen as could be, to this music; images that fit no possible conception of such a middle-class, adult life. The novel never quite manages to establish what might be called the antilife position with such force.

In due time, *Trainspotting* the film comes around to rejecting heroin rather forcefully as an alternative to life. But its cynicism never flags. It acknowledges no virtue, no dignity, little integrity. (Our hero makes his escape by cheating two of his friends.) It locates no grace or beauty, no essences. It places little faith in junk-free reality. It never quite buys into the logic of career-family-big television. The film's scandalous, electric instants in some sense won't let it. This film's real star—perhaps the great TV and motion-picture star of the coming era—is that nose-pierced, motionless bull, the subversive photographic instant.

One of the first devices for projecting moving pictures: Henry Renno Heyl's "phasmatrope," which in 1870 made a series of images of a waltzing couple (below), each posed separately, appear to move. (Heyl himself is the male dancer.)

(below) Developing new kinds of cinematic motion: three shots from D.W. Griffith's 1908 film, The Greaser's Gauntlet — a long shot showing an incriminating bandanna being discovered on the film's hero, José, while the guilty waiter (left) and the heroine, Mildred (right), watch; a long shot showing José and Mildred under a hanging tree as the men who were about to lynch him walk away; a "cut-in" to the couple talking under that tree.

In a moving image, what should do the moving? The traditional answer: the McGuire Sisters dancing in a 1959 Coca-Cola commercial.

Three shots from the video collage (produced with a design company called Number Seventeen) that introduces Mark Pellington's PBS series United States of Poetry: everything moves.

"free...

from human immobility":

moving pictures

those who argue that books or newspapers will long endure like to point to other forms of communication that have survived the arrival of new competitors; radio is their favorite example. They do not, however, mention clay tablets, papyrus scolls, handwritten books, printed ballads, town criers, the camera obscura, vaudeville, telegrams, typewriters, phonograph records or the magic lantern.

The magic lantern—a method for projecting images on screens— was the precursor of the motion picture and a powerful and venerable technology in its own right. A book recounting the history of these projection devices was first published in 1646. A lamp provided the light. The images—fictional characters, biblical figures, angels—were enlarged by a lens before they appeared on whatever served as a screen, usually a wall. Those who operated these machines, that book reports, "were not infrequently brought under suspicion of being magicians." If paper puppets, some flies attracted to a smear of honey or other objects that moved were placed between the lamp and the screen, then this "extraordinary and magical illusion," as a Boston newspaper called it in 1806, would also move.[1]

By the late 1840s a method was devised for preserving photographic images on glass. Light could be beamed through them, and they too could appear on-screen. "The dead appear almost to speak; the distant to overcome space and time and be close and palpable," a New York newspaper exclaimed about an exhibition of these early slides. The problem of making photographic images move proved more difficult, however. The magic lantern itself could be tilted, carried around or given a "sudden shake." Moving slides or multiple lanterns could be used.

But there was, it eventually became clear, a better solution: projecting a series of successive photographs of an action quickly enough so that "persistence of vision"—the eye's tendency to bridge gaps— would make it appear as if one were flowing into another. (This principle was borrowed from a children's toy called the zoetrope, in which the images on a spinning cylinder were viewed successively through slits.) The photographs initially were arranged on a strip or a wheel and moved, one by one, through the lantern.

"A semblance of life that can only come from motion" was added to the photographic image, noted a patent application by a Philadelphia engineer named Coleman Sellers in 1861; "the breath of life" was given to "statuelike forms." By 1870 a device like the one Sellers had patented was used by Henry Renno Heyl to make photographs of an actor playing Brother Jonathan (a precursor of Uncle Sam) appear to move, as an announcer advised the audience, "in most lifelike ways." In another sequences of photos, a couple appeared to waltz.

This is a book about moving images; that means it is most certainly a book about film as well as television. More than half the history of moving images took place *before* the arrival of commercial television in the late 1940s. Indeed, one day when this is all sorted out, Coleman Sellers or some earlier tinkerer may earn the title "Gutenberg of the moving image," and the modest invention that made Brother Jonathan appear to move may be celebrated as the instigator of humankind's third communications revolution.

To produce these bursts of movement, rarely more than a few seconds long, each step in a movement had to be carefully posed: waltzing couple with the man facing the camera, waltzing couple facing each other. Here is where Eadweard Muybridge makes another appearance. With his series of cameras aimed at a trotting horse, Muybridge had been the first actually to take successive photos of something in motion. By 1880 he had invented his own, relatively primitive device for projecting his series of images fast enough so that some moments of actual, not posed, motion could be re-created on a screen. Fortunately, Muybridge's name for his invention, "zoopraxiscope," did not catch on.[2]

This was a significant step forward. "A new method of entertaining the people," the *San Francisco Chronicle* labeled it after Muybridge's first demonstration. "We predict that his instantaneous photographic, magic lantern zoetrope will make the round of the civilized world."[3] The old, static magic lantern shows in the end would not be able to compete with the zoopraxiscope and the more sophisticated forms of film that followed. Unlike radio, the magic lantern would not find a new role for itself. Within a few decades it would die.

However, Muybridge's zoopraxiscope and its successors also represented, in an odd and mostly unnoticed way, something of a step backward. For once those images of a moving horse were projected, rapidly, one after another, they lost their strangeness, their grotesqueness.

The horses regained their grace, and we surrendered much of what we had learned about the instants that compose our lives, much of what we had learned from "fast seeing." "The effect was precisely that of animals running across the screen," the *Chronicle* reported.[4] Nothing more. Nothing revelatory.

Many of the most important issues raised by the moving image—issues that are crucial for the future of video—were already beginning to surface here in the beginnings of film. These chapters will look for them there. One of those issues is the essential conservatism of certain approaches to the moving image. In watching film of a galloping horse, we don't see anything more than we would see from a good seat at the racetrack—as long as the filmmaker is doing what Muybridge and his immediate successors did: simply aiming the camera at the horse or whatever else is doing the moving.

New communications technologies seem to arrive in our age at an astounding rate. In a twenty-one-year period, from 1975 to 1995, we greeted personal computers, home video games, CDs, home videotape systems, the World Wide Web, the Walkman, CD-ROMs. No other age, we assume, has seen anything like it.*[5] But in this we may be wrong. The case could be made that the inventions in a twenty-one-year period exactly a century earlier were comparable in impact: Alexander Graham Bell first patented and demonstrated the telephone in 1876. The first microphones were produced in the United States and Germany in 1877. Ottmar Mergenthaler invented the Linotype machine (which eased considerably the chore of setting books, magazines and newspapers in type) in 1884. The internal-combustion engine (which, like the railroad, rearranged patterns of communication) was first used to power vehicles in Germany in 1885. Guglielmo Marconi perfected wireless telegraphy—radio—in Italy in 1895. Indeed, the case could be made that the inventions in one workshop in New Jersey in those years were comparable in impact to all we have produced.

Thomas Alva Edison patented the first method of recording sound, the phonograph, in 1878. He perfected the first practical electric light in 1879. Edison met with Muybridge in 1888, studied his zoopraxiscope, then began considering the problem of moving pictures. After many false starts, Edison encountered the French photographer Étienne-Jules Marey. Inspired by Muybridge's work, Marey had devised a method of "shooting" a series of rapid pictures by feeding strips of film through a *single* camera (which looked like a shotgun).[6] The solution to the problem of recording and playing longer sequences of moving images began to come into focus.[7]

* Sven Birkerts, writing in 1994: "The rate of change, social and technological, has surpassed exponentially the gradually escalating rates of previous periods."

Edison's vision appears to have been actualized by W.K.L. Dickson, an inventor in his laboratory. (Film historians have continued to debate exactly who did or thought what, when, in and out of Edison's laboratory.) The result was two complementary devices: the kinetograph (*kinesis* is Greek for "movement"), which captured successive photos on a long, horizontal strip of film with perforations at the bottom, and the kinetoscope, into which the perforated, developed film was fed and viewed through a peephole. The citizenry had its first look in 1891: "They saw through an aperture in a pine box standing on the floor," the magazine *Phonogram* reported, "the picture of a man." The man was Dickson. "It bowed and smiled and took off its hat naturally and gracefully."[8] By 1893 Edison and Dickson had constructed the first film studio.

It did not take much imagination to see that a projection device — a version of the magic lantern—could put on a more impressive show than a peephole and entertain a larger crowd. Films were being projected for audiences in Paris by the Lumière brothers by the end of 1895 on the *cinématographe* (the root of this word is also the Greek *kinesis*). "With this new invention," a Paris paper exclaimed, "death will be no longer absolute, final. The people we have seen on the screen will be with us, moving and alive after their deaths."[9] Actions could now for the first time be reproduced and preserved; life could be replayed.

"Louis Lumière was another Gutenberg," the great French director Jean Renoir would later proclaim. (Comparisons to Gutenberg do tend to get tossed around rather freely.) Renoir's own initial experience with this new means for what he would call "the total transformation of the world through knowledge" came in 1897. It was not a happy one:

> Scarcely had we taken our seats then the room was plunged in darkness. A terrifying machine shot out a fearsome beam of light piercing the obscurity, and a series of incomprehensible pictures appeared on the screen, accompanied by the sound of a piano at one end and at the other end a sort of hammering that came from the machine. I yelled in my usual fashion and had to be taken out.

The future filmmaker, relying here on the recollections of his cousin and escort, was two.[10]

Older viewers, however, seemed well pleased with these first motion picture shows, though by modern standards they did not offer much. Films in the 1890s, like camcorder videos in the 1990s, were often seen as little more than moving photographs. When the Lumières' hand-cranked movie projector premiered in America in

1896, audiences rushed to see thirty- to ninety-second films such as *A Dip in the Sea* ("several little boys running...and diving into the waves"), *Washing Day in Switzerland* and *The Messrs. Lumière at Cards.* "The best picture," a New York newspaper reports, "was *The Arrival of the Mail Train*. The train came into the station, passengers alighted, met their friends and walked about, and all the bustle incident to affairs of this kind was shown to perfection." Later programs included *Feeding the Baby,* in which proud Lumière parents, displaying the requisite goofy grins, did just that, thus establishing in 35mm a genre that would go on to bore friends of parents in 8mm film and, now, 8mm videotape.[11]

Fin de siècle audiences, of course, were new to the pleasures of watching babies dribble on screen. Motion was still magic. Moreover, just the illusion of being there—of seeing that "far"—was a thrill, one nonphotographic art forms could match only with great difficulty. In 1924, the hugely inventive Russian director Sergei Eisenstein attempted to add verisimilitude to the play *Gas Masks* by staging it on location in the Moscow Gas Factory. This was Eisenstein's last play.[12] There was only one reasonable way to take audiences such places: via film.

Exciting as all this may have been, however, there remained room for an additional "metaphor," for a conception of what the moving picture might be that imitated another form of communication. The obvious choice, since motion picture audiences usually were sitting in a kind of theater, *was* theater—defined broadly.

The Edison studio initially produced films based on short scenes from musical reviews, circus acts, vaudeville routines, plays (including the climax of *The Widow Jones:* a kiss), and even a then-illegal prize fight (*Corbett and Courtney Before the Kinetograph*). Later there were passion plays and longer, multishot dramatic productions. In 1903 Edwin S. Porter directed a condensation of the well-known stage version of *Uncle Tom's Cabin* for Edison, using fourteen shots. That same year Porter shot the most successful film of the period, *The Great Train Robbery,* which was also based on a play.[13]

Theater retained its hold on early moving pictures—sometimes called "canned theater." In Paris, the *film d'art* movement formed in 1908 specifically to encourage filmmakers to aim their cameras at quality stage productions—with the original actors, even the original scenery. Critics, always in awe when a new medium dares to produce something respectably old, unloosed the superlatives. The movement spread through Europe. As television would half a century later, film grabbed prestige through this impersonation.[14] It also expanded its audience. In 1911 Adolph Zukor was sitting on a New York subway, contemplating the future of American film. He scrawled a note to himself on the back of an envelope: "Famous players in famous plays." Famous Players became the name of his film company; soon Zukor controlled Paramount Pictures.[15]

With theater as the model, the role of the camera in these first movies was simple: It occupied some version of the best seat in the house, and it filmed what it saw from there. Shots almost always changed when scenes changed; edits, perhaps covered by a fade to black or a title, were made where the curtain might have fallen. Sometimes the view presented was that seen from a seat on a train, but more commonly the camera was completely at rest.[16]

Multiple cameras were used to produce the hugely successful film of the Corbett-Fitzsimmons fight in 1897, but they were all standing in one spot. As one camera ran out of film another would simply take over. Angles were not varied. An Edison camera first turned to take in a wider scene in a fiction film in 1902. Pans then grew a little more common: *The Great Train Robbery* features two. But often this represented little more than the camera turning to follow the action as a head might turn in the theater. For the most part audiences saw what they would have seen from a seat in the theater because filmmakers could not imagine them seeing anything else.[17]

Each of the great late-nineteenth-century inventions initially raised questions (as our inventions certainly have and will): What, for example, was the purpose of the phonograph? (For years Edison saw it as a replacement for the secretary: Businessmen could now send a recording instead of a letter.[18]) Who would talk on the telephone: groups or individuals? Who would listen to the radio: individuals or masses?

The hundred-year history of film and television has remained haunted, in my view, by one basic question: *In a moving image, what should do the moving?* Indeed, this may be the largest of the questions currently faced by video's producers. The answer seemed obvious in the decade and a half after the kinetoscope: Whatever is being photographed should move—the horse, the actors, the boxers, the subject matter, that which is onstage. Such movement—on- or offstage—was, after all, the only kind of movement humankind had yet seen. In fact, this is the answer many people would give to this question today. I believe it to be profoundly wrong.

As a rule, I find the introductions to films and television shows more interesting than the films or shows themselves. That's often where the visuals are most densely packed.

In 1996 a series of programs Mark Pellington directed called *United States of Poetry* appeared on PBS. The idea, presumably, was to imbed

poems in the same lush, vivacious visual settings that have long flat-
tered rock songs and thus attract that audience for which all the older
arts now hunger: the young. The basic format of these programs is simple: Poets, looking rather naked without guitars, stand in some gritty
or surreal place and read their words (this traditonal mode of presentation rarely is escaped entirely here); cameras circle around them or
dive in at them from unusual angles; and images flash or sometimes,
deferentially, refrain from flashing. Most of the sequences in
Pellington's poetry series have a specific gravity sufficiently high to
grab my attention, but its introduction is particularly thick and rich. It
is perhaps the most attractive piece of video I have ever seen.

This introductory video collage seems intended to represent, in
fifty seconds, the poet's America.* It gives the feel, consequently, of
having been glimpsed from the road. More than one hundred images
race by: a motel, cows, blacktop, a weathered face, an eye, landscapes,
a dog, a kid, signs, lights, sky. But what is truly mesmerizing about
these roadside sights is the extent to which *everything* moves.

* It was pro-
duced with a
design
company called
Number
Seventeen.

The dog jumps, the eye blinks, the roads roll. But that is just a
small part of the activity. Pellington, to a driving beat, luxuriates in
other kinds of motion—kinds of motion that were absent in the earliest films, kinds of motion that don't fit our commonsense notion of
what should move in moving images, kinds of motion filmmakers had
to invent and then invent again.

The second shot of David Wark Griffith's seventh film, *The Greaser's
Gauntlet*, is typical of the earliest motion pictures. Griffith directed this
film in July of 1908, just four weeks after he directed his first. It tells
the story of a young Mexican man, José (the "greaser," alas), who is
framed and then saved from lynching by a young woman, Mildred.
Much of the plot unfolds in this one scene, a long shot of a barroom.

Here (based on film historian Tom Gunning's description) is what
the audience sees: While cowboys sit and play cards and a Chinese
waiter serves, José and Mildred meet and perhaps take a shine to each
other. The waiter secretly reaches into the pocket of a cowboy and
removes a bandanna filled with money. He then places the bandanna,
minus the money, next to José, who innocently picks it up. José steps
out of the shot—the same shot; there has been no edit. The cowboy
realizes his pocket has been picked. The waiter points offscreen, at José.
Our hero is pulled back into the shot, which still has not changed.
And, with Mildred watching, the bandanna is discovered on him.[19]

Now, viewers are certainly helped in following the various actions
here by the motion itself. When someone walks, meets, reaches,
removes, places, points or pulls, it tends to catch the eye. The scene is
to some extent "sorted," to return to Alan Kay's term, by these mostly

sequential actions. This alone gives moving images an advantage over static images in the effort to express meaning clearly. Nevertheless, this lengthy scene remains confusing.

Viewers watch it from afar without always knowing on which action to focus their attention; at times more than one person is moving. The limits of film as "canned theater" are here. Despite the motion, many of the limits of images in general as conveyers of meaning also remain here. However, the histories of both film and of image communication in general change after the second shot in *The Greaser's Gauntlet*.

Griffith (according to Gunning) now introduces two techniques he had not previously used: First, he begins "switching," or cutting, back and forth between two different sequences of actions. In one the cowboys drag José off to be lynched; in the other our heroine, Mildred, catches the waiter with the money. They alternate: José is mocked and manhandled; Mildred learns who the true villain is. Members of the lynch mob toss a rope over the branch of a tree; Mildred rushes to the rescue. The noose is fitted around José's neck; Mildred continues rushing to the rescue. Finally, as José is lifted off the ground, she appears. The two sequences of events merge in one shot: Mildred proves José innocent.

"Parallel editing," this is called, or "contrast editing." The meaning comes not just from within a scene but from the juxtaposition, the relationship of different scenes: poor, innocent José, villainous waiter; cool-headed Mildred, hot-tempered lynch mob. Griffith did not invent this technique. Industrious researchers have uncovered a few rough examples of parallel editing in films made a year or two earlier.[20] But Griffith developed it and established its importance.

The second new technique displayed in *The Greaser's Gauntlet* appears directly after the rescue. The lynch mob wanders off; hero and heroine are left alone under the hanging tree. They occupy, typically, just a small part of the screen, which also finds room for the dispersing mob and much of the tree, with its ominous horizontal branch. But Griffith, feeling that we should see this couple more clearly, does something almost unheard of: He cuts in to a shot showing Mildred and José from head to ankle, as he hands her a gauntlet his mother had given him. The audience in a theater could not have obtained such a view without leaving its seats and moving to the front. Griffith had started down the road to the close-up.

Again, this technique was not entirely new. Cut-ins can be found, the researchers inform us, on rare occasions in various movies from 1901 on.[21] But, again, this is a technique Griffith, the master, would make his own as he directed hundreds of films for one company, Biograph, from 1908 to 1913. When looking for a new job, Griffith placed an ad for himself in a trade publication in which he took credit, not unjustly, for "revolutionizing Motion Picture drama" and for innovating, among other techniques, the close-up and the "switchback."[22]

The close-up has received most of the attention. Some of the early reaction, typically, was negative: In 1909 *Moving Picture World* complained that these shifts in camera distance produced "a total lack of uniformity" and made a film look as if it were being performed "by a race of giants and giantesses."[23] But critical opinion came around.* "The marvel of marvels," Jean Renoir calls the close-up in his memoir. "From the technical point of view we owe [Griffith] something like the 'reinvention' of the cinema and its complete separation from the theater." Renoir loves the fact that "the enlargement enables us to delight in the texture of the skin." He finds delight too in the opportunity to see "a slight quivering of the lip" and thus learn "something about the inward life."[24]

Renoir, however, misses much of what is marvelous about the close-up. Not only did it provide opportunities to see more subtle motions; it made possible a new kind of cinematic motion. Griffith, to borrow the words of film historian Joyce E. Jesionowski, ended "the tyranny of physical activity" in moving pictures.[25] The world presents us with glimpses of quivering lips. Film, thanks to Griffith's "reinvention," could now present its audiences with something else. Now not only actors but cameras could move. They could pan and zoom, but more than that, cameras could instantly step in, step out, turn this way and that, focus on this and then that. And these different views could be knitted together through the editing. Scenes never before had been seen from a variety of angles. Because cameras moved, in other words, perspectives themselves moved.† Audiences were placed in the godlike position of viewing actions and reactions from multiple perspectives, almost at once.[26]

Through the close-up and the long shot, and by cutting between "a succession of" such "brief shots," explained the novelist André Malraux in 1952, film was able to do more than "merely...showing figures in movement." "Figures in movement" might be called the first kind of cinematic motion; these camera movements in and out, the second. They represent, Malraux concludeed, "the birth of the cinema as a means of expression."[27]

Griffith's other major innovation—the "switchback," or parallel editing—is less celebrated but even more revolutionary. Here the moving image moved not just between perspectives on a single scene but from scene to scene: from Mildred sneaking up on the waiter to José being hustled off by the lynch mob. Film suddenly could jump around in space. Early critics complained of "disconnectedness."[28]

* Hugo Münsterberg, writing in 1916: "The detail...being watched has suddenly become the whole content of the performance.... The close-up has objectified in our world of perception our mental act of attention."

† "The sequence of positional views which the editor composes from the material supplied him," Walter Benjamin concluded, "constitutes the completed film."

Nevertheless, within ten months after he made *The Greaser's Gauntlet,* Griffith directed, and audiences enjoyed, films that cut back and forth between three and four different scenes.*[29]

* Four in *Her First Biscuits;* then three in *The Lonely Villa.*

It was this third kind of cinematic motion that would truly "burst," using Walter Benjamin's words, the "prison-world" of physical location.[30] It became possible to be in more than one place at the same time. Consequently, instead of simply drawing meanings out of scenes, Griffith could draw them out of contrasts between scenes. Audiences were placed in the position of very powerful gods indeed— gods able to see the relationships among a variety of distant occurrences.

Griffith's *A Corner in Wheat,* produced in November 1909, cuts between the activities of a grain speculator, a farm and a bakery. The "Wheat King" is toasted at an extravagant dinner party after he corners the market; an old woman and young girl leave the bakery without any bread because the price has doubled; a farmer returns empty-handed after taking his wheat to the market. The director has constructed a simple but powerful disquisition on monopoly capitalism out of contrast edits.[31]

In Griffith's grandly ambitious 1916 film *Intolerance,* he dances between four different stories, set in four different eras: a contemporary story of union busting, the St. Bartholomew's Day massacre in France in 1572, a story set in ancient Babylon and the crucifixion of Christ. These are large "switchbacks" indeed—huge leaps in time as well as space. Griffith may not have actualized the potential of such juxtapositions in this difficult and ultimately somewhat confusing silent film, but he certainly indicated that potential.[32]

In 1923 the avant-garde Soviet documentary filmmaker and film theorist Dziga Vertov allowed the motion picture camera to do some bragging:

> I, the machine, show you a world the way only I can see it. I free myself for today and forever from human immobility. I'm in constant movement. I approach and pull away from objects...recording one movement after another in the most complex combinations. Freed from the boundaries of time and space, I co-ordinate any and all points of the universe, wherever I want them to be. My way leads towards the creation of a fresh perception of the world.[33]

Each of the different kinds of camera motion Vertov celebrated is found in Pellington's fifty-second introduction to *United States of Poetry.* His camera is "in constant movement," panning and zooming with abandon. It approaches for the tightest of close-ups—of an ear, a screaming mouth, a letter of the alphabet—and pulls away for long shots of people, bridges, pages of text. But what makes this short piece of video so dazzlingly kinetic is its "complex combinations" of cuts—a hundred or so of these abrupt leaps from one point in the universe to another.

Pellington's introduction, like similar recent examples of video, assumes the right to jump tirelessly, incessantly through time and space, without explanation, without bound. It is wildly disconnected by the standards of all art forms predating that celebrated by Vertov. And it is—at least in the view of this theory-laden enthusiast—fascinating to watch.

The camera, with the indispensible assistance of the editing machine, began to gain this unprecedented mobility with D.W. Griffith and the early experimenters in film. This mobility is now coming into its own in the work of Mark Pellington and other experimenters in video. But in the intervening four score or so years these lessons about the potential of moving images have often been forgotten or rejected.

For much of its history television has been stuck back on the first kind of cinematic motion. A Coca-Cola commercial from 1959 is a good example: It features the three McGuire Sisters, dressed in matching Spanish-cowgirl outfits, singing and moving in step. They dance; the camera, for the most part, simply watches.

The importance of changing camera angles and switching between scenes had to be rediscovered many times—in sound film and then again in television. In 1962 a Coke commercial finally stumbled upon the power of parallel editing: cutting (sluggishly) between a couple of preternaturally happy young Coke drinkers as they frolic on a beach, then as they glide, smiles intact, down some powdery slopes. Beach/skiing. Beach/skiing. Back and forth. (Another early and influential example was a "Go, Go, Go, Go Goodyear" commercial produced by Young and Rubicam that same year, which cuts, not at all sluggishly, between a car struggling with the snow, a commuter train arriving, and titles showing minutes ticking away.)* This technique seems so simple, but of course it is not. Many of those who talk or write about television today still think the trick is basically to aim a few cameras at an animated conversation, drama or sporting event and let them roll.

* Philip Dusenberry, now chairman of BBDO New York, credits this Goodyear commercial with interesting him in this technique.

Griffith's lessons have had so much difficulty sinking in because they contradict what had been learned from thousands of years of performances: that the McGuire Sisters move but the audience, and therefore its perspective, does not; that scenes appear one at a time and stay for a while. Nothing could be more obvious, and for the development of film, television and video, nothing could be more wrong.

The eagerness of American filmmakers to ape Griffith and bring to the box office *tours de force* of editing was also not helped by the fact that Griffith's most ambitious film, *Intolerance,* was a huge commercial failure. The director was paying off debts on it until he died in 1948.[34] However, filmmakers in another country, Dziga Vertov's country, proved more daring.

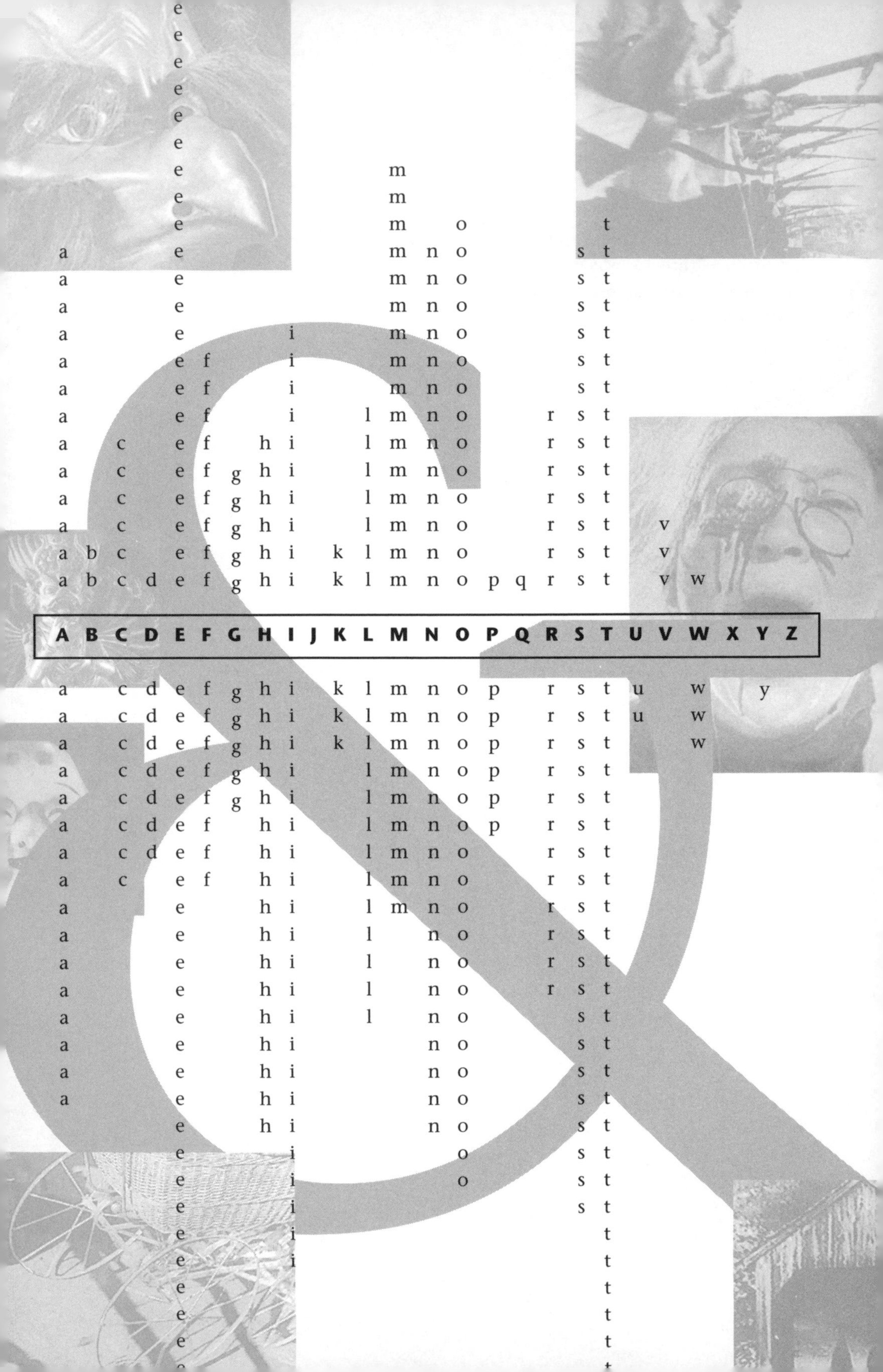
A B C D E F G H I J K L M N O P Q R S T U V W X Y Z

"Multiple Fragments ...Assembled Under a New Law"

M O N T A G E

[**Top Row** When the filmmaker has a more effective tool than the novelist: three shots from the Odessa-steps montage in Sergei Eisenstein's 1925 film *Battleship Potemkin*.
Center The fourth kind of cinematic motion: one of the series of different shots featuring modish young people in a 1969 Coca-Cola commercial.
Bottom Row An "intellectual cinema": three shots from the montage-of-the-gods sequence in Sergei Eisentstein's 1928 film *October*.]

i

have suggested that the true "curse" upon those who make images may be their difficulty communicating abstract thought. One of the most ambitious efforts to overcome this curse made use, interestingly enough, of images of gods—some of which *are* literally "graven images." In his 1928 film *October*, about the Russian Revolution, the Soviet filmmaker Sergei Eisenstein wanted to present a short critique of religion, under the banner of which anti-Communist troops had been marching. He did this in a sequence without plot and characters, as well as without words. Eisenstein simply cut between unmoving images of a series of religious symbols, including a baroque Christ, statues of Buddha, fierce-looking animal deities and a wooden Eskimo idol.[1]

This is a more extreme version of parallel cutting. Eisenstein "switches" not so much back and forth but *on and on*—producing a fourth kind of cinematic motion. New image follows new image, and each makes only a single appearance. "These shots were assembled on a descending intellectual scale," Eisenstein later explained, "and lead the notion of god back to a block of wood."[2] (This Soviet filmmaker did not display a respect for non-western cultures or for religion.)

The director had high aspirations for "the sequence of the Gods." He saw in it one of the building blocks of an "intellectual cinema."[3]

This is the kind of cutting—the kind of cinematic motion—that is crucial to the new form of video for which I have such high hopes. It has distinguished the work in the 1980s and 1990s of Mark Pellington on MTV and PBS, David Berrent on MTV and ABC, and Roberta Goldberg on ABC. It makes increasingly frequent appearances in films such as *Natural Born Killers* and *Trainspotting*. And it can be found in a more primitive and less distinguished form in a Coca-Cola commercial made in 1969.

By then such commercials had long ago left the McGuire Sisters behind. This commercial features a collection of modish, anonymous young people spilling out of a van, staring at a long field, fingering a guitar, strolling through a covered bridge—lots and lots of modish, anonymous young people. Instead of just switching between two scenes, this one-minute commercial jumps from scene to scene—on and on. It includes twenty-one different shots, each showing a different place or different images of the product.

Some of us have difficulty giving television commercials credit for their role in the history of video. Morality enters into it, since so many commercials are, at bottom, attempts to manipulate through oversimplification, distortion or appeals, whispered or shouted, to base instincts. Most of us have been seduced by one or another commercial into some form of vanity, conspicuous consumption, unhealthful living or profligacy. As a result, we have developed some ability, however imperfect, to resist their suggestions. (The alternative would likely be bankruptcy.)

Yet the most interesting images production assistant Mark Pellington saw on the TV sets scattered about the back rooms of MTV in the early 1980s appeared in the commercials. Television advertisements grew so visually interesting, even adventurous, because they have had to overcome so much resistance and because, in the effort to manipulate adroitly, so much money has been spent producing them. When Pellington began directing his own videos he hired a young film editor, Hank Corwin, who had been working on commercials. (Oliver Stone would hire the same editor to produce those jangled effects, universally described as "televisionlike," in *Natural Born Killers*.)

Commercials have often taken the lead in the development of video, and Coke and Pepsi have often taken the lead in the development of commercials. This is "because soft drinks are selling image, more than a product," *Ad Week* columnist Debra Goldman has explained.[4]

Of course, such efforts to sell the images of probably unneeded, perhaps unhealthy products have their limits as examples, particularly if you're trying to make the case that the techniques in question will advance art and thought. Coke commercials, no matter how stylistically advanced, don't seem to deserve mention in the same paragraphs as an "intellectual cinema" or an intellectual television or an intellectual anything. Nevertheless, they can't be excised from this history (any more than trade and commerce—in Sumeria, in Canaan, in Greece—can be excised from the history of a medium with manifest intellectual merit: writing).[5]

In its first decades, television seemed condemned to recapitulate the development of film. With this 1969 Coke commercial, TV can be said to have arrived—technically, not artistically—at the stage of montage, at the stage of Eisenstein.

Sergei Eisenstein belonged to a group of Russian artists who had been sufficiently stirred by their revolution (and had been left, for a time, sufficiently free) to be particularly susceptible to the revolutions in "Motion Picture drama" unleashed by D.W. Griffith. *Intolerance,* rereleased after the revolution, was said to have been a favorite of Lenin's and was a huge hit in the Soviet Union. It played there for almost ten years and influenced all the young Soviet filmmakers.[6] Many, like Dziga Vertov, became fascinated by camera movement and editing.*[7]

The Russians borrowed a word to express this ability to, using Vertov's phrases, record movements "in the most complex combinations," to place points wherever wanted, to create "a fresh perception of the world": *montage.*

This term, which would have so much significance for film, entered the art world primarily through photography. Beginning in the 1920s, especially in Germany, artists such as Hannah Höch and László Moholy-Nagy took to cutting up pieces from pictures—a delicate female head, a hairy male arm—and pasting them together to form often surreal photomontages. These were seen as reflecting the disjuncture and fragmentation of modern, fast-paced, urban life. Eisenstein was among those intrigued by this work.[8]

The essential experiment in film montage was conducted by Lev Kuleshov, the Soviet Union's most influential film instructor. He simply took old footage of the expressionless face of the well-known actor Ivan Mozhukhin and spliced into it three unrelated shots: a bowl of soup, a woman in a coffin and a girl playing with a teddy bear. When audiences saw this little film, they "raved about the acting of the artist," reports Kuleshov's student, the filmmaker V.I. Pudovkin. "They pointed out the heavy pensiveness of his mood over the forgotten soup, were touched and moved by the deep sorrow with which he looked on the dead woman, and admired the light, happy smile with which he surveyed the girl at play."[9]

The point of what became known as the "Kuleshov effect" is that the meaning of a shot is dependent upon the shots that surround it. The point of montage, the Russians realized, is that new meanings can be created through the juxtaposition of different shots. "Film-art begins from the moment when the director begins to combine and join together the various pieces of film," Pudovkin recalled Kuleshov teaching. "By joining them in various combination, in different orders, he obtains differing results."[10]

Eisenstein spent a few months in Kuleshov's workshop. He insisted, though, on a more radical, more "dialectical" interpretation of montage: not as a "linkage" between shots, but as a *"collision"** between them out of which *"arises"* a new "concept."[11] His most

* The shortage of film stock in the Soviet Union, which led to frequent use of leftover pieces, or "short ends," may have also encouraged directors to build scenes out of shorter shots.

* Eisenstein was free with italics.

renowned montage is the scene on the Odessa steps in *Battleship Potemkin,* released in 1925: troops marching down and firing into a protesting crowd; a mother, carrying the body of her dead son, climbing up; close-ups of screams, of blood spurting from behind shattered eyeglasses; a baby carriage bumping down the stairs through the bodies of the dead and wounded. (The average shot in this sequence is on-screen for only about two seconds.)[12] From the Odessa-steps montage, Eisenstein wrote, arose the "perception of an *oppressive regime.*"[13]

These six minutes represent perhaps the most praised segment of film in the medium's history. Whether some cinematic versions of thesis and antithesis are actually colliding here is questionable. Still, the Odessa-steps montage demonstrated, as nothing had before, the evocative power of changing camera distances and angles. It demonstrated how rapid "switchbacks" between different threads within a story—the mother with her dead son, the baby carriage—can produce something much greater than the sum of their parts. This montage remains, however, an exploration and expansion of techniques introduced by Griffith—of the third kind of cinematic motion. It also remains a kind of imitation—not so much of theater (no play could move around a scene in this way) but of the novel.

After hearing his plan for parallel editing in an early film, a Biograph executive is said to have complained to Griffith, "How can you tell a story jumping about like that? The people won't know what it's about." The director replied, "Well, doesn't Dickens write that way?"[14]

One of those most intrigued by Griffith's attempt to trace his ancestry to Charles Dickens was Sergei Eisenstein. The Soviet director had worked hard in his own writings to discover a pedigree for montage, finding, for example, a "shooting-script" in Leonardo da Vinci's notes for a painting and a "crowd of pictures" in a Pushkin poem.[15]

In a lengthy essay written in 1944, Eisenstein took it upon himself to justify Griffith's retort through a close reading of *Oliver Twist.*[16] He found details of lighting:

> There was a faint glimmering of the coming day in the sky; but it rather aggravated than relieved the gloom of the scene: the sombre light only serving to pale that which the street lamps afforded.

Eisenstein found Dickens employing close-ups: "The ground was covered, nearly ankle-deep, with filth and mire." He found a "progression of parallel scenes, intercut into each other" in the episode in which Oliver's benefactor waits with mounting despair for him to return from an errand, while the boy is waylaid by his old gang of thieves. And Eisenstein found numerous examples of montage—fast-cut montage, as in this description by Dickens of the sights and sounds of "market-morning":

> Countrymen, butchers, drovers, hawkers, boys, thieves, idlers, and vagabonds of every low grade, were mingled together in a mass; the whistling of drovers, the barking of dogs, the bellowing and plunging of oxen, the bleating of sheep, the grunting and squeaking of pigs; the cries of the hawkers, the shouts, oaths, and quarrelling on all sides; the ringing of bells and the roars of voices, that issued from every public-house; the crowding, pushing, driving, beating, whooping and yelling; the hideous and discordant din that resounded from every corner of the market; and the unwashed, unshaven, squalid, and dirty figures constantly running to and fro, and bursting in and out of the throng; rendered it a stunning and bewildering scene, which quite confounded the senses.

Point made. Filmmakers such as Griffith did owe a debt to novelists such as Dickens. And, to put a more controversial spin on it, novelists and filmmakers could be seen as playing at the same game. Griffith, while relying on only those words that fit on the occasional title, had come up with a new, novelistic method of telling stories. In the Odessa-steps scene Eisenstein demonstrated an even sharper novelistic eye for detail, pacing and, yes, narrative. Here images—moving images—are venturing into territories once explored only by words. By 1917 some moving pictures were even being described as "cinema novels."[17] This in itself was a great achievement: No other form of image communication—no painting, no still photograph—could presume to imitate the novel.

However, it is worth pausing longer over Eisenstein's reading of Griffith's reading of Dickens. We can proceed a long way toward an understanding of our current situation by looking deeper into this comparison of what the novel can do and what a montage of moving images can do. For what is being compared in this early Soviet filmmaker's analysis of a nineteenth-century novelist and an early-twentieth-century filmmaker is nothing less than this: the art through which the world *was* once seen and the art through which the world likely *will* be seen.

Few discussions of the relative merits of words and images get far without someone raising the quesion of imagination. Reading, they insist, requires it; watching doesn't. When we read, the assumption goes, scenes must be created in our heads. When we watch, that is not necessary; the scene is right there in front of us. I have problems with this argument.

This manner of reading, I must note, isn't my strong suit. Yes, like everyone else, I've experienced a shock when seeing actors playing characters from books I've read. They don't look right—which must mean I've been imaginative enough to form some image of how those characters should have looked. But I usually haven't gone much beyond "dark," "short" or "cute." And I do worse on scenes than on major characters.

Consider Dickens's description of the "glimmering of the coming day." Perhaps a whole early morning street scene appears in the conscientious reader's head as these lines are scanned. No such scene appears, I must admit, in mine: I can, if I concentrate, conjure up a greeting-card dawn, but a nineteenth-century London sunrise? Nope. When Dickens mentions "street lamps," maybe I recall one I noticed once. When he writes of "gloom," my eyebrows may lower and a hint of sinister gray may materialize somewhere in my head. That's about it. In reading Dickens I'm mostly involved in trying to follow Dickens, not in painting mental pictures in my head. Still, I respectfully acknowledge the potential for a decent-sized act of imagination here on the part of better readers than I.

Now let's assume this cloudy dawn has been captured on film. This time the light, street and pedestrians are in front of us all—conscientious or not. But what do we actually *see?* Most of us will get the feeling of early-morning urban life, but beyond that we're more or less on our own. Maybe we'll notice the street lamps; maybe not. Maybe our eyes will settle upon an interesting-looking person. Maybe we'll notice something about the light, the weather, the condition of the people or the nature of the times. Images provide no shortage of opportunities for creative seeing: making observations, divining significances, comprehending relationships—most of which the writer does for us when we read. The case could be made that interpreting images requires more imagination of us, not less.

I'm not convinced, however, that what I want from a work of art is another opportunity to use my own limited imagination. I doubt I could see that dawn as having "aggravated...the gloom" or see its light "only serving to pale that which the street lamps afforded." *That* takes a special imagination—the imagination of an artist like Dickens. Isn't the true test of the moving image not how much space it allows our own imaginations but whether it provides a means by which artistic imaginations can effectively communicate with us? The evidence on how well silent film can do this seems mixed.

Film sets scenes quickly, easily and powerfully: morning, cloudy, bustle, ankle-deep muck. It takes a skilled writer to give us the feeling that we are on a particular street at dawn. Once the extras are all in place and the lighting is right, film can communicate that impression in a few simple shots. It's when the imagination in question wants to do more than simply set a scene that the absence of words begins to be felt.

Six brilliant minutes of film can, as Eisenstein demonstrated, tell us with as much power as any piece of literature that a regime was brutally repressive. But silent film, because it tends to show and not describe, struggles with the offhand observations and characterizations that enrich just about every paragraph of a well-written novel. We can see that it's a dull, gray morning, but it would require a long, complex piece of film to tell us that the dawn has "aggravated...the gloom." A silent film would have to work even harder to make sure we realized, as Dickens explains later in this scene, that "it was as light as it was likely to be, till night came on again."

Literature makes many of its points through metaphors and comparisons ("as light as it was likely to be"). Eisenstein proved that it was possible for silent film to learn such tricks. His first production, *Strike* in 1924, cut between footage of workers being massacred and footage taken at an animal slaughterhouse. A bit heavy-handed, perhaps; nevertheless, a comparison likely to stick in the mind. Such leaps away from story line into overt metaphor have been rare, however, in the history of film.* More commonly directors have relied on less obtrusive—and therefore more ambiguous—attempts to comment on occurrences through variations in sets, angles or lighting. These are comments portions of the audience may sometimes miss.

* They are becoming less rare on TV. Embarrassing moments on Fox's *Ally McBeal,* for example, are often puntuated with a quick cut to a fat foot in an open mouth.

Film's tendency to show more than describe becomes a major handicap when it tries to capture feelings and thoughts. This, of course, is the novel's strong point. The narrator of *Don Quixote* speaks of authors who, when describing some hero's adventures, "not only recorded their actions, but described likewise their most minute and trifling thoughts."[18] Photographic images can't do that. What, besides such faint, enigmatic behaviors as a "slight quivering of the lip," is there for them to *show?* Film tends to be fascinated instead by surfaces: clothes, cars, chests and celebrity.

Emotions, it is true, have long had a place on the screen. Griffith's early motion pictures patterned themselves after late-nineteenth-century stage melodramas. They succeeded in communicating the requisite extremes of love, loss, fear or fury and drew the appropriate cheers, tears or boos. But subtler mental states are another matter. Consider how much time a silent film would have had to expend to say what

Dickens is able to say in this one sentence about a character's state of mind:

> Although Mr. Grinwig was not by any means a bad-hearted man, and though he would have been unfeignedly sorry to see his respected friend duped and deceived, he really did most earnestly and strongly hope at that moment, that Oliver Twist might not come back.[19]

Hidden hopes and complex hearts along with the feeling of being sorry (feigned and unfeigned)—like character, virtue and integrity—are not easily photographed.

Indeed, the increasing reliance upon *images*, which began with photography and accelerated with film, certainly seems to have contributed to a decreasing concern with our inner lives and an increasing concern with *image*—with style, possessions and public relations, with surfaces and appearances, with what Coke commercials are selling. Today we attribute this rise in vanity, materialism and phoniness to television, but this phenomenon too can be traced back to film. For many decades it was summed up by the name of the town in which D. W. Griffith began wintering his movie crew in 1910: Hollywood.

Sergei Eisenstein spent some months in Hollywood in 1930 (living in a hilltop Beverly Hills house). He found what he later called "somewhat unusual social circumstances": studio heads fighting for the services of "the world's greatest director" but then berating him because he wouldn't direct a "whodunit" with "sex appeal"; press agents responding to allegations that this Soviet director was what he in fact was—a "Jewish Bolshevik"—by photographing him with Charlie Chaplin and Marlene Dietrich and publicizing his friendship with Douglas Fairbanks; Greta Garbo asking him who that man Lenin was; a studio president inquiring if he thought Trotsky might write a film script. Eisenstein, who himself was photographed shaking hands with Mickey Mouse, found a town where hardly anyone he met seemed serious *except* Chaplin. The two uses of the word *image* had begun to converge in the American movie industry by 1930. Eisenstein spoke of retaining his "integrity as an artist" and left Hollywood without making a film.[20]

Moving images certainly created Hollywood, the industry. Because of the emphasis they—unlike novels—place on appearances, moving images also deserve substantial credit for the "unusual social circumstances" associated with Hollywood. A type of seriousness *has* been lost with this switch from words to images and has remained lost. Still, moving images were and are too powerful to be contained by Hollywood in either sense.

Independent films (such as *Trainspotting*) have always managed to bubble to the surface. Independent television or video was more difficult than film to produce; soon it will become much easier. Plenty of films that have insisted on various varieties of seriousness—that critique Hollywood, the mind-set—have also found their way into theaters. I will argue that we can expect video that challenges, with seriousnesses of its own, the manipulations and commercialism currently associated with much television. (Pellington's series *Buzz* and *United States of Poetry* may contain the germ of such a challenge.)

Part of the power of moving images comes from the technique Eisenstein championed: montage. Here the tables turn in the contest betwen the novel and moving images, for in switching rapidly between perspectives, it is those who share their imaginations with us by writing who are at a disadvantage.

Because writers must work to make each view they present believable, it is very difficult for them to present a rapid series of such views. Dickens, with his marvelous alertness, succeeds as well as any writer has: "the whistling of drovers, the barking of dogs, the bellowing and plunging of oxen, the bleating of sheep, the grunting and squeaking of pigs; the cries of the hawkers, the shouts, oaths, and quarrelling on all sides." But when attempting to capture the energy and chaos of this "stunning and bewildering" market-morning scene, Dickens is often reduced to lists: "Countrymen, butchers, drovers, hawkers, boys, thieves, idlers, and vagabonds of every low grade" or "crowding, pushing, driving, beating, whooping and yelling."

Such processions of words have their power; nonetheless it would take a reader of quick and formidable imagination indeed to get from them much of what Dickens saw. The word *pushing,* for example, doesn't provide the conscientious reader with a whole lot of guidance. In the same amount of time it takes to read those words, film, on the other hand, can present a procession of energetic and detailed views of the scene. We could witness three-quarters of a second or so of a particular angry, aggressive push. At these speeds, film's ability to communicate impressions rapidly comes to the fore.

Eisenstein stood at the Odessa steps, Dickens at a London market. It is hard not to conclude that in these circumstances the filmmaker, even without sound, had the more effective tool. Which is to say simply that montage works better on film than in print. The literary theorist Erich Auerbach, writing during World War II, was blunt about his opinion on the subject:

A concentration of space and time such as can be achieved by
the film (for example the representation, within a few seconds

and by means of a few pictures, of the situation of a widely dispersed group of people, of a great city, an army, a war, an entire country) can never be within the reach of the spoken or written word.[21]

This is a significant disability. Circumstances fast and variegated enough to lend themselves to montage are everywhere. We can see them not only in the diasporas, battles and urban vistas mentioned by Auerbach, but at sporting events, crime scenes, beaches, cocktail parties, malls, aerobic centers and mosh pits. Among the many occasions Dickens found for montage was a description in *Nicholas Nickleby* of how London shops and their wares "seemed to flit by in motley dance" when viewed from a stagecoach.[22] Nowadays we spend a good portion of our lives in vehicles, virtual and not, that cause things to "flit by" faster still, in dances that are often unabashedly, even aggressively "motley."

The speed and style of montage also can be seen in dreams (the subject that once was most likely to inspire traditional filmmakers to hazard a montage),[23] and it can be found, as Eisenstein notes, in the motley stream of thoughts that flits through our minds.[24] This latter is crucial. How can the scenes that pass before our mind's eye be communicated without recourse to montage?

And capturing the pace of modern and postmodern life and thought is not the only task for which montage is suited; it can present us with new ways of imagining those lives and thoughts. For there is another form of montage, one seen only rarely in print or the physical world. *October,* the film Eisenstein completed after *Battleship Potemkin,* includes segments—nonnarrative segments—that jump rapidly not within a scene but from scene to scene, from image of god to image of god, for example.

In his idea-dense writings about montage Eisenstein sometimes mentioned hieroglyphic. That's a giveaway, a sure sign that the subject of a language of images is being raised once again. This ambitious Soviet director was indeed ready to face the largest challenge for any form of communication: abstract thought. Eisenstein announced that he was moving toward "a purely intellectual film, freed from traditional limitations, achieving direct forms for ideas, systems and concepts."[25]

He had a major new weapon at his command: this new kind of montage, the fourth kind of cinematic motion—a silent version of the kind of montage that would be used in that 1969 Coke commercial and that is now being experimented with by Pellington and others. By cutting rapidly between images taken from different contexts, Eisenstein was no longer limited, as Griffith and most novelists had been, to presenting one or even a few scenes at a time. He could quickly juxtapose, compare and find meaning in the relationship between numerous different scenes. Images of gods from all over the world, for example, could be thrown up on-screen in a short period of time. The message was no longer in one god or another but in humankind's age-old efforts to represent divinity.

Eisenstein was so confident of his ability to express abstract thought through montage that he announced as his next project a film version of nothing less than *Das Kapital* itself, from, as he put it, "a 'libretto' by Karl Marx."[26] Shortly after releasing *October* he boasted, "The hieroglyphic language of the cinema is capable of expressing any concept."[27]

It is clear that considerable progress had been made toward solving the problems that had defeated other attempts at an image language. In the earliest films it was difficult even to tell a simple, usually melodramatic story with some clarity. Now here was a director ready to grapple with "ideas, systems and concepts." Still, Eisenstein's ambitions may have exceeded the techniques then available to him. His images of images of gods are certainly presented in the order in which he wanted us to view them; they are sorted. Nevertheless, the meaning of these images is not always clear. Film historian Gerald Mast, for example, has explained that all the gods are meant to be seen as "ugly." However, Eisenstein himself wrote that the initial Baroque Christ is "magnificent."[28] The ambiguity problem had not yet been entirely solved.

October was delayed five months while Eisenstein removed all references to Leon Trotsky, whom Stalin had expelled from the Communist Party. When it was finally released, audiences in Russia and the United States were perplexed by its abstract montages.[29] Alexander Bakshy, writing in the *Nation* in 1928, expressed awe at Eisenstein's attempt "to build the language of cinematic images." Still, Bakshy concluded that critics were right to label the film "confusing and sometimes even boring."[30]

The Russians were not the only filmmakers experimenting in those years. In France, Jean Renoir had been, as he put it, "ravished" by *Le Brasier Ardent,* a dreamy, experimental, fast-cut film starring, written by and directed by Ivan Mozhukhin (then living in France) who had appeared in Kuleshov's famous montage experiment. Renoir's directoral debut in 1924 was an often dreamy, experimental film called *La Fille de l'Eau.* In one sequence, where the heroine falls into a delirium, Renoir splashed on the screen in just a little more than three seconds a montage of seventeen shots, most taken from earlier in the film. "Rapid cutting fascinated me," he later explained.[31]

La Fille de L'Eau, like *Intolerance* or *October,* qualified as a fascinating experiment rather than a commercial success or a complete artistic success. For these techniques to be used without confusing or boring the audience, for moving images to truly challenge the novel, something additional had to be added to the mix. Eisenstein understood this. "The tasks of theme and story grow more complicated every day," he wrote in 1928; "attempts to solve these by methods of 'visual' montage alone...force the director to resort to fanciful montage structures, arousing the fearsome eventuality of meaninglessness and reactionary decadence."* The solution, Eisenstein argued, was sound.[32]

Few are quoted more frequently in this book than Walter Benjamin, the German-Jewish critic and theorist who killed himself with an overdose of morphine in 1940 when his efforts to escape the Nazis seemed to have been frustrated. Almost all those quotes, including the one from which the title of this chapter is taken, are from Benjamin's still widely discussed essay, "The Work of Art in the Age of Mechanical Reproduction." I won't pretend that Benjamin, writing in 1936, was saying what I am saying, or even what Eisenstein was saying. Yet at times he seemed remarkably sensitive to the special nature of the moving image, whose art, he explained, "consists of multiple fragments which are assembled under a new law."[33]

Eisenstein was indeed exploring the capabilities of "multiple fragments"—fragments of perspectives, fragments of scenes. In its less inspired way, that 1969 Coca-Cola commercial begins to exploit these same capabilities—with, of course, very different purposes and the significant additions of music and color. We are still experimenting with these hugely promising assemblages; indeed, we have barely gotten started.

The full potential of such collections of fragments clearly could not be realized under old laws borrowed from theater and print. Photography, film and television began to smash, however hesitantly and erratically, those laws and the view of the world they preserved. Benjamin spoke of "the dynamite of the tenth of a second" and "its far-flung ruins and debris."[34]

The development of "new laws" has begun, but it will take time.† That development has been slowed typically and understandably by a reaction against all this destruction. Partisans of the Ancients have been trying their best to preserve the old laws. Like Eisenstein, they placed some of their hopes on the addition of sound to film. Initially it helped their cause much more than his. For once that missing element arrived, filmmakers were thrown back—away from fast-cut montage, in the direction of the McGuire Sisters.

* From "A Statement," a manifesto, presumed to have been composed by Eisenstein, signed by him and two other Soviet filmmakers.

† I will present an interim report on the lawmaking process in chapter 12.

9

The dream of a sound film has come true [but] sound recording is a two-edged invention.

—Sergei Eisenstein, 1928

"GIFTS

Television and social life: France now has less than a third as many cafes as it had in 1960.

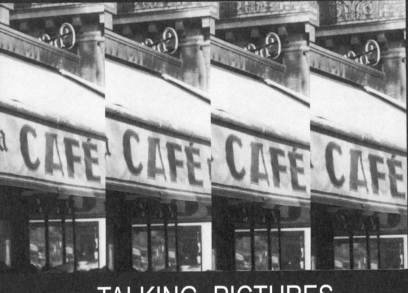

TALKING PICTURES

OF PARALYSIS"

AND COUCH POTATOES

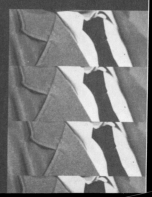

An early "couch potato": Jackie Gleason as Ralph Kramden in *The Honeymooners*.

t he first episode of the classic Jackie Gleason situation comedy *The Honeymooners,* is entitled "TV or Not TV." At the insistence of wife Alice, the Kramdens choose the former. In short order husband Ralph is entranced—planted in front of their new set, snacks by his side, until one in the morning.[1] Although the term was not in use when this show first aired in 1955 and he sat in a chair, Ralph Kramden has been transformed into a "couch potato."

A year earlier the singer and television star Perry Como acknowledged, even bragged of having reached a similar state. His "favorite home pastime," Como reported, "is to create a still life consisting of TV set, bowl of fruit, paring knife, cigarette, and Como stretched out on couch."[2] Many of our fears about the ascendency of the image can be found in Ralph Kramden's fictional transformation and Perry Como's eerily still life.

Men and women have always had reason to stretch out: to read, to sleep, to rest, perchance to daydream or even copulate. Perhaps chores needed to be done; perhaps this was not the appropriate person with whom to lie. But for the most part these were happy circumstances: straw in mouth, leafy oak overhead, soft bed below.

Now, following Como and sometimes still watching Kramden, we spread ourselves out for another activity, and the scene it evokes is considerably less sylvan: chips (not Como's fruit) in a bowl, beer can in hand, belly protruding. This seems an activity (to continue to paraphrase Hamlet) that loses the name of activity.[3] We're not holding up our end of a conversation. We're not clapping. We're not even transforming letters into sounds. Sometimes we concentrate on what we are watching; sometimes we don't even manage that. Our eyes are half open; everything else appears to be shut down.

Usually we envision the worst offenders as being, like Ralph, male, white and middle- or lower-middle-class. But substitute pretzels or organic baby carrots for the chips, a soft drink or Merlot for the beer, and who among us has not adopted this posture? Television—some evenings—does make couch potatoes of us all.

That is not a self-image to which we aspire. What we won't do to escape its sting, to place some distance between ourselves and the couch potato's stagnant limbs, glazed look and social isolation. This helps explain the Nautilus machine and all the new Barnes and Nobles. This helps explain the on-line "chat room" and the self-help group. But inevitably we succumb—some evenings, many evenings.

William Paley, who played as large a role as anyone in the development of television, was initially pessimistic about its future: "Man is a social creature," the longtime chairman of CBS noted when the early television experiments were being conducted; "he likes to rub shoulders with his fellows."*4 That may be true, but it turned out, to William Paley's great good fortune, that most men and women like to watch television even more. They are content to sacrifice the caress of all those shoulders for a good lie on a well-situated couch.

What draws us to the couch? The dozens of channels that can be pulled in by a thick cable certainly help, as does the remote that enables us to "surf" through them without repeatedly having to lift ourselves to our feet and slog, grunting and sweating, across that yard or two between us and the set. But Kramden and Como required neither of the above to receive what the novelist Thomas Pynchon has dubbed television's "gifts of paralysis"—its quietus.5 All they required was the opportunity, in their own homes, to experience the formidable combination of moving images and sound, to have both of their dominant senses stimulated.

Some improvements in the mix were still possible: color and a larger screen (which most of us have), more convenient access to the shows we want to watch (which we can expect). Programming forms remained in their infancy. (I argue, of course, that they still aren't much more than toddlers.) Nevertheless, in their living rooms in the 1950s Kramden and Como received a nice little taste of the magic.

Moving images and sounds were first combined, of course, on film more than a quarter of a century earlier. Difficult aesthetic issues must be wrestled with if we are to perfect this potent brew and develop new, nobler forms of programming. This chapter locates those issues in the early history of the sound film. Making use of some tricky parallel editing of its own, the chapter also considers what the consequences of regular ingestion of this apparently highly addictive potion might be— for early filmgoers, for Kramden and Como, for all of us who have followed them to the couch. That is among the most troubling of this book's questions.

At one point in *The Jazz Singer* Al Jolson says to a nightclub audience, "Wait a minute...wait a minute...you ain't heard nothin' yet!" That plus one other snatch of dialogue (added to an orchestral score, some

* Others agreed. "One thing is incontestably certain: the family is not going to stay at home all the time because there is a television receiver in the living room," Robert E. Lee concluded in a book on television published in 1944.

Jewish music and seven songs) qualified this as the first major Hollywood film to begin to make realistic use of sound in telling its story. *The Jazz Singer* premiered in 1927, at a time when the size of the audiences attracted to movies had been declining. It was a spectacular success. By the spring of 1928 in just about any town in the United States any sound film, no matter how bad, would outdraw any silent film, no matter how good. The major Hollywood studios rapidly overcame their resistance to this new technology, spending hundreds of millions of dollars to retool for sound. From 1927 to 1930, weekly movie attendance increased by 50 percent.[6]

Like all such innovations, the sound film distressed many of those who had grown attached to the form it replaced. In 1930 the English film historian (and later filmmaker) Paul Rotha decried "the attempted combination of speech and pictures." He insisted they are "two separate mediums, which appeal in two utterly different ways."[7] Like all previous steps forward in the presentation of images, the sound film also occasioned references to the supernatural: "No closer approach to resurrection has ever been made by science," a Columbia University physics professor exclaimed.[8] The question, as always, was what forms might best exploit the problematic yet undeniably magical combination of moving images and sound.

Jean Renoir had no doubt (often a dangerous sign). In his memoirs he recalled welcoming "the talkies...with delight, seeing at once all the use that could be made of sound." The use Renoir, who made his first picture with sound in 1931, saw was similar to that the rest of the film industry rapidly settled upon: presenting people, in dramas, talking. "After all," Renoir wrote, "the purpose of all artistic creation is the knowledge of man, and is not the human voice the best means of conveying the personality of a human being?"[9]

In 1934, with a number of sound films under his belt, Renoir wanted, as he put it, to "experiment with theater people." Such experiments were going on throughout an industry suddenly in need of intelligible voices as well as attractive faces. A producer offered Renoir a new project. Renoir said he accepted because it had "certain phrases that you know must be spoken by lips accustomed to speaking words." The project was a film version—the second of the five that have been made as of this writing—of *Madame Bovary*.[10]

However, not everyone was convinced that "talkies" were the proper result of the addition of sound to film. In a statement written in 1928, Sergei Eisenstein worried that the "line of least resistance" would be taken and that sound would produce little more than "talking films." The Soviet director and theorist called the addition of sound "two-edged" and expressed particular concern that artistic energies would be channeled into "'highly cultured dramas' and other photographed performances of a theatrical source." Eisenstein foresaw, in other words, a step back to the "canned theater" days. He feared that the potential of sound as an additional element in more original uses of film—in montage—would be lost.[11] Eisenstein was right to worry.

Renoir's original three-hour version of *Madame Bovary* was rejected by distributors (too long to fit in a double feature) and lost. A 117-minute version is all that survives. In it Renoir, once a great experimenter in various forms of cinematic motion, used a total of perhaps half a dozen close-ups. Scenes are viewed instead as if in a theater, from afar. Motion is confined, for the most part, to the characters. Camera angles change relatively infrequently. Many shots are held on-screen for the better part of a minute, some for longer than a minute. Parallel editing is used only twice.[12]

In the next two decades, most film embarked upon a similar journey into the past: It rediscovered *film d'art*; it forgot Eisenstein and to an extent even Griffith; it repressed the revelations of photography and crawled back to the security of word-oriented narrative. What had happened? Well, there were technical considerations: When presenting sentences on film, not only did it seem to make sense to allow them to finish before cutting, but it made it easier to keep picture and sound coordinated; dialogue, therefore, tended to be cut more slowly. And the need to keep the clatter of early motorized cameras out of the reach of early nondirectional microphones forced those cameras into soundproof glass-paneled booths; for a time they were unable to move around after different angles and perspectives.[13] But more significant was the fact that sound had allowed words to enter what had once been the province of images, and the word *culture* was still so strong that what it entered it tended to dominate.

Writing in the same year in which Renoir made *Madame Bovary*, Eisenstein expressed his dismay at the abandonment of the visual techniques he championed, then added, "At this point some viper must be hissing: 'Aha! the old devil is going to gallop about montage again.' Yes, montage."[14]

But montage was out of fashion. The esteemed and influential French film theorist André Bazin raved that Renoir "forced himself to look back beyond the resources provided by montage and so uncovered the secret of a film form that would permit everything to be said without chopping the world up into little fragments."[15] Grace and beauty returned. The McGuire Sisters danced and sang. The world—as presented on film, at least—was restored, reassembled; its meaning could once again be found in stories that made heavy use of words.

"Today we can say," Bazin proclaimed in the 1950s, "that at last the director writes in film."[16]

&   &   &

To experience the power of moving images and sound in 1930 required some effort. To begin with, it was necessary to leave the house. You had to get dressed, face the elements and the public, and find your way to a theater. A companion or date, while not a necessity, was a comfort. An admission fee had to be paid. Nevertheless, in 1930, when the population of the United States was a little less than 123 million, 80 million people went to the movies each week. Increasingly they were presented with double features, occasionally triple features. Some portion stuck around to see the show twice.[17]

Those who were sitting in those motion picture houses were not, for those hours at least, reading Cicero or Dostoevsky. They were not, for the most part, seeing Shakespeare.*[18] Movie patrons were also not, for the moment, reading poetry or staring at paintings or listening to symphonies. For some, like the French novelist Georges Duhamel, this was a great shame:

> Beethoven, Wagner, Baudelaire, Mallarmé, Giorgione, Vinci— I'm citing randomly, I've named six, there are a hundred— that's truly Art. To understand the work of these great men, to get to its core, I've made and continue to make efforts that elevate me above my self and belong to the most joyous victories of my life. The cinema has sometimes entertained me, sometimes even moved me; it's never asked me to surpass myself. It isn't an art, it isn't Art.[19]

As many of us have discovered late at night on television or at our video stores, some classic films were produced in these first decades of sound.† Yet film historian Gerald Mast has suggested that of the seventy-five hundred or so movies made by Hollywood from 1930 to 1945, only about two hundred still stand up.[20] Even if we overrule Duhamel and rate some of these films as "Art," art on screen remained a rare and elusive phenomenon.

People went to the movies primarily for the same reason they had once gone to Elizabethan plays (large numbers of which were also not by Shakespeare): for entertainment.[21] And what a great new source of entertainment this was. Travel to London or New York was not necessary to enjoy it. Although the Depression did cut attendance, at most times in the United States the price of admission was within reach of the vast majority of the population. And these masses found in the talkies tried and tested forms: stories, tragedies, comedies.

Entertainment has always been a somewhat suspect activity. "Nothing is as ruinous to the character as sitting away one's time at a show," wrote the Roman Stoic Seneca almost two thousand years ago, "for it is then, through the medium of entertainment, that vices creep

* The first two talkies based on plays by Shakespeare were made in Hollywood in 1935 and 1936, with great publicity and big stars— James Cagney as Bottom with Mickey Rooney as Puck. *Variety's* verdict: a "B.O. [box office] Washout."

† *The 39 Steps,* directed by Alfred Hitchcock; *Stagecoach,* directed by John Ford; *The Rules of the Game,* which Renoir directed five years after *Madame Bovary;* and *The Philadelphia Story,* directed by George Cukor, are examples.

into one with more than usual ease."[22] If the assumption is that character can be damaged by an excess of pleasure—an assumption that
has outlived Stoics and Puritans—then watching actors on a screen
may indeed be unwise. At times in the 1930s theater owners concluded that it did not matter what movies they showed; audiences would
come anyway. Observing interesting characters (played by actors who
were interesting in their own right) as they moved and talked through
a couple of suspenseful, humorous or emotional narratives for a few
hours once a week was simply fun.

The threat to the character of television viewers like Ralph
Kramden and Perry Como would prove even more severe, of course:
They indulge in similar hours of what seems to pass for fun up to seven
nights a week. Indeed, this is among the most terrible of the sins for
which couch potatoes must answer. They aren't struggling or elevating
themselves or even, the argument goes, using their imaginations.
They're just—more or less, in their sleepy-eyed way—being entertained.

In the early 1950s a group of writers discussed the implications of
that new arrival, television. "We write one play," Moss Hart reminded
the others.

> It takes months to put it on, and then, if it's a success, we play
> it eight performances a week, two hours a performance. When
> we sell out, we reach a weekly audience of perhaps nine thou-
> sand customers...*if* we sell out. But the day is coming when
> that two-hour play can be seen once—by millions of people.
> And when that happens, the networks will have to be looking
> for people to supply them with thirty-six of those plays—or
> seventy-two hour-long plays—*each week*!

Impressive, if disconcerting, arithmetic. Hart's fellow writers thought it
over. Finally one spoke: "Where was it ever decreed that man had to
have so much entertainment?"[23]

The British communications theorist Raymond Williams suggested in 1974 that "in societies like Britain and the United States more
drama is watched in a week or weekend, by the majority of viewers,
than would have been watched in a year or in some cases a lifetime in
any previous historical period." Williams made an additional comparison: "Most people spend more time watching various kinds of drama
than in preparing and eating food."[24] And these calculations were
based on mere broadcast television. Videocassette recorders and cable
have further swelled our drama consumption.

Which leaves us...? Diverted, certainly. In itself that may not be
not such a bad thing. "However sad a man may be, he is happy for a

time if you can only get him to enter into some diversion," Blaise Pascal noted; "and however happy a man may be, if he is not amused and occupied by some passion or entertainment, which prevents the spread of boredom, he will soon be peevish and miserable."[25]

In the end I don't find those evenings on which I have succumbed to the seductions of television in its current, mostly unchallenging form hugely enjoyable. Many people I know don't. This may reflect a Puritan streak; it may reflect good taste. Still, I would never deny TV's ability to paint its pastel hues over dark hours of disquiet and discontent. Moving images with sound can, undeniably, ease some kinds of boredom and divert our minds from certain kinds of pain.

In 1977 the *Detroit Free Press* decided to conduct an experiment on television deprivation. It took some effort to come up with people willing to serve as subjects: The paper offered five hundred dollars to 120 different families before finding 5 who would agree to give up television for a month. These families, like others who have participated in such experiments over the years, found that life without TV led to increased boredom, nervousness and depression—Pascal's point.[26]

But is there not something, besides sadness and ennui, we are being diverted from? Are there not things we *ought* to be doing besides taking in all this drama? Sure. We could always be using our time better. The Greek word for "leisure" is *scholē*—from which comes our word for school. A bit of education, a bit of elevating Art squeezed into our leisure hours couldn't hurt. But there's nothing to say that diversion can't arrive with art, and vice versa. Shakespeare certainly diverted. Does the fact that moving images can entertain mean that they cannot educate and inspire?

Whether merely having some fun, vibrant or pastel, is on its face unconscionable is a matter for each of us to settle within our own heart. But if we can abide the presence in our lives of some activities engaged in for a little pleasure, for a little diversion, then the issue is not how much entertainment we are getting but how much artistic stimulation accompanies that entertainment. The issue is whether we're sometimes stretched, educated. This book argues that we might be—by new forms of video. The route to an understanding of how this might happen passes through talking pictures.

In such films as Howard Hawks's *Scarface,* Luis Buñuel's *Land Without Bread,* John Ford's adaptation of John Steinbeck's *The Grapes of Wrath* or Preston Sturges's *The Miracle of Morgan's Creek,* movie audiences in the 1930s and 1940s were asked to question pat moral judgments or ponder social issues. Movie audiences were not, thanks to the retreat from montage, forced to confront a world that had been chopped "into little fragments."

      &   &   &

One of the shots in Renoir's 1934 *Madame Bovary* presents a rare happy moment between Emma and her husband. Charles drapes a new scarf over Emma's shoulders, admires the way she looks, then surprises her by announcing that he has purchased a coach. He walks to the window. She does too. The shot has not changed. The camera moves slightly to look over Emma's shoulder at the coach across the street. She runs out of the frame. Charles follows. The camera can now see clearly through the window to the street, where Emma and then eventually Charles reappear hurrying to the coach.[27]

Such a lengthy shot has some advantages. It gives us, to begin with, a chance to study what we are seeing. Here's what one extremely conscientious and sensitive viewer—Renoir's friend, film and philosophy professor Alexander Sesonske—discovered in this shot:

> The overall pattern of movement is balanced, nearly symmetrical. The movements of Charles and Emma are nearly identical; each repeats the movement of the other as if they were quite in harmony. And the doubling of this repetition, first in the large frame of the screen, then within the small frame of the window, brings them even closer together.

Elsewhere in this film Sesonske noticed how "Renoir frequently divides his frame with a central vertical and balances his composition on either side," how "our eye moving into the depth of the space is drawn toward the center of the screen rather than a corner," and how "the overall tendency is toward static, balanced composition, pictorial stillness rather than movement."[28]

This is the sort of vocabulary I encountered during a brief immersion in film school some decades ago. It is a vocabulary borrowed—except for the talk of movement—from art criticism, which is appropriate in this case since Renoir, the son of the painter Pierre-Auguste Renoir, did indeed look through a camera with a painter's eye. Lengthy shots ask to be seen like paintings, moving paintings. They allow us to appreciate the verticals, the symmetries, the frames within frames, the repetitions and the doubling of repetitions. Montage would distract us from these pleasures. (Renoir used this technique only once in his classic *The Rules of the Game*.)[29] In explaining why he gave up his "experiment" with "rapid cutting," Renoir wrote, "I now consider that the best editing is the kind that is not noticed."[30]

Lengthy shots also allow life to be shown on screen in a close approximation of the way it normally appears before our eyes. In that long shot from Renoir's *Madame Bovary,* people move as they move in life. Time flows as it flows in life: We actually wait for the actors to walk outside to the carriage. And we see no more than we would see in life—if we, like the camera, had been inside that room with Emma and Charles.

All this "realism" pleased André Bazin no end. For Bazin "total cinema" would be a "complete imitation of nature" (Baudelaire's nightmare). The goal of the medium, he argued, is to come as close to achieving that as possible. And Renoir lauded Bazin as the person who "made us feel that our trade was a noble one."[31]

Here are some guidelines for filmmakers distilled from Bazin's analyses: "Take a close look at the world, keep on doing so." Create "dramatic effects" out of the "movements of the actors within a fixed framework," not montage. Play no "tricks with time and space." Avoid the close-up, "the too violent impact of which would make the audience conscious of the cutting." Evaluate an image "not according to what it adds to reality but what it reveals of it."[32]

Bazin's camera position of choice was the "depth shot"—a long shot in which meaningful actions occur, in focus, in both the foreground and background of the scene. Renoir developed the potential of this shot. In 1941 Orson Welles made brilliant use of it in *Citizen Kane* (which, nonetheless, fails to resist dazzling lapses into montage and other attention-getting editing techniques). Depth shots are necessarily ambiguous: We don't know exactly what *we* are to focus on. We're back to wondering whether to watch the waiter, the cowboys or the young man meeting a young woman. But Bazin loved this ambiguity. He announced that he preferred the expressionless film of the actor Mozhukhin *before* Kuleshov gave it various meanings by mixing it with other images. Life, after all, is ambiguous, and the purpose of film, intoned Bazin, is to try to reproduce "the flow of life itself."[33]

This is a seductive point of view. Life certainly has its interest. But is producing an exact copy of it the most ambitious purpose we can imagine for moving images?

Photography and film are often credited with inspiring a revolution in the arts. Once it became clear that any amateur photographer could produce a reasonably realistic image of a scene, artists began experimenting with new, less obvious realities—not all of which presented themselves in scenes. Artists also began seeking out some of the revelations of photography and film: odd instants pulled out of systems of meaning, cut-ins and cut-aways, liberties taken with perspective.

Cubists began "chopping the world up into little fragments," to use Bazin's dismissive phrase. Surrealists shocked with impossible, dreamlike photomontages. Abstract expressionists renounced the pictoral representation of reality. Pop artists invited flat, glossy, commercial images onto canvases once occupied only by solemn Art. Throughout the art world traditional notions of grace and beauty were being subverted; traditional notions of reality were being disassembled.

Even the two forms that moving images were most busy imitating set off on "modernist" excursions. In the theater of the absurd, narrative and traditional meanings were subtracted. And novelists such as Virginia Woolf and James Joyce began exploring the ways in which thoughts and images rolled and tumbled in front of a lively consciousness. In his insightful historical analysis of the novel, written during World War II, Erich Auerbach described how these writers mixed "many fragments of events," "mere splinters of events." He too sensed film's influence here: "One might feel inclined to assume that it was the writer's purpose to exploit the structural possibilities of the film in the interest of the novel."[34]

In Paris in 1930 Sergei Eisenstein met James Joyce. The two men quickly discovered a common interest: the stream of consciousness. The Soviet director was a great fan of what he called "the immortal 'inner monologues' of Leopold Bloom in *Ulysses*,"* which are presented, in large part, as montages:[35]

> Houses, lines of houses, streets, miles of pavements, piledup bricks, stones. Changing hands. This owner, that. Landlord never dies they say. Other steps into his shoes when he gets his notice to quit. They buy the place up with gold and still they have all the gold. Swindle in it somewhere. Piled up in cities, worn away age after age. Pyramids in sand. Built on bread and onions. Slaves. Chinese wall. Babylon. Big stones left. Round towers. Rest rubble, sprawling suburbs, jerrybuilt, Kerwan's mushroom houses, built of breeze. Shelter for the night.[36]

Joyce read out loud from his book for Eisenstein. Eisenstein discussed his own theories, including his belief, recorded in an article written two years later, that the stream of consciousness "finds full expression, however, only in the cinema. For only the sound-film is capable of reconstructing all phases and all specifics of the course of thought."[37]

Eisenstein was convinced that the normal film vocabulary of "knitted brows, rolling eyes" and worried conversation was insufficient for communicating the mind-set of characters. He envisioned instead a montage of aural and visual sensations that captured the "race of thoughts" that pass before our excited minds. "And how obvious it becomes," he wrote in that article, "that the material of the

* In 1928 Eisenstein called *Ulysses* "the Bible of the new cinema."

sound-film is not dialogue. *The true material of the sound-film is, of course, the monologue."*[38]

Joyce, although his eyesight was fading, asked to view the more experimental sequences of *Battleship Potemkin* and *October*. Ideas were exchanged on a film version of *Ulysses*.[39] This might indeed have been elevating, to use Duhamel's word. But, of course, no Eisenstein-Joyce film was ever made.

Despite numerous proposals, scripts and even some completed reels, Eisenstein was able to finish only one sound film, *Alexander Nevsky* in 1938. His ideas had managed to disturb both capitalist studio heads and Communist apparatchiks. Other adventurous artists, among them Buñuel and the surrealist Jean Cocteau, were at times able to grab hold of a sound camera in these decades. But for the most part the sound film remained in the hands of Bazin's forces. It was replicating a familiar view of reality, not finding new ways to understand reality.

This, of course, is the irony I'm after: The medium perhaps most responsible for spurring the twentieth century's challenges to traditional presentations of reality has spent most of the century trapped in them. It seemed as if everyone was exploiting "the structural possibilities of the film" except filmmakers. "Other kinds of writer, such as playwrights or novelists, may for the moment be able to work in a more cinematic way than film people," Bertolt Brecht observed in 1931.[40]

The movies had the excuse of often having to please large audiences—larger than those required by painting or sculpture, theater or literature. But in those years, those decades, even many of those filmmakers able to make do with smaller audiences managed to convince themselves that the more difficult lessons on cinematic motion taught by Eisenstein and Griffith could be forgotten.

While older art forms, and even life itself, were straining to look like movies at their wildest, most movies were still relying upon familiar artistic conventions and straining to look like life—or at least a spiffed-up, more violent and romantic version thereof. The editing was tame and unobtrusive. People talked. Credible stories were told. The "verticals" were in order. Actors moved. Cameras stared. Balance reigned. Audiences were pleased. Studio heads and apparatchiks of all stripes were pleased. Even film-school professors with an eye for composition were pleased. A comfortable, glamorous world of lifelike, well-photographed moving images was created.

We misunderstand moving images when we think of them merely as a form of communication, a type of entertainment, a means of informing or an art form. Perhaps books, newspapers or radio can squeeze under such headings. Moving images with sound, because they occupy both of our major senses, cannot. They are more than that. They are a place we go.*[41]

The world of moving images, which most Americans have been entering weekly or daily for most of the twentieth century, has many attractions. First and foremost are its beauty and visual interest. Color helped. (The first successful Technicolor film was released in 1922; more than 50 percent of Hollywood films were shot in color by 1954; the key moment in television's conversion to color, heralded by the NBC peacock, may have been the success of *Walt Disney's Wonderful World of Color* on NBC in 1960.)[42] Film and television, particularly color films and color television, are full of what Emerson called "eye-traps."[43]

I was trying to persuade a group of unusually bookish undergraduates recently that moving images have a formidable visual pull, and they were, as happens with disturbing frequency, resisting. A TV set was in the room. I turned it on and began flipping through the channels. "Yeah, there's a lot to look at," one student said, "but that's just because you're changing channels so fast." I kept the set on a single channel for a while, turned down the sound and tried to resume the discussion. A few students began smiling. I began smiling. Soon everyone was smiling. Although the students made efforts to look in my direction, they could not divert their eyes from the screen for more than a moment.

Something similar occurs at sporting arenas nowadays, where eyes seem instantly to turn away from the playing field as soon as images—replays, highlights, bloopers, advertisements—begin to move on the giant video screens. Something similar has been happening in concert halls too as more and more screens have been placed on or around the stage. What's on-screen often looks more intriguing than what's not.

"For us of the minority, the opportunity to see geese is more important than television," wrote the conservationist Aldo Leopold during television's infancy.[44] That is a small, ever-shrinking minority.

To clarify this point, let me borrow a parable from the historian Daniel Boorstin. He was leafing through an advertising brochure in 1960 when he saw a picture of a man preparing to look into a Viewmaster, a small slide viewer. The man was sitting in a convertible parked next to what appeared to be the Grand Canyon. This man, Boorstin reported, "with the Grand Canyon at his elbow," is choosing instead to look at images.† "Here, if ever, is a parable of twentieth-century America," Boorstin concluded.[45]

What is the lesson of this parable? Boorstin's book *The Image* is a

* Baudrillard had a characteristically provocative take on this: "There is no longer any medium in the literal sense. It is now intangible, diffuse and diffracted in the real."

† I have pared down Boorstin's parable somewhat: The

☞

thoughtful and impassioned critique of the culture created by images, particularly those carried by the Viewmaster's big brother, television. He saw waste in this scene: the great energy and technological know-how of the American economy occupying itself with the creation of images when we have the real Grand Canyon to look at. And Boorstin saw a kind of moral decay here: Clearly he would have liked to drag that man out of his convertible, throw away his silly slides and turn his head toward that spectacular canyon. Most of us would. Cursed be the man who looks at an image instead of natural beauty!

I interpret this parable somewhat differently, however. If moving images merely imitated nature, as Bazin wanted, they wouldn't captivate us so. The fact—a sad one for all us nature fans—is that images often look better than nature.*[46] I won't push this point too hard for the Viewmaster, though undoubtedly the slides that man was about to look at were well lit and well composed, while canyons can have their bad moments. The real competition for nature came when those well-lit, well-composed images began to move and talk. What window, overlooking what canyon, showcasing how many gaggles of geese, can pull the majority's gaze from screens that can show dozens of the world's best vistas and gaggles of walking, talking, spectacularly attractive and talented members of our own species? These screens do not, with all due respect to Mr. McKibben, offer a low-fat visual diet; they offer a feast!

Our Viewmasters and screens grab our attention for an additional reason: because they take us, as E.B. White once put it, "elsewhere."[47] Most art has this capability, but moving images with sound can make such leaps through time and space particularly persuasive and compelling. Much of the seductiveness of their world comes from the ability we gain there to leave behind instantly whatever classroom, stadium, concert hall, canyon rim or living room currently traps our body.

The world of moving images also is rich in drama: At any given moment someone is likely in peril, in love or stumbling into some droll situation. And the people we encounter in this world have certain advantages over most of our acquaintances: Not only are they great-looking and often witty, but they never disdain our company.

Moving images share their entertainments with us without demanding anything in return; this is another of the attractions of their world. We don't have to be presentable; we don't have to hold up our end of the conversation. No wonder we have been visiting this world so often, losing ourselves in it so completely.

Unfortunately, the world of moving images has a few drawbacks. The first relates to the question of free will: the extent to which we are free to influence our circumstances rather than beholden to fate. In the world of film and television things clarify themselves considerably: We have absolutely no influence whatsoever, free or otherwise, on anything that transpires. Movies and television shows proceed entirely without us. As the pawn of such large, intractable forces, a viewer can end up feeling somewhat small.

"One looks more and more and *does* less and less," concluded a participant in an early British examination of television.[48] The pictures do the moving for us. The act of watching moving images, consequently, does not require much of our appendages or muscle groups. Since that which is unused in a living organism tends to atrophy, this is an additional drawback. And something similar is happening to our social skills.

Movies fit reasonably comfortably into older, bourgeois social patterns. Going to the movies was not that different from going to a dance or to the theater. No previous social pattern, however, can accommodate the vast amounts of solitary, silent time we spend in front of the tube.

Harvard political scientist Robert D. Putnam has fingered television as the "prime suspect" in the "strange disappearance of civic America," by which he means participation in community groups and even bowling leagues.[49] He has a point. Time spent with television isn't any more solitary than time spent reading books. But we spend an awful lot more time with television, and therefore an awful lot less time joining bowling leagues, attending meetings and talking with each other. Consequently our civic life has declined; so has our social life. Putnam concluded that we devote about one quarter less time to socializing than Americans did in 1965.[50] His calculations may be controversial; the trend, however, seems beyond contention. Those two and a half to five hours a day had to be subtracted from something. This is perhaps the largest of the drawbacks.

We used to say we were watching shows "together," "as a family"—though social interaction on those occasions rarely extended beyond demands that one or another family member "shush!" The arrival of the remote control has pretty much put an end to this pretense. It is becoming difficult for any two people, no matter how much in love, to agree on what channels are to be selected, in what order, during what commercials. Television, now more than ever, is a solitary pleasure. We surf alone.

Not only does television cut down on time spent with others, it cuts down on the need for others. Here books, no matter how devoted we are to them, just can't compete. Jerry, Elaine, George and Kramer; Regis and Kathie Lee; Dave and Paul—they all visit us regularly, every week or every day, for years and years; Emma and Charles never did that. The faces and voices of these television personalities grow familiar. They are consistently clever and cheery. They are always tolerant of our foibles. They make fine friends—if we overlook the fact that they don't have the slightest awareness of or interest in us.

What effect does the presence of these new friends have on our lives? Andy Warhol was characteristically blunt: "When I first got my television set, I stopped caring so much about having close relationships."*51

Here's Alan Coren, a British television critic: "Television is simply more interesting than people. If it were not, we should have people standing in the corners of our rooms"—or at least sitting on our couches or across from us at a bar or café. Pubs are closing in England. France now has less than a third as many cafés as it had in 1960.52 Is there any doubt why? And as television takes over, people actually grow less interesting—less skilled at the conversational arts because they are less practiced at them.

Novelist David Foster Wallace has explained that the art of conversation has changed for his generation: "In younger Americans' experience, people in the same room don't do all that much direct conversing with each other. What most of the people I know do is they all sit and face the same direction and stare at the same thing and then structure commercial-length conversations around the sorts of questions that myopic car-crash witnesses might ask each other—'Did you see what I just saw?'"53

The writer Vivian Gornick was walking with an Israeli journalist on a quiet evening in Tel Aviv in 1977 when she was confronted by one of the more dramatic of the social implications of television: streets without people. "A few years ago they would all have been out in the cafés," that Israeli muttered. "Now they're home watching *Dallas*." Gornick asked where the journalist and his friends gathered to talk. "People didn't talk anymore, he said."54

We return from our now frequent and lengthy sojourns in the world of moving images feeling smaller, more solitary and less socially adept. This is where Ralph Kramden's decision to purchase a set and Perry Como's placing of himself in a still life with television have led. We pay a price for watching the equivalent of a double feature most nights; we pay a price for watching it mostly alone in our homes. We pay that price as individuals and as a society. If I continue to risk charges of hypocrisy by monitoring, however ineffectually, the television consumption of my children, that price is my excuse.

This is, as you have undoubtedly noted, an optimistic book. But I have little optimism to contribute here. Can we survive this sharp decline in opportunities "to rub shoulders with [our] fellows"? Undoubtedly. The species has survived worse. Are our social impulses sufficiently strong to force us to find new ways of engaging each other—perhaps on-line, perhaps by forming even more interest or support groups, perhaps by hiring, even more frequently, people to hear out our anxieties? I wouldn't be surprised. Might a backlash develop? Might it become fashionable to push the off button and go out and pay some calls? This too appears possible. Still, it is difficult not to conclude that the days of widespread gregariousness are behind us. Would we be a more vigorous people, though less well entertained and informed, if we were still on the streets in the evening, shooting the breeze? I would think so.

That's the bad news. In fact, you have just completed the most depressing collection of paragraphs in this book. (Those convinced we're in decline may find them the most congenial group of paragraphs.) I can't pretend that the new form of video I am heralding will transplant our couch potatoes. The good news—the message of the final four chapters of this book—is that this new form of video may occasionally "elevate" them.

Video has a chance to accomplish this and become Art only if a few unusual conditions are met: It must more frequently abandon the effort to merely replicate life that has characterized most talking films and most television; video must disobey Bazin and once again dare to reimagine life. It must relocate some of the techniques, verve and bravado once displayed in the silent film. It must reclaim some of the avant-garde impulses it released into other art forms; future Joyces must collaborate with future Eisensteins in video. Video must confront and try to harness the anarchic energies of the photographic instant. It must unleash that force that has been so long feared, so long scorned: the power of the image, not in lieu of words but in partnership with words.

This sounds like a radical prescription, particularly for a popular, intensely profit-oriented medium. However, these conditions are slowly beginning to be met, not so much in art films or art videos but on television. Jean Renoir caught a glimpse of the change: In a book first published in 1974, the French director acknowledged that the "device" of "rapid cutting," which he had abandoned early in his career, "was to make a brilliant reappearance half a century later in American television."*[55] Orson Welles, who directed the classic of the talking-film era, also noticed that something was changing: "I see a lot more interesting things in television than I do in movies," he explained in one of a series of interviews with Peter Bogdanovich that began in 1968:

> The minute I arrive in America, or any country, I sit right down, turn off the sound, and stare at the commer-

* Renoir gave as an example the variety show *Laugh-In*.

cials...because I think some of the most interesting moviemaking is in the commercials. I don't mean they're all good, but every once in a while you see something that's staggering. And the more fast-cut commercials are made, the more sophisticated the public's eye becomes.[56]

The remainder of this book will be devoted to the techniques that are responsible for, and are taking advantage of, this growth in sophistication of the public's eye. It will consider the potential of these techniques and speculate on what they might bring—to couch potatoes, to art and to thought.

Part III

The New Video

Some exercise in complex seeing is needed...it is perhaps more important to be able to think above the stream than to think in the stream.

—Bertolt Brecht, 1931

One of the thirteen hundred still images in Chuck Braverman's three-minute-long 1969 film *American Time Capsule.*

One dramatic image after another: two shots from Bruce Conner's 1958 film *A Movie.*

10 "A Forced Condensation of Energy":

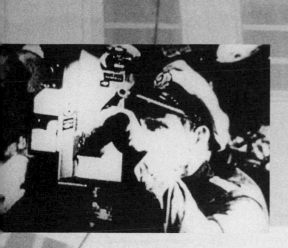

"A new dissolution of literary forms": one "whooshingly entertaining" moment (featuring Tom Cruise) from Brian De Palma's 1996 film *Mission: Impossible*.

Fast Cutting

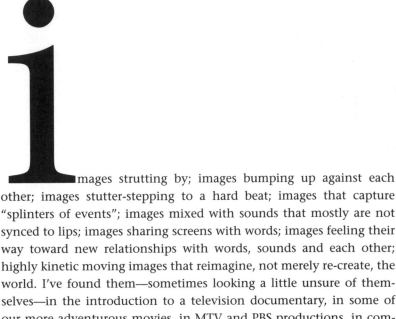mages strutting by; images bumping up against each other; images stutter-stepping to a hard beat; images that capture "splinters of events"; images mixed with sounds that mostly are not synced to lips; images sharing screens with words; images feeling their way toward new relationships with words, sounds and each other; highly kinetic moving images that reimagine, not merely re-create, the world. I've found them—sometimes looking a little unsure of themselves—in the introduction to a television documentary, in some of our more adventurous movies, in MTV and PBS productions, in commercials.

The final section of this book will describe more of these new, still immature swarms of images: a brief rush of animation by the filmmaker Jeff Scher, a short film made by Mark Pellington about his father's struggle with Alzheimer's, a public-service announcement edited by Hank Corwin for a children's charity, and intriguing segments from a variety of additional films, music videos, television productions and commercials. In them I will try to discover an art form that is currently in the process of being born, an art form capable of exploiting the full potential of moving images with sound, an art form I call—to distinguish it from the imitative groupings of moving images that currently plod through most of our channels, multiplexes, VCRs and Web sites—the *new video*.

I have tried to trace the ancestry of the new video back to painting, photography and, particularly, the use of montage in silent films. Aquinas and Eisenstein serve as prophets, Muybridge, Griffith and Eisenstein (again) as patriarchs. Bazin represents the unbelievers. However, the new video itself is a more recent phenomenon. It cannot live up to its capabilities without audio—primarily music and spoken words. So this form can be said to have entered the world and taken its first tentative steps forward only *after* the arrival of the sound film.

The history of the new video begins, then, as a tiny countermovement to the large step back to theatrical drama and narrative taken by the talkies. It would be nice if I could locate this small beginning for what I believe to be a major art form in the work of some pipe-smoking cineast, some philosophically inclined, preferably French, visionary. Instead I find it in a Marx Brothers film.

It would also be nice if the chain of influences I am about to construct were sturdier. But influences are often nothing more than scents on the breeze, and techniques this elemental and this effective are stumbled upon almost as frequently as they are sniffed out. It is equally difficult to reconstruct the history of the techniques embodied in, for example, the novel.

It would be nice, too, if this movement were neatly contained in some bohemian circle. Instead, it drifted all over film and television—wafting back and forth between the avant-garde and the resolutely commercial.

To recap: Television advertisements helped influence Mark Pellington, who would help MTV develop its style in the 1980s and thereby begin the process of spreading the techniques of the new video throughout the universe—even as far as ABC News. Advertisers had become aware of these techniques by the end of the 1960s, as evidenced by that Coca-Cola commercial in 1969, which featured a montage of still images of modish young people. To extend the chain we need to know who influenced the advertisers.

Some ad executives may have been familiar with Eisenstein; *Battleship Potemkin* occasionally preceded *Duck Soup* and *Citizen Kane* at the film festivals that were de rigueur at universities and art-film houses in the sixties. However, advertisers—not known for their fascination with deceased Bolsheviks—had a somewhat more congenial source for these techniques: experimental film.

Those who stood behind 16mm projectors on Manhattan's Lower East Side in the 1960s occasionally seemed a little paranoid: Television advertisers, they suspected, were stealing their ideas. It was true, of course. The admen were appropriating not just the ideas of underground filmmakers, mind you, but also the freewheeling camera movements and syncopated editing introduced by French New Wave directors, particularly Jean-Luc Godard in the film *Breathless*. (The French, fortunately, are not entirely unrepresented in this history.) Advertisers imitated, too, some of the energetic, attention-getting, occasionally highly *visible* methods of shooting and editing introduced by a new generation of Hollywood directors who had trained in television, including John Frankenheimer and Sam Peckinpah.[1]

"We paid attention to it all," acknowledged Philip Dusenberry, who made Pepsi commercials for BBDO then and is chairman of that advertising agency's New York office now. "We borrowed from them all. We borrowed freely." Advertisers did not get much from the long-winded, Bazin-like attempts to stare down reality underground filmmakers often produced. (When Andy Warhol and Paul Morrissey began pointing unblinking, unmoving cameras at their more unusual acquaintances, these attempts gained the opportunity to bore larger audiences on larger screens.) But ad executives were particularly taken with films that attempted to distinguish themselves by moving in the other direction, that were, as Dusenberry put it, "the opposite of dull."[2]

Perhaps the most influential experimental film of the 1960s was originally produced for the much-watched, much-argued-about *Smothers Brothers Comedy Hour* on CBS. Chuck Braverman, a twenty-three-year-old film-school graduate working as a messenger at CBS, had shown some of his student films to Tom Smothers. When Smothers found himself with three minutes to fill on an upcoming show, he and Braverman decided it would be cool—this *was* the sixties—to fit the history of the United States into those three minutes. Smothers forgot all about it, but in due time Braverman presented him with the film *American Time Capsule*—a remarkably fast-cut collage of stills, precisely coordinated with a drum solo, showing most of the major events in American history. Length: as promised. Number of cuts: thirteen hundred, Braverman reported. (I haven't undertaken the task of counting this one myself.[3])

Here's what happened next, as Braverman remembered it:

> Smothers said, "The show is already all locked up." But he looked at the film. Then he called all his producers and his brother to look at the film. They kicked a singer or someone off the program, and showed the film. This was the weekend before the 1968 election, and the program was at the height of its controversy. They got the largest positive mail response they ever had. And they hired me as their resident filmmaker.

Braverman's next film, on the year 1968—a whole four and a half-minutes long—was broadcast in one week on both the *Smothers Brothers* and the new *60 Minutes.*

"Everybody said that you wouldn't be able to see the two-frame cuts I did," Braverman explained, "but you can. There's a scene in *American Time Capsule* of Truman holding up the Dewey-victory headline, and it's not on long enough to see. If you were from Mars, you wouldn't know what it is, but since it comes in chronological sequence and you know the scene, you figure out what it is." I've shown this film myself to dozens of people; most see President Truman holding up that newspaper.

"Agency people really picked up on Braverman's film," Dusenberry remembered. "He was cutting so incredibly fast. The reaction was, 'Holy cow!'"[4] That "Holy cow!" makes the connection between Chuck Braverman and Pepsi and Coke commercials. But one of the weak links in my chain of influences is the next connection: between Braverman and an earlier experimental filmmaker and artist, Bruce Conner.

Mark Pellington labeled Conner "an influence." "Bruce Conner was one of the keys; Braverman too," added Hank Corwin, who has edited many of Pellington's videos, many of the most interesting commercials and much of *Natural Born Killers*.[5] Dennis Hopper's *Easy Rider*, released in 1969, has experimental, "psychedelic" sequences that have a role in this history, and Hopper is quite direct about it: "Bruce's movies changed my entire concept of editing," he said.[6] Braverman, however, while acknowledging that he had seen some experimental films, did not mention Bruce Conner's name. We'll have to call Conner's influence on Braverman, then, one of those that was floating on the breeze.

Bruce Conner probably deserves credit for having introduced the technique Braverman used, and commercials and MTV continue to use: cutting fast to a driving beat. In his 1961 film *Cosmic Ray*, Conner first mated a rock beat (Ray Charles singing "What'd I Say") to what the critic Greil Marcus described as a "barrage of fast cutting and superimposition." Marcus explained, "In the sixties he made a series of music-based short films that all but invented the language music video has plundered ever since."[7] Conner had first unleashed that "barrage," minus the rock beat, in his first film, called *A Movie*, in 1958.

Conner shot no footage for *A Movie;* he couldn't afford a camera. A friend had lent him a film splicer, however, so he taped together shots from reels of 16mm film (some of which were erotic) he had purchased or filched. "Found footage" (a kind of found art) is the name the cineasts later attached to the technique. "There would be shots I thought were curious or interesting, absurd or peculiar, or maybe they touched a reminiscence in my mind," Conner explained. "I would cut out all the footage in between, and the reels would keep getting shorter and shorter."[8] A car crashing, a suspension bridge wiggling itself apart, the *Hindenburg* burning, a man looking through a periscope, a submarine firing a torpedo, some female nudes, a mushroom cloud forming ("Nobody had ever used the image of the atomic bomb in this way before," Conner said); one dramatic image on the heels of another.[9]

Alfred Hitchcock's thriller *Psycho*, made two years after *A Movie*, includes a section that is also cut incredibly fast: the famous shower sequence. Janet Leigh (or a body double) is stabbed to death in forty-five seconds and eighty-seven shots.*[10] That's about a half second for each shot—a rate that would do a 1990s Mountain Dew commercial proud. However, unlike Conner's film, or Mountain Dew commercials,

* Saul Bass said he conceived of this scene. Hitchcock, however, denied it.

Hitchcock's shots are all of the same scene. *A Movie* employs the fourth kind of cinematic motion: Scene follows scene, on and on, without anything resembling a traditional narrative to connect them.

In these years the graphic arts were embarking upon similar experiments in the power of compression, overlap, composite and pastiche.*[11] And Conner noted that a similar disjointedness can be found in news shows, which not infrequently leap from the catastrophic to the cute, from the instructional to the sensational.[12] Television news learned to shove items together like this from radio news, which learned it from newspapers. In fact, news had been extracted from narratives or other contexts and jumbled together in the weekly handwritten "gazettes" distributed in sixteenth-century Venice—the oldest direct ancestors of the modern newspaper.[13] One way of looking at *A Movie* is as a kind of "news summary" or "gazette" of cinematic moments—speeded up, with moving pictures and sound.

Conner has come up with some suitably lofty theories about what it all means. One or two film theorists have developed equally lofty, though different, theories.[14] But the crucial message of *A Movie*—a message now echoed thousands of times a day by TV highlights and commercials—is simply that a bunch of interesting moments, edited together can produce a new, often fascinating way of looking at the world. Conner himself had first received that message while watching a Marx Brothers movie. This is where the chain that leads to the new video begins.

The arrival of sound had forced film studios to find comics who sounded as well as looked funny. The Marx Brothers, veteran vaudeville comedians, certainly qualified.† Their fifth film, *Duck Soup,* released in 1933, featured an extraordinary collection of witticisms in an almost entirely ordinary talkie format. Most of the action—vaudeville bits, characters breaking into song—might as well have taken place onstage. The scene that made an impression on the young Bruce Conner, however, is a glaring exception.

Near the end of the film, with both the country he leads and the building in which he is holed up under attack, Groucho dramatically announces, "Help is on the way." At this point director Leo McCarey inserted a montage consisting of what we now know as found footage: fire trucks, runners, boats, swimmers, apes, elephants, dolphins—all behaving as if they are in a great hurry. Eleven shots in just under seventeen seconds. We are supposed to see a joke here—these various vehicles, people and animals rushing to Groucho's rescue. Bruce Conner, who reported getting "bored with most movies after fifteen or twenty minutes," also saw a new technique, one that was the opposite of boring. "In my mind I was thinking of a sequence where you could add

*In the work of, for example, such designers as Herb Lubalin, Armin Hofmann, Seymour Chwast and Milton Glaser.

† Harpo, of course, was a special case.

even more images to this rush," he recalled.[15] In Conner's mind while watching *Duck Soup,* in other words, was a rough outline of *A Movie, American Time Capsule,* MTV and modern television commercials.

"Some of the people who now do this have never even heard of me," Conner noted with more bemusement than chagrin. Yet if the first phase of experimentation in montage, the silent era, began with Griffith and developed with Eisenstein, a second phase can be said to have begun with this joke in *Duck Soup* and developed with Conner and Braverman. This is the stage that is leading to the new video. Conner called the fast-cut, video-plus-audio montage technique he helped invent, develop and release out onto the breeze "a forced condensation of energy."[16]

For a time Nam June Paik, who helped start a different line of experimentation with moving images, slept on a mattress supported by three old black-and-white RCA TV sets. The future of art too, he believed, rested on television. Paik purchased the first relatively portable videotape recorder, made by Sony, the day it went on sale in New York, in 1965. "I was very naive," the Korean-born artist reported, in still-accented English. "I thought the first man to own videotape recorder could become best painter of the age."[17]

Paik, probably the first *artist* to own a videotape recorder, produced some influential art videos in the 1960s and 1970s. His best-known, *Global Groove,* includes electronically distorted images of dancers and shots of such avant-garde figures as John Cage, Merce Cunningham, Allen Ginsberg and Paik's longtime collaborator, the cellist Charlotte Moorman. However, for all his enthusiasm for the artistic possibilities of video, Paik's ideas—fiddle with the electronics and show interesting artists—do not seem to have contributed much to its development. The truth is that few of the video artists who have followed Paik into museums and galleries have.

Moving images, the way I see them, are in large part an editor's medium, and until the late 1970s videotape remained difficult or expensive to edit. The frames of film, meanwhile, could be cut and spliced easily and cheaply by hand. That's why the early experiments that led to the new video were completed on film.

When video artists finally began to get hold of precise, relatively inexpensive editing equipment, they had difficulty competing with the spectacular effects already being produced for commercials and music videos, so most did what artists are always wont to do: They set off in the opposite direction. "Serious avant-garde art here is always in opposition to American mass culture," Paik acknowledged. "You have to define what you do against what they are doing. We want to make more crude if they are perfect; we want to make more boring if they are exciting."[18] American mass culture has, if nothing else, been visually exciting; hence, much of the video in museums and galleries, particularly that projected onto sculpturelike "installations," isn't. It features lengthy, repeating shots of stagnant scenes. The question of how this qualifies as art I'll leave to others. It does not qualify as part of the new video.*

Nor does the bulk of what we currently see on television programs or in movies. While two of the most awkward attempts at mimicry— the TV variety show and the movie musical—have for the most part been put to rest, imitation continues to overwhelm originality in most television programs and movies. Take as an example the popular, long-running situation comedy *Home Improvement*. Watched with the sound on, it is an unimaginative collection of awkward situations and childish-dad, clumsy-home-repair-expert jokes, distinguished only by the additional irony of a television show within a television show in which Dad stars. Watched—as Orson Welles recommends—with the sound off, this program is dominated by the standard shots of the filmed stage play: one camera on Mom as she launches a gently sarcastic comment; cut to another camera on Dad, star Tim Allen, as he quips back puppyishly.

This is the camera work that dominates most television programs. One camera on Ted Koppel from the chest up, another on the guest. *Take camera one. Ready camera two. Take camera two.* A third camera is looking over Koppel's shoulder at an image of the guest. *Ready camera three....* Elsewhere a camera provides a long shot of the operating table. *Cut.* Then it moves in for a close-up of the surgeon's face. One camera on the pitcher, a second on the batter. A close-up of Jay Leno's face as it bobs to the beat of his chuckles. A long shot of Oprah Winfrey standing amongst her audience. A two-shot of Larry King and his guest. One, two, three or more cameras manipulated by skilled technicians to facilitate our stares. True television: "far seeing." The mechanics of a kind of voyeurism.

Actors, reporters, athletes, talk-show hosts, special guests, contestants, MTV "VJs" and chefs move. Camera angles move. That, on most of the programs we see on our dozens of channels, is all that moves. Film too continues to rely primarily on this same ballet of moving actors photographed from moving camera angles.

But a different kind of motion—the fourth kind—is beginning to appear more frequently on our screens. It is most visible on the edges and in the interstices of television and film. Title sequences, promos, trailers and introductions mix slices of themes, characters and settings into thick new concoctions. The introduction to *Home Improvement*, with its amalgam of animation and live action, is as good an example as any of this new style; so are the "wipes" the show uses to switch between scenes, in which a shot of the family's kitchen might suddenly be covered with a wall of bricks that is rapidly disassembled, brick by brick, to reveal a shot of the local hardware store. Elsewhere sports highlights sprint from impossible catch to impossible catch, barely pausing for scores and standings; documentaries compact an hour's worth of news into high-energy overtures less than a couple of minutes long. And then, of course, there are the commercials.

NBC's coverage of the 1996 Olympics was known, and sometimes attacked, for emphasizing the personal stories of the athletes more than their feats. Less noticed was the extent to which that coverage reflected changes in the style of television. It began with a lengthy montage cut to the beat of a rock song. The various athletic events, especially those shown live, were still mostly presented by switching between a few cameras. Some of the cameras slid about on wires; still, the athletes (fittingly, I'll concede) were allowed to do most of the moving. However, those ubiquitous profiles of the performers, the highlights of completed events and even extended accounts of events that took place earlier in the day, such as cycling or the long-distance races, were edited at a Bruce Conner-like pace.

The edges and interstices, in other words, are growing larger, the familiar three-camera programs between them gradually eroding. The flow of giggly conversation on late-night talk shows is increasingly interrupted by staff-produced comic tapes sometimes as frenetic as music videos. Movies drift off into fast-cut montages at the slightest pretext—a recollection, a summary, a dream. (For *Trainspotting*, one excuse is the protagonist's arrival in London.) Screens are filling with more and more collections of past, present and coming attractions.

MTV's case is an interesting one. Yes, music videos have lost some of their freshness and vitality. Pellington said he now declines most opportunities to direct them because of the pressure to focus the camera on the product: the lip-syncing faces of band members. Yes, many fewer music videos are being played, and a whooping, hooting remake of *The Dating Game*, called *Singled Out*, lounges salaciously across valuable half hours of air. But many of the techniques pioneered in music videos have made casual and frequent appearances in MTV's new generation of documentary shows. *The Real World* and *Road Rules* have placed young, not previously famous people in staged situations (apartments in a city, RVs driving across the country) and then recorded intimate details of their "real"—not fictional—adventures. These shows shift, as easily as songs move to a chorus, from quick scenes of the participants enjoying or explaining themselves to even quicker collages of a day's activities.

And this new kind of motion—celebrated on MTV, scattered around and within films and programs on more traditional networks—

has also begun to transform the films and programs themselves. Some movies are still just filmed novels or dramas, but many hop from peak moment to peak moment like trailers or highlight films. Excepting intros and wipes, *Home Improvement, Seinfeld* and most situation comedies still mostly plod along, but *NYPD Blue,* for example, and others of the more adventurous drama series sometimes leave the studio and skip and jump around the streets at a speed unimaginable to eyes used to theater or life, even urban life. *Oprah* and PBS's *NewsHour with Jim Lehrer* present their canned conversations at a leisurely pace, but most television news reports—on the evening news, on the magazine shows—are now cut at a speed that would have seemed appropriate in a soft-drink commercial just ten years ago. I recently watched four images appear in four seconds during an otherwise unremarkable political report on the *CBS Evening News.* "Fortunately or unfortunately, the MTV style of editing has become the norm," commented Beth O'Connell, director of political coverage for NBC News.[19]

The new video—if you'll forgive an image borrowed from horror films—has been oozing out of the cracks and spreading.

> *"Why do you have to talk so much about fast cutting?"*
> *"That stuff just gives me a headache!"*
> *"Isn't fast cutting what you do when you can't think of any other*
>   *way to get people to watch?"*
> *"It's for kids. After a while you outgrow MTV."*
> *"You're not really serious about this fast-cutting stuff, are you?"*

And this is just what I hear when I discuss these ideas with my friends. Even Conner, Braverman and Dusenberry have qualms. Each is unwilling to limit his legacy to fast cutting. Each in turn insists that it is just one technique among many.

Those who write about what's happening on contemporary screens can be much harsher. Bill McKibben sees fast cutting as a sign of cowardice: "In its immense fear that we might grow bored, TV has not yet acquired the courage necessary to show an unmoving picture for very long.[20] Susan Sontag concluded, in a recent article about film, that "the unprincipled manipulation of images (faster and faster cutting) to make them more attention-grabbing, has produced a disincarnated, lightweight cinema that doesn't demand anyone's full attention."[21] The political theorist George F. Kennan's great complaint about television is that "attention is constantly being abruptly yanked from one thought or image to a wholly different one"; he labeled this "a massive abuse of the capacity for concentrated thought on the part of countless millions of people."[22]

These indignant voices seem to swell into a great chorus, tens of millions strong, when the issue is framed in terms of "sound-bites"—the amount of time television newscasts give newsmakers for uninterrupted speech. Indeed, just about everyone in America—whether queried by barber, pollster or talk-show host—seems prepared to expound upon the menace shrinking sound-bites pose to journalism, to politics, to you name it.

"This is an age of fifteen-second sound-bites," the scientist and science writer Stephen Jay Gould complained in 1992.[23] He was wrong, of course. This is an age of sound-bites little more than half that length. The average sound-bite from presidential candidates on network evening newscasts in 1968 ran more than forty seconds. By 1988 these newscasts allowed candidates to speak without interruption for an average of 9.8 seconds. Four years later another 1.4 seconds had been lopped off, and the returns for 1996 show the average sound-bite for presidential candidates down slightly once again—to 8.2 seconds.*[24]

"Sound-bite," once merely a term of art, has become a term of derision since being dragged into common parlance. H. Ross Perot, for instance, recently listed among his political hopes that people "not allow themselves to be manipulated by little...sound-bites."[25] Political discourse is threatened, it is everywhere assumed, by TV's taste for the short and pungent rather than the long and thoughtful. Conniving politicians, the argument goes, have now been granted the power to lead the public astray with snappy little distortions. American politics has grown superficial; we have lost the willingness to face our problems—all because these quotes have grown so short. And the threat extends beyond politics. For Gould, short sound-bites—even at fifteen seconds—are indicative of a culture that prefers entertainment to factual truth.[26]

Those who work in television, always prone to bouts of self-flagellation, are apparently as vulnerable to this argument as everyone else. "They're picking out a few words that don't even have nouns and verbs [among] them," moaned former *CBS Evening News* anchor Walter Cronkite in 1996, while fighting for free air time for candidates. "That's no way to present the issues of the day."[27] CBS's chief Washington correspondent, Bob Schieffer, spoke for many of his colleagues when he admitted, "I do long for the longer sound-bite."[28]

In 1992 Dan Rather and the then executive producer of the *CBS Evening News*, Erik Sorenson, actually made an attempt to satisfy that widespread longing: They decreed that no statement from a presidential candidate could be broadcast on their newscast unless it ran at least thirty seconds. "No more of those cute eight-second sound-bites," Sorenson was quoted at the time as promising. "What we're experimenting with is trying to get away from the sound-bite journalism that

* The statistics on sound-bites in this section are from the Center for Media and Public Affairs in Washington, D.C.

we have been criticized for in the past." In a recent conversation he added, "Our point was to make the candidates talk longer, to make sure they didn't escape with brief platitudes."[29]

CBS executives pointed proudly to a story on H. Ross Perot in early July of 1992 that featured a full thirty-four seconds of the then-undeclared presidential candidate talking.[30] The words that filled those thirty-four seconds are worth quoting in full:

ROSS PEROT   Can we agree we have work to do?

CROWD   Yes!

PEROT   Is there anybody here that's not willing to put his or her shoulder to the wheel and do it?

CROWD   No!

PEROT   Is there anybody here that can live with the fact that we are no longer the number-one economic superpower in the world?

CROWD   No!

PEROT   Is there any question in your minds that, if we get off our seats and get in the ring, you and I can make the words "Made in the USA" once again the world standard for excellence?

*CROWD   Yes!**

* CBS Evening
News, July 2,
1992.

This extended sound-bite certainly gives us a chance to spy on Perot as he rallies the troops; it gives us a sense—not conveyed by a mere transcription—of his energy and charm. However, even though it runs thirty-four seconds, this sound-bite does not move us beyond "brief platitudes" or contribute much to our understanding of the issues. It does not, in other words, add a lot of substance. That would be a lot to ask of a sound-bite of any length taken from a campaign appearance.

The argument that long sound-bites would return seriousness to journalism and politics has many weaknesses: It ignores the fact that a century before television, politicians were elected on such lengthy and deep slogans as "Tippecanoe and Tyler too." It assumes that giving politicians more time to speak will somehow deter them from manipulating, distorting or, in Perot's case, simply filling the air with a series of "brief platitudes." In assuming politicians will dispense disproportionately more truth and meaning in thirty seconds than in seven, the argument gives too much credit to mere length. "A sentence doesn't have to be long to have impact," Bob Schieffer conceded. "One of the most powerful statements in the English language, 'I love you,' is three words long."[31]

This argument also conveniently ignores the length of the quotations that appear in even our most sober and exhaustive newspapers (or books), which are also, on average, only a sentence or two long. Martin Plissner, executive political director at CBS News, once sat down and counted the words in newsmagazine and newspaper quotations—"ink-bites," he dubbed them—and found them to be at least as short as television sound-bites.[32] Indeed, publications (including this book) frequently use partial quotes, which, to echo Cronkite, "don't even have nouns and verbs in them." How would newspaper or magazine writers react if someone dismissed their work because all the quotes in their stories do not fill at least two paragraphs?

In addition, the argument for plumping up sound-bites ignores the many other places on what used to be called the "television dial" where audiences sometimes can hear politicians chat, campaign, filibuster, change the subject or occasionally even outline what they might do if elected—at much greater length.*[33]

Sound-bites have not grown short because gigantic and gluttonous global media corporations are eager to feed lazy audiences aural and visual "candy" rather than substantive accounts of the issues of the day (though those corporations are certainly profit obsessed and those audiences certainly impatient). Sound-bites have grown short primarily because this medium communicates more effectively that way.

I am as disappointed as the next journalism professor by the cavalcade of murders and fires that our local newscasts have become.†[34] I stopped tuning in at six and eleven long ago. But the evening newscasts on ABC, NBC and CBS present their summaries of the day's events with some skill and intelligence. The videotape stories they broadcast now explain issues and events by combining a series of often fast-cut moving images with some carefully phrased sentences from a reporter, plus, increasingly, some computer graphics and on-screen wordings. Granted, perspicuity, comprehensiveness and wisdom are not always attained. This remains a relatively new form; standards are still developing. Nevertheless, in competent hands it is a form of significant power. Much more can be said in the allotted time.

In thirty-four seconds—the time CBS handed over to Perot—the houses, cars and faces of some of the wealthiest and poorest 10 percent of Americans might be contrasted. We might be presented with examples of the occupations and investments that have favored the former, as well as the machines and foreign factories that have displaced the latter. We might watch various measures of the share each group has of the nation's wealth wiggle further apart. And we might listen to a trained journalist's studied attempt to explore the causes and conse-

* These include C-SPAN, CNN and various other cable networks, public television's *NewsHour*, ABC's *Nightline* and the network morning shows.

† As someone who has written about the *long* history of sensationalism, I am, however, less surprised.

quences of this growing economic disparity. (Don't get me wrong: I'm not saying discussions of such important issues should be limited to fractions of a minute. I'd be happy if a network gave this subject hours. I'm just saying that there are more efficient uses of whatever time is made available.)

Sound-bites, by contrast, give us only a chance to examine the faces of newsmakers as they speak—usually extemporaneously, generally in unpolished sentences. Sound-bites have their place; like quotations in a newspaper, they buttress a story with other voices—expert, eyewitness or opinionated.[35] Occasionally, when sentences of unusual pith or portent are being enunciated, it makes sense to allow a newsmaker to go on. Sometimes it's more interesting to layer a newsmaker's voice under the visuals—cinema-vérité style—rather than rely on the standard reportorial equitone. Still, television news is usually at its best when it relies *least* on such "talking heads."

"If you want to get the main element of, say, a welfare proposal out to people in any reasonable amount of time," CBS's Plissner explained, "to simply have its proponent speak into a camera is nowhere near as effective as using graphics and using the economy of language you get by writing a script."[36]

Sound-bites, in other words, generally *should* be short.[37] This realization is rarely expressed, but for anyone who has sat behind an up-to-date videotape editor it is pretty much unavoidable. At the risk of sounding a tad mystical, I'll suggest that the medium itself seems to be speaking here. The sound-bite is a borrowed device—an imitation of conversation or public speech. Just as forcing the symbols in a writing system to resemble objects as much as possible did not make sense, giving over large chunks of television news reports to sections of conversation or speeches does not make sense. It is not a particularly efficient use of this medium. Long sound-bites belong to the first era of video. The fury unleashed by their disappearance is a result of a lack of understanding of and a consequent fear of the new era of video we are entering.

By September of 1992, according to the *New York Times,* CBS executives had dropped their minimum sound-bite length from thirty to twenty seconds and made clear that even that was flexible.[38] By the end of the campaign, those sound-bites from the presidential candidates on the *CBS Evening News* were running an average of 8.3 seconds—the same, give or take some tenths of a second, as on ABC and NBC. CBS executives said they continued to push for longer sound-bites in 1996. Theirs did average slightly longer than sound-bites on NBC and ABC, but they still ran an average of only 8.8 seconds.

Different CBS producers and executives supplied different explanations for the failure of that thirty-second rule. "It was because the candidates didn't speak in thirty-second bites," said Susan Zirinsky, former head of the political unit at CBS News.[39] Sorensen recalled that "it became trickier with three major candidates in the race to find time for three thirty-second sound-bites each night."[40]

Martin Plissner acknowledged that there is truth in both these explanations, but he added another that is blunter and more telling: "It was an interesting experiment, but after we tried it, we didn't really like the stories. The pieces, when you got them, weren't as good."[41]

The choice in television news, of course, is not always whether to let a sound-bite run long; sometimes it's whether to let a reporter stand before the camera for an extra fraction of a minute or whether to hold a shot ten seconds longer. However, I believe a lesson can be drawn from CBS's failed experiment with sound-bites that applies in most—certainly not all—circumstances across television news and across television in general: This medium works better at higher speeds.

In 1980 I published the first edition of a textbook called *Broadcast News*. It was filled with guidelines on how television news stories were to be shot and edited—suggestions on "composition," "balance," "framing" and the "sequence" in which stories should be approached (long shot, medium shot and then close-up). And it included some hard and fast rules:

> **Pans and zooms**. "The camera must be moved slowly and steadily or the result will be a jerky blur."
>
> **Visual continuity**. If a fireman is wearing a hat in one shot, the hat can't be off in the next.
>
> **The line**. When reporting on events that move in set directions—such as "parades, football games [or] conversations"—the camera should stay on one side of a line running through the action. "Otherwise, when the shots are edited together, the parade will keep flip-flopping—moving from left to right on the screen, then from right to left."
>
> **Jump cuts**. Were two nearly identical shots—close-ups of a person being interviewed, for example—edited together, the picture would appear to jump somewhat at the point of the edit. "It would be disconcerting to the eye and unprofessional-looking." The solution is to edit in a "cut-away"—perhaps a shot of a reporter nodding her head—between the too-similar images.
>
> **Cut length**. "Silent cuts should be on-screen just long enough for the viewer to comprehend whatever information is in them."[42]

I had learned all these guidelines from more experienced television journalists. Most were originally borrowed from film, which had handled the on-scene reports for television newscasts before being displaced in the 1970s by videotape. These are more or less the same suggestions and rules that were assimilated by a couple of generations of film school students. All of them, however, are now routinely violated.

Anyone examining a television screen nowadays will spot shots that are oddly framed, wildly asymmetric, even purposely out of focus. Scenes are more often simply visited than "approached" in proper sequence through long "establishing shots." Jerky, blurry "swish pans" and abrupt zooms are used to add energy and pace. (See *NYPD Blue,* for instance.) Hats sometimes are allowed to pop off and on just for fun. And "the line" is routinely crossed. "I got into an argument with an editor I was working with who kept insisting that we had to honor that line," Hank Corwin recalled. "The rules work, I guess, if you're telling a certain kind of story, but otherwise these rules are absolutely useless. It doesn't matter."[43]

By the second edition of my textbook, published in 1986, I was noting that jump cuts were beginning to step out from behind those forced cut-aways in some television news stories and show themselves. I cited a study that found no evidence that viewers were disturbed by such "editing discontinuities."[44] This too, it turned out, doesn't matter.

The example of an edited news story I included in the first edition of that textbook featured some shots that were five seconds long; most ran for ten seconds.[45] On network newscasts today—edited not by renegades from MTV or advertising but by mainstream broadcast journalists—the average shot is held for about three or four seconds. Sound-bites are, in fact, now the longest shots in television news video. (I don't agree with McKibben that this represents a lack of "courage." The sentences in McKibben's book are reasonably short and punchy. Did his courage fail? Or was McKibben, like most television journalists, looking for the clearest, most engaging style in which to present his material?)

I often show my students the renowned 1960 CBS documentary *Harvest of Shame* by Edward R. Murrow, David Lowe and Fred Friendly. We're all disposed to honor and respect it, and it's true that this crusading documentary on migrant farm workers is exceptionally well reported and well written. Yet sections of it have become difficult to watch. Shots are sometimes held on-screen a painfully long time.

Fast cutting has arrived not as a tic or an affectation, but because it makes video of all sorts more interesting to look at and potentially more informative. The rule that we must stare at each shot long enough to comprehend everything in it turns out to be just as misguided as the rest. It doesn't matter. A quick impression is usually sufficient, and since many more shots can now be squeezed into the same period of time, it is usually more stimulating. We get to see a lot more.

The rules have also been changing at a rapid pace outside of news. Two early milestones were the arrival of *Rowan and Martin's Laugh-In* in 1968 and then *Sesame Street* in 1969. Both were structured more like collections of commercials than like traditional programs. They jumped enthusiastically, almost haphazardly, from comic bit to comic bit—in one case with educational value, in one case not. It turned out that variety-show hosts did not need to introduce each act; that television viewers, old and young, wanted to see the funny moments, not the lead-ins to the funny moments; and that they wanted those moments to come fast.

These changes were felt eventually even in more traditional programs. Here's Quinn Martin, producer of two popular television dramas, *The Streets of San Francisco* and *The Fugitive*, from an interview published in 1983:

> We used to play everything out; the exit walk, the long dissolve. I mean, people were very literal minded fifteen to eighteen years ago.... They couldn't absorb if you moved quickly. Well, as commercials got people so used to absorbing information quickly, I had to change my style to give them more jump cuts or they'd be bored.... Now we tell them in twenty seconds what we used to tell them in a minute. The whole art form has speeded up.[46]

Let's focus for a moment on Martin's example of the "exit walk." Onstage, unless a curtain intervenes, characters are seen entering and leaving scenes. In television, naturally, actors were given entrances and exits, too. Indeed, early television, like most movies of the period, seems obsessed by doors. But, as Martin learned, it's enough to show the tearful goodbye; audiences don't need to see the retreat out of the room that everyone knows will follow.* It turned out that in imitating theater television was squandering an awful lot of time. Show the romantic reunion; don't show the train arriving. Pick up the pace. Cut to the fight. Cut to the chase.

The Streets of San Francisco and *The Fugitive* were not examples of the new video. Most television news reports don't quite qualify yet, either. But they have been affected by the same forces that are leading to the new video. In other words, the fast editing I annoy my friends by talking so much about—the fast editing that is only one technique among many and only for kids—is already beginning to take over much of television.

"The war is over," is how Corwin put it. "The kids have won."[47]

      &   &   &

* Those familiar with the techniques of rhetoric will pick up echoes here of *metonymy.*

Film has certainly not escaped these influences. Editing speed has been ratcheted up, as it has throughout television. For instance, a quick look through the first James Bond film, *Dr. No* from 1962, finds many shots held longer than half a minute, with the typical shot running about six seconds (fast for the time). The typical shot in *Goldeneye,* a James Bond film from 1995, is on-screen about half that long, and there are many sequences in which the cuts come every second—or faster.

Film also has been freeing itself of a similar set of rules. The one that has fallen hardest, perhaps, is that most sacred of rules, that test of each director's humility and good taste: Thou shalt not call attention to thy editing! In 1969 Pauline Kael, perhaps the most influential film critic to take on flashy editing since Bazin himself, derided it as an "insanely obvious method" of keeping "the audience jumping," "a disguise for static material," "expressive of nothing so much as the need to keep you from getting bored and leaving."*[48]

Artists in most media, it is true, are cautioned against technique for technique's sake. But few other artists have been ordered, like this, to simply disappear. Shakespeare, dare I say, indulged in some rather flashy wordings. Van Gogh was not so humble that he tried to efface his brush strokes. To insist that artists whose medium is moving images must avoid distinctive arrangements of those images—that it is somehow unseemly of them to, in Kael's words, "juxtapose startling images"[49]—is just another way of pretending they are still working in theater or print.

Can such "startling" editing be obvious? Of course. The supply of originality is as limited here as in any other art form. But it certainly doesn't have to be obvious. Does attention-getting cutting tend to show up more frequently in empty-headed productions like television commercials? There's no denying it. But that doesn't mean these visual splendors can't also enrich works of intellect and sophistication. (It wouldn't be the first time serious artists had followed a path cleared by less talented experimenters in technique.)

Is it more "unprincipled," as Sontag charged, overtly to "manipulate" images like this than it is overtly to "manipulate" words, as all writers do? Is it more "unprincipled" to try to achieve, through clever editing, "attention-grabbing" arrangements of images than it is to achieve "attention-grabbing" sentences? In talented hands creative, unexpected editing can *add* to the meaning of a film in the same way a creative, unexpected style can add to the meaning of a piece of writing or a painting. Martin Scorsese is one of those who have pampered and surprised our eyes; Welles, Godard and now Pellington and Corwin are others. The rule that editing should be unnoticed was wrong; it needed to be overturned.

* Despite this harsh language, Kael did rate as at least "debatable" the proposition that this editing style might occasionally be used "responsibly"—she offered the films of Alain Resnais as a possible example.

Many of these rules can be seen in retrospect to have been attempts by tastemakers steeped in older forms to reign in this new form. Others seem merely to have been impositions of ill-considered standards on a medium too young to have developed considered standards. Chuck Braverman recalled asking one of his professors in film school whether he should cut to the beat of the sound-track. Under no circumstances, he was told. It isn't done.[50] But most of Braverman's *American Time Capsule* is cut precisely to the beat, as are the tens of thousands of television commercials and music videos that followed. It turns out *that* does matter.

This ongoing challenge to old views of how we should communicate with moving images runs deeper still. I write in early summer, as this year's presumptive summer blockbusters seek their fortunes in the multiplexes. The debate about them—in the press, on the sand, over iced cappuccino—is a lively one, but it boils down, as it has for many summers now, to one issue: Is it legitimate to praise a film that flouts most traditional standards of narrative development?

Let *New York Times* book critic Michiko Kakutani, in her role as surveyor of the larger culture, speak for all those who can't believe anyone could find anything worthwhile in that drek. "Not only are old-fashioned stories with beginnings, middles and ends on their way to extinction," she groaned, "but basic principles of dramatization, character and structure are in danger of becoming endangered species as well." Kakutani focused her indignation on one film, Brian De Palma's *Mission: Impossible* (released in 1996), which she dismissed, in essence, as *Story: Impossible*. The "battle cry" of these movies, and of other works of art that ape them, is, Kakutani charged, "Stop making sense."[51]

This argument remains compelling for those of us who resist turning our minds off when the theater lights go down; nevertheless, each year more and more apparently thoughtful people seem willing to take the other side in the debate. Here are phrases snatched from *New York Times* critic Stephen Holden's review of *Mission: Impossible*: "whooshingly entertaining...zooms along...exhilarating...the wildest movie ride of the year...a delirious rush." Emboldened by his enthusiasm, Holden tackled the larger question: "If [the] story doesn't make a shred of sense on any number of levels," he wrote, "so what?"[52]

This debate between Kakutani and Holden is sure to be echoed over new thrillers in future summers at a beach or barbecue near you. It seems inevitable in a period of transition such as ours. Contemporary films are often dazzlingly visual and unflaggingly energetic. The form is young, however. These films are not yet accomplished enough to bring such obvious attributes to the service of a new kind of sense. Meanwhile, shoulders are being shrugged at some formidable and venerable rules: A believable plot? *So what?* Developed characters? Dramatization? Structure? *So what?* The remnants of print and theater, which dominated film since the arrival of the talkie, are being expunged. The sense we had come to expect movies to make—a print kind of sense—is being abandoned.*[53]

"The movies made possible a new dissolution of literary forms," lamented Daniel Boorstin.[54] I understand why we find this upsetting; something of great significance is certainly being lost. But why do we find it surprising?

That dissolution of literary forms can be seen in a sequence from *Mission: Impossible*: Our wilier-than-life hero, Tom Cruise, has assembled a couple of lapsed secret agents to attempt some barely motivated, suitably impossible caper. He outlines its mind-boggling difficulty. His cohorts grumble. Courage is tested. End of scene. In novels, or in most films at least fifteen or twenty years old, this would be followed by scenes of preparation and planning, during which relationships would develop and character would be revealed. (I think of movies like *The Great Escape,* which is about three quarters preparation and one quarter escape.) In *Mission: Impossible* this scene is followed directly by the caper itself. Just *bang;* not lull, buildup, stretch-it-out-for-a-while, *bang.* Most of the slow stuff has simply been deleted. What's left after these subtractions is Conner's "forced condensation of energy": the "whoosh," "zoom," and "delirious rush" of intense, fast-paced moving images.

Such "special-effects extravaganzas," Kakutani muttered, "resemble nothing so much as marathon trailer sequences." Exactly. Movie producers have gotten wise to a secret long whispered in the back of theaters: The coming attractions are often more entertaining than the films. (Bruce Conner listed movie trailers as another of his influences.)[55] It is amazing what can be gained with film, with television, simply by—as trailers do—cutting out everything that doesn't "whoosh."

This, of course, was the crucial insight of the early experimenters in fast cutting. Conner cut and spliced his 16mm reels of film, then cut and spliced some more, and found that as the reels got shorter they became more interesting to watch. Jean-Luc Godard had a serendipitous and similar experience with his first film. "I remember very, very clearly how this famous montage, which you see today in every commercial, was invented," he writes. *Breathless,* released in 1960, originally ran about two and a half hours, and the contract allowed for only ninety minutes. "We took all the shots and systematically cut everything that could be cut without completely destroying the rhythm," Godard reports.[56] The result? Well, Godard's use of the word *invented* can be questioned: He began cutting rapidly within scenes two years after Conner had already begun cutting rapidly, as so many commercials now do, among numerous different scenes. Nevertheless, Godard's accidental discovery in what became a hugely influential film placed jump cuts, that frantic pace, a peek into the future, before hundreds of thousands of pairs of eyes.

Hank Corwin was handed his first professional editing assignment in the early 1980s. It was a commercial for the drink mix Tang, scheduled to be shown only in the Middle East. Someone else had shot the film and "it was terrible," Corwin recalled. "I cut the film into two-frame pieces, mixed them up and spliced them together. And it was spooky it was so good. I saw the power."[57] This is the power of condensation, of fast cutting, of the new video. Mark Pellington, David Berrent and Roberta Goldberg have seen the same power. Chuck Braverman saw it; so did Godard and Conner. "It just works," testified Don Schneider, who has produced some groundbreaking commercials at BBDO.[58]

Is something lost to all this hurry and razzle-dazzle? Yes, of course. I don't mean to dismiss the laments of Kakutani or Boorstin. A kind of art—a leisurely, narrative, justly revered, often brilliant kind of art—has been under assault; a logic, a way of looking at the world, is threatened. The pain we feel when something accomplished and beloved begins to die is not alleviated by the birth of something immature and unfamiliar. But the new video will mature, and it will accomplish. There will be gains. There already have been gains.

For a glimpse of the benefits of fast cutting, I turn once again to an unlikely place: a commercial for General Electric airplane engines, produced under Schneider's supervision by BBDO in 1991. This commercial is, to begin with, unexceptional. Turn on television at any time of day now and you'll see one that does the same thing just as well or, since techniques have continued to improve, better. I use this example, however, because no one can accuse an advertisement for airplane engines of being aimed at kids.

The commercial features seventy-seven different images in sixty seconds. They include shots of a hockey goalie, a mother kissing a child, a computer screen, fast-motion traffic, a group of kids lifting a sumo wrestler and, oh yes, airplanes. Some of the images are sepia-toned, some feature bright primary colors; in some the camera zooms, hurriedly pans or shifts focus, in some it remains still; some are close-ups, some long shots. A peppy if saccharine ditty—more Gilbert and Sullivan than rock and roll—is playing. The song, at one point, lists places GE airplane engines fly: "St. Petersburg and Uruguay and Malibu and Paraguay...," while the images present a scene from each of those places.

There's plenty of "whoosh" here as all these pretty scenes speed by, but that is not the commercial's only virtue. "Cutting that fast," explained BBDO's Dusenberry, "allows you to communicate vast amounts of information in a very brief period of time."[59]

Now, I know it is difficult for some of us to conceive of television commercials actually communicating any *information*. Sometimes their goal seems to be dazzle us with images to the point where we disregard what we do know—about the nutritional value of sodas, about the unlikelihood of a car or a sneaker changing our social status, about the irrelevance to most of our lives of one or another brand of airplane engine. It is true that most of what Schneider, Dusenberry and company are in the business of communicating belongs instead under the heading *impressions* (not in itself an unimportant category). But there are occasionally some honest-to-goodness facts in those commercials: thirty destinations to which General Electric airplane engines fly, for instance. And this commercial does manage the considerable trick of introducing those thirty places to us, in pictures and in song, in only twenty seconds. Perhaps the skeptical reader could keep in mind other less manipulative uses to which such a capability (minus, perhaps, the ditty) might be put (a news report noting the cities hardest hit by welfare cutbacks, say), while we hear one more adman out.

John Bergin is a retired advertising executive who worked on early Pepsi commercials then later, after changing agencies, moved to the Coke account. He talked of the "pace and excitement" achieved by these quick commercials, which often ended up with as much editing tape on the reel as film. But Bergin emphasized their ability to communicate efficiently: "With quick cutting you could get forty people into one thirty-second spot."[60]

Few viewers, to be sure, would be able to focus on each of those soda-drinking young people or on each of the places visited by GE engines. But, as Quinn Martin noted, continual exposure to series of images like these has made us—even the adults among us—much more adept at "absorbing information quickly." CBS's Bob Schieffer made an assertion that few in his business would question: "The human mind can now absorb a lot more information in a shorter period of time than at any other point in history."[61]

We frequently bemoan the shrinking of attention spans; we almost never celebrate its corollary, which is the expansion in the amount of information or impressions that can be taken in in a short span of time. Let's give ourselves credit: We have learned to grasp quickly. We can read signs, change lanes and avoid other vehicles at seventy miles per hour while also listening to a song and planning our weekend. We can click our way through complex programs and thickening forests of Web sites. We can chart a course through the masses of alluring merchandise packed into a mall. We can sample and reject dozens of channels in half a minute. We can listen to the radio, step in and out of a conversation and thumb through a magazine simultaneously.

Things come at us at a rate our ancestors could not have imagined, and we handle them. Maybe we don't absorb everything that is aimed ‚our way. Maybe we would not be able to pass a viewing-comprehension test asking us to name all the places to which GE airplane engines fly, but most of us would have noted quite a few of them in those twenty seconds. And the message—the feeling, the realization—that these engines power planes to a plethora of places, all around the world, certainly gets communicated. A lot does sink in—quickly.

Fast cutting has helped develop this skill, and fast cutting takes advantage of it. It allows impressions *and* information, not just "energy," to be "condensed." That's how Roberta Goldberg can touch on most of the main points of a one-hour ABC documentary in ninety-six seconds. This is a clear benefit of the new video—one that should be of less use, in the end, to advertisers than it will be to those who really do have truths to tell (future documentary makers, say, or video essayists). They will be exploring how much can be packed into videos 30, 60 or 120 minutes, not seconds, long.

And as this form matures, we can expect an even larger benefit: ideas too being communicated with this efficiency.*

Let me add one more historical analogy: Our suspicion of fast cutting brings to mind the suspicion that greeted the arrival of rock and roll. In the fifties and sixties just about everyone above a certain age moaned that melody, subtlety, sense and beauty were being sacrificed to that big, fast beat.

> *"Why does it have to be so loud?"*

> *"That stuff just gives me a headache!"*

> *"They only scream like that because they don't know how to sing."*

> *"You'll outgrow it!"*

> *"Why can't they write real songs?"*

And they were talking about Chuck Berry and the Beatles! But rock 'n' roll had power. It worked. It triumphed.

Sometimes I think it's 1955 all over again, and Hank Corwin is Little Richard.

* I realize I have dropped a few portentous but enigmatic hints about the new video's potential contributions to thought. Please bear with me; this subject is chewed over at some length in the book's final chapter.

chapter eleven

"Increasingly Complex Media"
New Technologies

The Parisia
one of th
paintings i
film Milk

Company Number Seventeen.
produced by the graphic-design
TNT program/ American Dreamers,
introduction to the 1996
some of the images in the
A product of digital editing:

Caption: The first
videotape recorder
the VRX 1000,
built by the
Ampex Corporation

We must expect great
innovations to transform
the entire technique of
the arts, thereby affect-
ing artistic invention
itself and perhaps even
bringing about an amaz-
ing change in our very
notion of art.
—Paul Valéry, 1928

p (slide)
rtists' model/ Kiki

housands of individual

Jeff Scher's 1992

of Amnesia:

a kind of cubism of motion.

"milk of Amnesia"

decades later, are
videotape editors
beginning to become
inexpensive
enough and easy enough
to operate so that
nonprofessionals can
finally "speak" in moving
images

J eff Scher, who is in his early forties, bridges two generations. He studied under the late avant-garde filmmaker
Warren Sombert, a buddy of Bruce Conner's and another
early experimenter in fast cutting. But Scher, whose own
films mostly employ animation, also makes some television
commercials and knows Mark Pellington and the MTV generation of
directors. Sometimes he finds the view from this bridge a little upsetting: "When I watch MTV, I'll think, 'Oops, that's borrowed from Bruce
Conner; oops, that's from Warren Sombert,'" Scher reported with some
bitterness. "Those guys couldn't afford to pay their rent, and now these
kids are driving BMWs. Another rape of the avant garde, I guess."[1] Still
Scher is not oblivious to the talents of this new generation. "Sparks of
epiphany seem to come off of the boy," he said of Pellington.

Enough members of the MTV generation had mentioned Jeff Scher's
own work to make me want to see it. The best way of doing that, it
turned out, was to take the subway to the artist's own studio in
Manhattan for a private screening. This filmmaker is resolutely low-tech.
An old 16mm projector, just about as loud as the one that frightened the
young Renoir, began clacking away and a reel of Scher's short films
played. The one that seemed the most interesting for my purposes was
Milk of Amnesia, a 1992 film shown at the New York Film Festival and on
PBS. It offers yet another glimpse of the potential of techniques introduced by Conner and employed by Pellington among others.

Milk of Amnesia is a collage of dozens of brief movements—each of
which Scher has painted, frame by frame. (The film runs four and a half
minutes; it features, the filmmaker said, thousands of individual, index-
card-sized paintings.) To the accompaniment of an Argentine tango
from the 1930s, a woman makes a bed; a cow turns its head; the famous
Parisian artists' model Kiki turns her head; a woman prepares to jump
awkwardly off a diving board; et cetera, et cetera. Motion painting, it
might be called. There is something lovely, even poignant about these
movements. I tried to make an analogy to dance, but Scher stopped me.
"These are motions from everyday life," he explained. "That's much

more interesting to me. I'd rather watch a fat man and a dwarf walk down Fourteenth Street than go to the ballet."

And there is much more going on in Scher's film than lovely, interesting, everyday motions. That woman poised on the diving board, though her movements seem realistic, changes color with each frame; her clothes come off, then back on; the pool she hovers above fills with swirls, dots, colors, patterns, writings and even golf tees. In similar fashion, dozens of abstract patterns and newspaper collages explode around and over Kiki's slowly turning face. Motions are not only being re-created here; they are being reconstituted into a multiperspectival series of one-frame instants. Dance can't do that. Theater certainly can't. This is a kind of cubism of motion. It is as if Muybridge's horse had found a way to move and be frozen in revelatory instants at the same time. It is a kind of "fast seeing" in motion.

Milk of Amnesia partakes, too, of the power of montage. Scher spoke, Eisenstein-like, of how the "collisions" among these short scenes "create this other event." That clumsy woman on the diving board is surrounded, for example, by images of acrobats and fancy divers and watching eyes. Her awkwardness and self-consciousness deepen.

Jeff Scher is the son of a painter and a sculptor. "Film was the only thing left," he quipped. But Scher left no doubt that he is happy with his choice. "Film is the culmination of every medium man has worked in," he declared. "It has the ability to incorporate painting, architecture, stage performance and story telling. It's an Aladdin's cave of treasures." My view, of course, is that it is also more than that; that there are new, unopened boxes in that cave; that moving images can do things no other art form could manage, such as quote or reconstitute motions and bump those short bits of motion up against each other.

It turned out *Milk of Amnesia* had been transferred—with erratic quality, Scher cautioned—onto the medium that is in the process of incorporating film: video. I don't own a film projector, and I wanted to watch it some more times, so this was good news. Scher, though he is capable of waxing poetic on the virtues of celluloid, did acknowledge one advantage to seeing the film on video: The pause button would allow me to easily examine individual frames—the swimming pool filled with golf tees, for example, or a Kiki collage.

I walked out with the video in my bag onto a mid-Manhattan street still soaked from a spring afternoon's heavy rains. A pink light from somewhere over New Jersey spilled onto the gray clouds. (You note these kinds of things after an afternoon with an artist like Scher.) I was thinking, as I often am, about what else could be done with such techniques. Scher has created a beauty and a poignancy. With some words and some more didactic orderings, couldn't he also do more than that?*

I had another thought on my mind on those wet streets: Why must

* When I had hinted at this possibility in

Scher's studio,
his response
was to encour-
age me to
make that film
myself.
a collection of moving images like that Scher had produced be so difficult to access? Why couldn't I view it, any part of it or the work of any
other experimental filmmakers on my TV at any time I wanted?

Imagine deciding to pick up a book and facing a choice only of the
handful of most popular books in America. Imagine having to go
through every story and advertisement on the first few pages of the
newspaper word for word, in the order in which they appear. Imagine
reading a magazine article without being able to reread any sentences
that are difficult to follow. These are the logistic handicaps video has
lived with in its childhood, during the television years.

Anyone who has been following the business or entertainment
news lately knows that television, the computer and even the telephone
are increasingly becoming the same thing. One day we learn of a Baby
Bell contemplating offering cable service; the next it is television sets
being connected to the Web; then it is telephone calls via the Internet.
Perhaps our media behemoths are really itching to trespass on each
other's turf and compete. That would be refreshing. But there is a larger,
mostly overlooked story in this "convergence": With help from these
other technologies (primarily computers), video's handicaps are finally
being overcome. Our means of accessing video are finally coming of age.

This chapter is about those means, about technologies, not the
works of art and intellect that might take advantage of them. The new
video might eventually arrive even without most of these spiffy new
technologies. Scher's film, which is as fast and thickly layered as any
video, was produced on a homemade rotoscope device—essentially a
16mm camera, capable of shooting one frame at a time, with a built-in
light and fan. "There's no technology here that wasn't around in 1930,"
Scher said with satisfaction. These new technologies, therefore, are not
my primary story. But as we are constantly being reminded, they are
arriving rapidly, and they will certainly contribute to the development
and dominance of image communications. These video-related technologies (most will not appear on old broadcast television or in movie
theaters) are a part of this revolution.

The first step was actually a step backward technologically: a retreat
from Marconi's magic (wireless transmission) to Morse's (the use of wires
to carry signals). Television signals first abandoned the air in favor of
cables in a few geographically isolated towns. By erecting one large
antenna in a high place and then wiring each house to it, the residents
could receive all the channels available in the nearest city. "Community
antenna television," this was called. By 1960 the United States had about
640 such CATV systems.[2]

But someone soon realized that the television-deprived were not the only viewers with a hankering for additional channels. The people of San Diego could choose among three clear local VHF television channels in 1961. But after an entrepreneur erected a powerful antenna and began laying some wire, they could choose among all the Los Angeles stations too, for less than six dollars a month.[3]

Another realization followed: "Cable television," as it was being called, could attract larger audiences by producing some original programming. There were plenty of extra channels with which to play. The great advantage of using a wire, rather than transmitting signals through the air, was that additional channels were easy to add—just squeeze another signal through the cable. CATV systems had been filling unused channels with cameras aimed at weather dials, stock tickers and even some local events. In New York City cable operators contracted to broadcast the home games of the local basketball and hockey teams. By 1971 cable had more than eighty thousand subscribers in New York.[4]

The next realization was that television viewers would pay extra for early and frequent opportunities to watch movies. Time Inc.'s Home Box Office (the metaphor it relies on is apparent in its name) debuted in 1975. HBO is a "premium service," subscribers pay extra to obtain it. More national networks, most free to cable subscribers, followed. An Atlanta businessman, who probably saw cable's potential as clearly as anyone, took a money-losing Atlanta UHF station, WTCG, filled it with old movies and the games of the Atlanta teams, and in 1976 began making his station available by satellite to cable systems around the country—it became the first "superstation," now WTBS (the *T* is for Turner, Ted Turner). C-SPAN (live broadcasts of the House of Representatives), ESPN (sports) and Nickelodeon (children's programming)—all non-premium services—debuted in 1979. Turner followed with Cable News Network the next year.[5] Dozens of other cable networks as well as some distributed directly into homes by satellite then began seeking channels of their own.

In most of the rest of the world, new networks—comedy networks, food networks, court networks—have not sprung up at nearly this rate, and it may indeed be some time before the economics justify a comedy network in Swedish, a cooking network with Vietnamese recipes or a network devoted to trials in Senegal. But American networks are easy to pull off a satellite.* And as production costs drop, non-English, non-U.S.-based sources of television programming should also multiply.

To fully exploit the choices these networks are beginning to provide, however, another technological breakthrough was needed: "the timely invention—not a minute too soon!" Thomas Pynchon wrote, "—of the remote control."[6] The first device to transmit our will from couch to console through the ether actually was introduced in 1956:

* I was watching MTV on broadcast TV in southern Russia in 1994.

Zenith's Space Commander, which used high-pitched sounds as its invisible agent.[7] But it was in the 1980s, when channels started madly proliferating, that the Styrofoam in which most new TVs were packed began to contain a slot for an infrared remote. You couldn't really "surf" without one.

With "zapper" in hand, a cable subscriber in most of the United States now has easy access to about as many different possibilities as might be found on an average magazine rack. The point is not that we watch all these channels; the research indicates that we each choose an average of about seven to bounce among.[8] The point is that we now can each choose seven or so channels that interest not everyone but *us*. We certainly don't read all the magazines on the rack, either.

Sony further expanded viewers' control over what they watched with the first successful home videocassette recorder, the Betamax (initial price: $1,300), in 1975. JVC followed with the first recorder using the videocassette format that would eventually dominate, VHS, in 1977. "The VCR is one of the most successful consumer devices ever invented," noted Michael Bloomberg, whose understanding of the potential of new technologies has helped him construct a major new cross-media business-news empire. "But it never has been used for the purpose for which it was designed. It was designed to time-shift."[9] We don't use our VCRs much to record and replay; we do use them to play not-so-old movies secured at the new video-rental stores that began opening in the 1980s.

Old broadcast television often left us—the masses of us who do not always share mass tastes—watching "other people's programs," as Leo Bogart, who produced an early study of the effects of television, once put it.[10] Nothing else was on. The selection of movies in theaters at any one time—even after the arrival of multiscreen cinemas—wasn't much larger. Cable and the VCR increase the chance that we might watch programs or films of our own choice, as we read magazines of our own choice. That's a beginning.

The number of available channels, like the number of movies available to rent, undoubtedly will expand further. Computer-supervised compression of signals will help. Additional advances in direct transmission from satellites will help. The application of telephone lines to the task will help, especially as more and more of the branches of those lines are replaced by high-capacity fiber-optic cables. The selections available to us are becoming and will continue to become more diverse. "In a five-channel world it is probably bad for your health to be too different," explained Canadian television entrepreneur Moses Znaimer, "but in a five-hundred-channel world you better be different."[11]

Those difference are as likely to involve variations on successful formats (HBO, CNN, ESPN, MTV) as truly original programming. They are as likely to involve excesses of sex and violence as excesses of intelligence. "There is no reason to assume that with greater diversity video would become, on the average, a higher quality medium than it is today," MIT media scholar Ithiel de Sola Pool contended in a book published posthumously in 1990. "It is a standard illusion to believe that new options will somehow advance culture and taste."[12]

Perhaps quality will not advance—on average. Nevertheless, five hundred channels, the number most frequently bandied about, would begin to solve the problem of where to display the artistic and intellectual experiments in the new video heralded in this book. There would be room for 490-odd channels of imitative talk, drama and sports, or mindless fast cutting, *and* also a few channels to satisfy those who occasionally do hunger for more stimulating fare. There are already channels for independent films; there might also be channels for fast-cut independent films and videos like Scher's.

Obviously, unlike Pool, I see culture as rather headstrong. It found its way, despite Plato's misgivings, into writing. It found its way, despite Pope's misgivings, into modern forms of print. And it will find its way, in more challenging forms than public broadcasting's *Great Performances,* onto our proliferating channels. Indeed, if moving images ultimately frustrate human intellect and human creativity, it would be a first; no other medium this large has.

Many critics have announced that we don't need all those new channels. The truth is we need more. Five hundred channels would still not provide us with a selection of alternatives comparable to that available at any decent bookstore. And we still would not have anything approaching the control over video that we take for granted in print. For that television will have to converge a little more with the computer.

The printed word had been going through a particularly dispiriting period when the computer began showing up on desks: Newspapers, after the exhilaration of Watergate, were beginning to confront their declining popularity, particularly with the young. Book publishers were merging and cutting costs. Cable networks and videocassette recorders were providing even more excuses to stare at TV screens.

Most word lovers initially greeted this latest tangle of transistors with predictable suspicion: The computer seemed a toy for the techies. If civilization was to be redirected by this green-screened, boxy data cruncher, it would undoubtedly be away from privacy and poetry, toward uniformity and numbers. As it became clear in the 1970s and early 1980s that articles, even books, were among the data that could be crunched, how many normally cynical writers suddenly began to declaim the glories of their pens or typewriters? Even that grim moment when a sheet of paper had to be crumpled and tossed was romanticized.

But gradually the literati began to wake up to two encouraging facts: First, here was a technology, as advanced as they came, with the letters of the alphabet inscribed upon its input device. And second, here were screens, increasingly watched screens, that were filled in large part by intelligible combinations of those letters. Indeed, it turned out that besides manipulating spreadsheets and managing databases, there wasn't a task for which computers proved better suited than cutting, pasting, spell-checking and choosing type fonts for words. It turned out, too, that many of the databases and networks computers were managing and accessing could be filled with interesting collections of words—every issue of most of the major English-language newspapers in the world, for example, or every word written by Shakespeare.

Had that white knight, a good technology capable of doing battle with brain-depleting television, finally galloped onto the scene? It began to seem so.

This feeling may have peaked in the first half of the 1990s as the Internet and the World Wide Web began making larger and larger amounts of information available to larger and larger audiences—mostly in the form of words. On the chat lines, above the smileys, a miracle seemed to be occurring: People, especially young people, were sitting at desks instead of lying on couches, and they were not only reading but writing to each other once again! Digital cheerleader Nicholas Negroponte began to speak of "the post-MTV generation."[13]

What about moving images? On the rare occasions when videos did show up on computer screens in those years, they looked like kinetoscopes: small, short and jerky. Neither computer processors, computer memories nor computer connections were burly enough to manage the multitudes of bits that make up the frames of moving images. Computers, the Internet and the World Wide Web, once you got a few clicks beyond the graphics-intensive home pages, belonged safely, securely, miraculously to the domain of words. The momentum, for the first time since Daguerre, seemed to be with the word.

That feeling is, or at least should be, fading now. Those limitations in computer processors, memories and connections are rapidly disappearing. "Our computers finally have enough power to deal with images as naturally as we do type fonts today," announced Intel's Lew Paceley while introducing a new generation of microprocessors in 1995.[14] Soon it will be moving images. The standards for digital television approved in the United States in 1996 anticipated that day. In other words, video and computers are ready, like two huge corporations, to work out a merger.

Since there are two relatively new technologies to misunderstand here, there have been lots of odd statements not only about the potential culture clashes and synergies but about which partner will end up dominating the joint enterprise. "The computer industry is converging with the television industry in the same sense that the automobile converged with the horse," media theorist George Gilder has proclaimed in one of the brashest of such statements.[15] It seems more accurate to say that the computer is converging with video in about the same way the chariot converged with the horse. Computers will make video significantly easier to use, but our eyes will still be focused primarily on moving images. That will be the source of most of the creative energy.

Names like *compuvision* or *telecomputer* have been proposed for the entity that will result from this merger. My candidate remains *video*.

"By the year 2000 I believe that as many homes will have a computer as have a TV," Negroponte declared, perhaps a bit overenthusiastically, in 1995. Negroponte's prediction of victory had a second part, however: "In fact, many Americans will be watching TV in the upper-right-hand corner of their P.C."[16] A Pyrrhic victory indeed!

One way of looking at this merger is that moving images, which long ago established their power in photography and broadcasting, are now beginning their conquest of computers. A brash prediction of my own: Someday the computer revolution will be understood in large part as a stage, a crucial stage, in the process of harnessing the potential of video and therefore as yet another blow to the word.*

For most of their history to date—their early history, in other words—moving images have been only half a medium. The original, genetically programmed form of human communication is two-way: We both hear and speak. Since the Greek alphabet made possible widespread literacy, large numbers of people were also able to produce and understand written symbols.†[17] But for almost all of us, (edited) film and television can only be watched, not produced. The equipment has been too expensive, too complex, and too bulky. Reporting for television is like writing with "a one-ton pencil," former CBS News President Fred Friendly used to complain. Most film and television, consequently, has been controlled by a caste: the high priests of Hollywood and Sixth Avenue—a caste almost as closed and as narrow as that of the scribes of ancient Egypt. (Many independent filmmakers are also connected with that caste through financiers and distributors.) Except for some primitive home movies, in moving images most of the rest of us have been, to use a formulation of Alan Kay's, only half "literate."**[18]

This partially explains, perhaps, the sobbing relatives who somehow find the strength to satisfy sound-bite-hungry television reporters, the bystanders jumping up and down in the crowd behind them, the victims of unfortunate circumstance who seem all too eager to reveal all to

* Am I doing what I accused others of doing: calling for a new medium—the Internet—to imitate an older medium—television? I hope my view of digitally distributed video is expansive enough to refute that charge.

† Literacy, of course, declined again in Europe during the Middle Ages.

** I purposely do not use the term video "literacy" to describe the ability to follow fast-moving images or a familiarity with works of film or television. It seems too early to hazard these analogies. However, Kay's relatively limited use of the term seems comfortable here.

* Some kinescope films of earlier shows survive. Still, for those who live in the world of television this is an important date, for it is, more or less, when recorded history begins.

Oprah Winfrey or Ricki Lake, the fans in the stands who seem to lose all composure once a camera with its red light on deigns to point their way. We have been living with the frustrations of a one-way form of communication, the frustrations of the mute. One response is this compulsion to get *on* TV.

Having once had the experience of writing a book on a typewriter, I would never underestimate what the computer has meant for the writing process. But it will mean much, much more for video. It will, to begin with, make it possible for most of us to "speak" in moving images.

The struggle to gain in video the power we have with other forms of communication has been a long one. A successful videotape recorder was first demonstrated publicly on April 14, 1956, at the convention of the National Association of Radio and Television Broadcasters in Chicago. "Pandemonium broke loose," recalled Charles P. Ginsberg, who headed the team that developed the Ampex VRX 1000. (The Ampex Corporation had beaten RCA, the BBC and Bing Crosby Enterprises in the race to record pictures and sound on tape.) What most excited the broadcasters was the solution the videotape recorder represented to one of their largest problems: How to rebroadcast shows on the West Coast that had been seen live three hours earlier on the East Coast. (Kinescopes—essentially off-air films—had been used, but the quality was low and the process slow and expensive.) On November 30 of that year a television show, CBS's *Douglas Edwards and the News,* was for the first time taped and rebroadcast.* In 1967 an Ampex recorder, able to replay quickly and in slow motion, made possible the first "instant replay"—on ABC's *World Series of Skiing.*[19]

Ampex's first videotape recorders cost $75,000 each.[20] However, videotape recorders, cameras and the videotape itself began to get smaller, cheaper and more efficient (cassettes instead of reel-to-reel, for example). In the late 1970s it became possible for middle-class American families to contemplate owning a videocassette recorder and then even a video camera of their own.

Camcorders, like 8mm movie cameras, do not by themselves cure our muteness. Moving images, as I have been arguing, gain most of their meaning, not to mention most of their entertainment value, from the editing. An unedited videotape, whatever charm it may hold for its subjects, is as primitive a use of video as a yell or a chant is of speech. Homemade, unedited videotapes, again like home movies, are rarely used as anything but a record of family events.

Videotape, as video artists had discovered, was initially almost impossible to edit. You had to get two tapes rolling at once, push some buttons and hope you had everything lined up more or less correctly. That began to change in the late 1960s and 1970s as electronic controllers first took command of the recorders and made possible pinpoint edits. Now a new generation of film and tape editors that convert video signals into digital bits is making it as easy to store, recall and rearrange moving images on a computer as it is to do the same with words. I don't recall any pandemonium having broken loose, but no invention is as important to the development of the new video.

You can see the products of these computerized editors all over television and movies now—but rarely in such an intriguing and attractive form as in the introduction to a 1996 TNT program, *American Dreamers*. Bonnie Siegler and Emily Oberman originally produced these forty-seven seconds for their design company, Number Seventeen, on an Avid digital editor—a machine too expensive at the time for their company to own one of its own. (They would move to an even more sophisticated machine for the final version.)

The Avid "captured" from videotape the dozens of scenes, taken from well-known movies or shot for the program, that were being considered for this introduction and then transformed them into digital images that could be manipulated on the computer screen. Siegler and Oberman had in mind a rather complex manipulation: They wanted all these moving images, one after another, to drift from right to left across the screen. The idea was to create a truly complex dance, one I doubt Eisenstein, let alone Griffith, could have imagined.

There was motion within each of the scenes themselves: Gene Kelly spun with his umbrella; Sylvester Stallone's Rocky pushed up with one overmuscled arm, then the other; Orson Welles's Kane turned his head to the side; a row of swimmers from the Esther Williams movie *Million Dollar Mermaid* tilted to the right into a pool. All these scenes simultaneously moved against and with the scenes surrounding them, and they moved against and with the backdrop of that constant right-to-left glide. To accomplish this, the computer had to get every image, including titles displaying the names of the people who would appear in the show, gliding at exactly the same pace.

"We could have done all this without digital video," Siegler explained, "but it would have been so much more expensive and less flexible."[21] Even with computer editing, Number Seventeen's forty-seven second digital production took a month of work. (Scher, who insists that "paint is much more seductive than electrons," said that for him a good day of painting produces four or five seconds of film animation.[22]) But on the computer screen and then, when *American Dreamers* was broadcast, on hundreds of thousands of cable television screens, still more of the potential of the fourth kind of cinematic motion was revealed. We saw a new dance.

All that's necessary for increasing numbers of us to become fully literate in video and begin experimenting with this new kind of motion ourselves is for these digital editors to complete the familiar trek up in

* As I write, a
few hundred
dollars will buy
a video-capture
card and such
software—not
yet broadcast
quality but cer-
tainly show-to-
friends quali-
ty—for use on a
reasonably
powerful per-
sonal computer
with a few
gigabytes of
free hard-disk
space.

capabilities and down in price or—an even more likely scenario—for affordable personal computers to gain the power and the software to perform these tricks themselves.*

Sometime in the next few years all those homes with personal computers Nicholas Negroponte is so excited about will be able to hook them up to their camcorders and videocassette recorders. They'll then be able to chop up moving pictures of a walk downtown or an evening hanging at the mall into video as fast and lively as anything on MTV. They'll be able to mix in music, narration, stills and on-screen text. And they'll be able to experiment with many of the same otherworldly effects that have been gracing television commercials.

Most Americans can take photographs. Shooting a video won't be much more difficult, and the range of expression possible in video is considerably broader. Many Americans have mastered word-processing programs. Editing a video won't be much more difficult, and it will open newer and fresher forms of expression. I'm not suggesting the majority of us will rise from our couches and begin to manipulate moving images. But many of us will.

Producing video is no longer going to be a skill mastered only on the job. It should become an art form kids learn at about the age they learn how to draw a face, play the guitar or navigate the Internet. Video should no longer be the private tool of professionals in the employ of advertising agencies and media conglomerates or of well-funded artists. Teenagers should be playing with it; friends should be staying in touch on it; radicals may challenge the status quo through it; academics should eventually be warned to produce it or perish.† Video will be shot by amateurs and freelancers; it will be edited in basements, in garrets.

† This is the
development
that may take
the longest.

Bookkeepers, record keepers and the pharaoh's scribes once produced most of the world's writings. Their monopoly eventually faded; the pharaohs eventually faded. Advertisers now produce the bulk of the world's fast-cut video, but their monopoly too is about to fade. A heavily capitalized team will no longer be needed to work in moving images. Videos, like writings, should increasingly be the product of noncorporate minds, of creative individuals.

Some of those creative individuals now allow themselves to be buffeted by the image culture and then crawl over to their word processors and attempt to squeeze the experience into sentences:

> She was watching the world news of the day.... She sees people caught in strangleholds of no intent, arms upflung, faces popping out at her, hands trying to reach the fence but only floating in the air, a man's large hand, a long-haired boy in a denim shirt with his back to the fence, the face of the woman with the tresses hidden behind her own twisted arm, nails painted glossy pink.[23]

Soon such experiences—this televised horror is described in Don DeLillo's *Mao II*—will instead be analyzed in video. That's a better place for them. And as more and more creative individuals grab hold of this new form, we should see new dances created out of such experiences, unexpected dances.

The development of the new video has, to date, been slow. One reason for that is the small number of talented, thoughtful people who have been able to participate in that development—perhaps a few dozen. Soon there will be tens of thousands. I have made myself a bore with my students and my children by repeatedly advising that they beat the rush. Perhaps I should be telling them that it's 1595 and someone is going to be Cervantes. Instead I tend to say that it's 1955 and someone's going to be Bob Dylan.

After noting that "cinematic or televised images" are "extremely difficult to produce," Umberto Eco concluded that "ease of execution is a notable argument in favor of verbal languages."[24] This is another argument in favor of words that will no longer hold.

Writing about the digital world today is as perilous as writing about the cinematic world must have seemed a century ago. It is difficult to keep up. New terms, techniques and devices seem to take possession of the cognoscenti every couple of years. In the first decades of film it was the zoopraxiscope, then the kinetoscope, the *cinématographe*, the nickelodeon, the switchback and the close-up. In the first decades of the computer we have had, among other items, the workstation, then the video-display terminal, the PC, the Macintosh, Windows, multimedia, the Internet, the World Wide Web and, as I write, the network computer. The last four items on that computer list are worth discussing in detail, although another new term or two will undoubtedly have swept everyone away by the time you read this.

In 1995 I rushed out to buy a new CD-ROM, *Bob Dylan Highway 61 Interactive,* hoping that I could keep my understanding of computers, if not my musical tastes, up to date. Multimedia, this was called. It was then all the rage. What I found, once the program was properly loaded, was lots of intricate graphics, extensive lists of songs, some interesting clips from audio interviews and, after much frustrating pointing and clicking, a few small, short, flickering videos, which seemed to have been made purposely difficult to find, of a recent Dylan performance. I listened to as many of the audio tapes as I could locate, watched the videos three or four times (dedicated fan that I am), then never opened the thing again.

I know that the CD-ROM has (or had; it is on its way out as I write) some real strengths, but those strengths seem to have revealed themselves mostly in games and reference sources. I've made wide use of the latter; my children enjoy the former. But otherwise multimedia, as a new form of communication or entertainment, seems something of a bust.

It should be noted that the new video itself incorporates, along with moving images, a bunch of other media: music, sung or spoken words, printed words and still images. Computers will soon add depth to this on-screen mix: Click here and you can read the lyrics, click here for a video history of the band. But the multimedia available at local computer stores for much of the 1990s likely will prove to have been little more than a way station. Most of those motionless graphics and audio clips on CD-ROM are there only because the technology has not yet been capable of presenting fully realized *moving* graphics and *more* video clips. DVD, the anointed successor to CD-ROM, should have little problem dealing with bit-hogging moving images. The future, it seems to me, does not belong to that primitive multimedia; it belongs primarily to a single, inclusive medium, the one for which humankind has repeatedly demonstrated a preference: video.

The Internet, of course, is of much greater significance. This global network of computers has done wonderful things for words: It can speed them around the globe with an efficiency telephones and post offices can't approach. It can allow us to dig words out of databases on the other side of the planet more easily than we might find them on our own bookshelves. And the World Wide Web's ability to make connections available between material on disparate computers—hypertext—gives words added context and depth. However, the Internet, particularly the Web, will do much more for video.

Words have been relatively easy to access for centuries now. It wasn't long after the arrival of paper and printing that they began traveling light, accumulating on shelves and lending themselves to indexing. Much of the more reliable information now available on the Internet could be found—more slowly and clumsily—at a university library.

Video has had much larger problems. A satisfactory collection of old movies has already settled in video-rental stores. Those of us who can master the controls of a VCR can record programs to view later or store in our own tape libraries. Cable, pay-per-view and direct-broadcast satellite services have bolstered selections. Nevertheless, it is still difficult or impossible to view, at a time of our *own* choosing, a report on the president's day, a favorite episode of a situation comedy, the latest REM video, the highlights of last night's Bulls game or one senator's recent speeches on the Mideast. It is still difficult or impossible to view a Jeff Scher film without making it to the right film festival, tuning in to PBS at just the right time or using the excuse of writing a book to wrangle an invitation to his studio.

While most of us, in other words, can arrange with a little planning to read what we want when we want, this has been impossible with video. No video store or library can provide us with this basic level of access to a wide range of moving images. But the World Wide Web or its successors will be able to.

As hardware and software improve and larger-capacity wires (such as coaxial cable) are used to connect to the Internet, it is safe to assume that increasing numbers of clicks on Web pages will start videos. Every music video REM has produced should be available on the Web or a similar network; so should every news story shown on the evening newscasts this evening or this decade. At some point every speech on C-SPAN should be there, along with highlights of all NBA games and libraries of movies and television shows voluminous enough to make the offerings on five hundred channels look sparse. Those interested in attempts to explore ideas through the techniques of the new video will find them there too.

This might be called the "library metaphor." The Web or its successors will provide viewers what libraries have long provided readers: choice, indexed access, control. The lack of these basic powers has been responsible for a portion of our frustration with television. When whatever magazines, newspapers and books are around the house leave us bored, we tend to accept the blame ourselves. "*I* have to get down to the library"—or newsstand or bookstore. However, television, because it is still so scheduled, draws most of our ire itself. "Fifty-seven channels and nothing on," Bruce Springsteen grumbles. We rarely direct similar complaints at videotapes—which, like print, we select ourselves.

These new computer-accessed video libraries—the ultimate in "video on demand"—should improve the medium's reputation considerably. Programming of all sorts should be available at all hours, if *we* have the energy to seek it out. We will be free, finally, from the television schedule. The frustrating feeling that there is nothing on worth watching should finally disappear. And another of the advantages words have had over moving images will be gone.

The turn-back-and-reread-a-section-*within*-a-story advantage won't last, either. Patrons of such on-line libraries will be able to rewind (or whatever the digital equivalent), replay, skip, slow down, speed up and search. Consequently there will be no limit to the number of times it will be possible to puzzle over the woman-on-a-diving-board scene in Scher's *Milk of Amnesia* or watch the New York Yankees flop on top of each other after winning the World Series. Another way of looking at this is that in terms of accessibility, moving images will move from the scroll stage to the book stage.

One argument against the new, quick form of video has always been

[handwritten margin note:] doubt the library effect will really happen because we are all motivated by $ ... Napster for example was a library squelched due to profit or lack of it

[handwritten margin note:] —TIVO

that it deprives viewers of the right to examine an image as long as they would like. Now they will be able to moon over pictures indefinitely, as readers have always been able to moon over words. All they have to do is press pause (or whatever the digital equivalent) until they are ready once again to step into the cascade.

A note on time: If the clock was indeed invented to keep monks from missing their prayers, its main use lately has been to keep us from missing our shows. We have been living for many decades now under the tyranny of the schedule and therefore of the minute hand: "Oh no! It's after ten! *ER*'s started!" The VCR has helped, allowing us to rent and watch when we want or, less frequently, to record and time-shift. VCRs even make it possible to stop a rented or recorded program should the phone ring or nature call. Cable and the remote have also helped: Channel surfing is an activity that can begin at 8:07 and end at 10:43 (or in my case 1:35). "Television time is no longer the linear and uniform commodity it once was," Thomas Pynchon has suggested. "Not when you have instant channel selection, fast-forward, rewind and so forth. Video time can be reshaped at will."[25] Our ability to gain control of video time will advance much further with the arrival of computer-accessed video libraries. This particular form of tyranny should end.

The network computer is that much-anticipated, stripped-down, five-hundred-dollar machine that will find most of its data and storage capacity on computer networks, particularly that largest of computer networks: the Internet. This may be the computer that realizes Negroponte's dream of entering as many homes as television.

But as more and more video is produced, with the mass marketing of digital video editing, and as more and more video is stored in data-bases and accessed on Web-like networks, it seems inevitable that the screens of those network computers will be filled much of the time with moving images. Not just with Negroponte's "TV in the upper-right-hand corner," but with a whole range of full-screen videos—tracked down in archives, discovered through hypertext (hypervideo?), forwarded by friends, crafted by artists, assigned by professors.

In fact, give this network computer a sufficiently large screen and access to cable as well as Internet programming, throw in maybe a videophone (one you can switch off on bad-hair days) and a set of remote controls that can be manipulated from a nearby couch, and it begins to look an awfully lot like that television-computer-telephone hybrid.

Or upgrade the screen further, miniaturize the computer's innards even more and use remote connections to the network, and the network computer becomes a means of watching video that can be carried to the beach, to bed, to let's just say anywhere a book can now go. And another of the advantages of print disappears: its portability.

The network computer begins to look like the computerized, well-connected, reasonably priced access device that will help video finally reach maturity.

The crowd trying to peer into the future of television—my cohorts, if not coreligionists—has failed to keep pace with the droves of digital prophets. It has, consequently, produced a smaller group of buzzwords. I've already discussed the most significant: *convergence* (a term this crowd must share) and *five hundred channels*. One remains to be grappled with: *interactivity*.

For some time now it has been cheering to imagine our couch potatoes bestirring themselves sufficiently so that they actually *interact* with their televisions. This is envisioned as the solution to the problem, actually first recognized back in the early years of radio, that broadcast audiences don't *do* very much. They don't applaud or jeer; they barely even chuckle.

Devotees of the theater were among those who concluded that this can't be good. Bertolt Brecht's "positive suggestion," proposed in 1932, was to turn the radio back into some form of wireless telephone, to "change this apparatus over from distribution to communication," "to bring [the listener] into a relationship instead of isolating him."[26] Unfortunately, certain economies of scale were achieved by having one station broadcast to thousands of listeners, economies that Brecht's one-to-one model could not match.*

In the 1970s the coming of cable television once again raised the hope that audiences might, if not actually take a full share in the communicating, at least contribute something. More than one forward-looking media conglomerate has experimented with allowing groups of viewers to send signals *back* over television cables. The messages that might be sent "upstream," as the Federal Communications Commission called it, included opinion-poll responses, game-show answers, orders for pizza, answers to quizzes about televised lectures and suggestions for plot development. This is something less than true one-to-one communication as, say, Socrates might have understood it, but it seemed an improvement on the typical TV trance.

Perhaps the most extensive of these experiments was Qube—a two-way cable service begun in 1977 by Warner Communications and American Express in demographically representative Columbus, Ohio. A powerful computer stood ready at the other end of the cable to listen or at least tabulate. Some viewers, mindful of their role in creating the future, played along. Many changed the channel. Being counted pro or con was apparently not that great a thrill. The plug was pulled on Qube in 1984.[27]

Less heralded forms of interactivity did succeed in gaining a

* Until, perhaps, the arrival of cellular telephones.

foothold while Qube and its cousins failed: video games, for example. A whole generation has grown up dodging karate kicks, bullets and poison mushrooms. The video-game player is still mostly to be found on a couch but is generally sitting on the edge of that couch. The Internet too, of course, is a hotbed of interactivity, providing opportunities to write, research, click to learn more, download, order, "chat" and "flame" (a version of the jeer). And cable does offer the home-shopping networks, though orders to buy whatever trinket is currently on camera travel "upstream" by telephone, not two-way cable.

All these forms of interactivity, not just the Internet, have some growing ahead of them. Video games, still rather cartoonlike, will get more realistic and will be able to be played with friends next door or on the other side of the planet. As the technologies continue to improve and converge, home shopping undoubtedly will also gain strength. Soon we will be able to move with ease, without leaving our living rooms, through whole shopping centers' worth of goods and services— examining clothes, in all sizes, from all angles, observing how they might appear on computer images of ourselves; checking out all models and colors of automobiles, inside, outside, under the hood; calling up demonstrations of various brands of fly-fishing equipment.*

The motivations that inspire game players to "beat" a "board," shoppers to call in a credit-card number or Internet users to employ a search engine have not been available, however, to most television viewers. No matter how small all this inactive watching may make them feel, when tuning in a show they have continued to evidence a distressing lack of interest in exerting themselves. In this they have, it must be admitted, company: Movies where audiences choose endings have not caught on. Book readers also seem content merely to lose themselves in the proffered entertainment. They don't seem to be demanding that their novels be interrupted by multiple-choice quizzes or requests for assistance with the plot. They seem quite content, despite Plato's concerns, to receive information without the chance to engage in a dialogue with its source.[28]

"People don't want to be active when they watch television," TV critic Marvin Kitman has suggested. James Wolcott, writing in the *New Yorker,* made a similar point in lusher terms: "When there's beauty and talent and driven vision on the screen, passivity can be a form of ravishment."[29] This is the ravishment of the audience enthralled, the ravishment of art. It can be experienced while listening to an epic poem, sitting in a theater, strolling through a museum, or lying on a couch—book in hand or screen across the room. Button pushing and certain categories of decision making seem extraneous to the experience.

Time Warner's latest experiment in interactive television, which

Margin notes:

Video networking a reality now

* An example included in a surprising number of discussions of interactivity.

debuted in Orlando, Florida, in 1994, had some legitimate selling points. It was promoted as potentially featuring the chance to play advanced video games against others on the system; the chance to wander the "virtual" aisles of supermarkets, pull items off the shelf and inspect their packages; the chance to get movies "on demand" and rewind or fast-forward through those movies; the chance to select individual stories from earlier newscasts; and the chance to have the system automatically collect information on specific stocks.[30] However, in 1997 Time Warner gave up on this expensive system, too.

Part of the problem remains clarifying what activities viewers really want to expend energy on. Part of the problem is getting the cost per household of such a system sufficiently low and its ease of operation sufficiently high.[31] But some such system—perhaps not owned by Time Warner, probably on the Internet and available on inexpensive computers—should eventually succeed. And our control over moving images, when we're in the mood to control moving images, will further expand. Moving images, the point is, should finally be competing against words on a level playing field.

That is what we can expect from the technology. If people can actually be convinced to want it, it will undoubtedly be quite wondrous. On this point most of us prophets, digital and video, agree. However, the superlatives usually stop when the articles and books that outline all this have to come up with some predictions about the sorts of programming these mighty systems might actually carry. At that point, grand visions suddenly become rather small.*[32]

Here are the dreams of George Gilder, author of one of the more starry-eyed of these analyses, *Life After Television:* "You could watch your child play baseball at a high school across the country, view the Super Bowl from any point in the stadium that you choose, or soar above the basket with Michael Jordan." There's more: encounters with "the best teachers in the country," meetings with the boss at home, sightseeing from our living rooms, "interacting on the screen with Henry Kissinger, Kim Basinger or Billy Graham."[33]

These seem rather modest advances. I have, of course, my own, less modest view of what programming might take best advantage of these wondrous technologies—the view I had begun to contemplate once again on the wet mid-Manhattan streets outside Jeff Scher's studio.

Bertolt Brecht, writing in the early years of sound film, concluded that artists were being forced to "speak through increasingly complex media."[34] He was correct; with each subsequent decade he appears more correct. However, Brecht seemed to suspect that this technological complexity would make it more difficult to produce the complexity of thought he was after. My view is that it will make it easier.

* Marshall McLuhan tried to sell the idea for a television show that would dramatize business problems and reward the viewers who came up with the best solutions.

Confident excursions into the unreal: an image from Young and Rubicam's advertisement for the U.S. Postal Service's Global Priority Mail.

A shot from Peter Greenaway's 1991 film Prospero's Books, showing one of Prospero's magical volumes: "Intellectually challenging and shockingly beautiful."

Background image: sustaining multiple thoughts simultaneously—one of the images, a strikingly

You could tell an incredibly complex story in an hour and a half or tw

12

"Complex Səəing"
A New Form

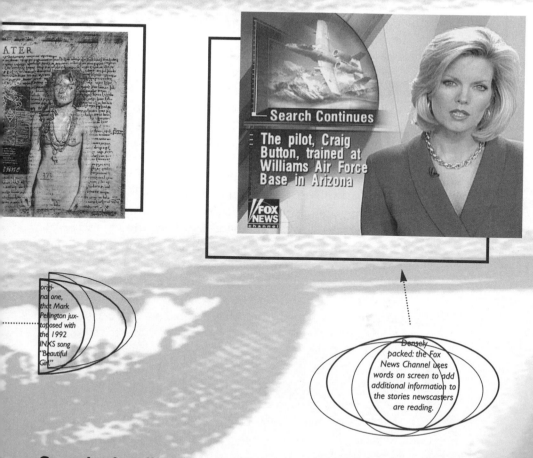

ATER

origi-
nal one,
that Mark
Pelington jux-
taposed with
the 1992
INXS song
"Beautiful
Girl."

Search Continues

The pilot, Craig
Button, trained at
Williams Air Force
Base in Arizona

FOX
NEWS
channel

Densely
packed: the Fox
News Channel uses
words on screen to add
additional information to
the stories newscasters
are reading.

urs. Somebody will do it well soon. —Ridley Scott, film director

O nce again we are imitating—using moving images to present a play by Shakespeare, as so many have before. But it is a visually adventurous, unpredictable, crowded adaptation. In the reviews of this 1991 film based on *The Tempest,* there are mentions of MTV. *Prospero's Books,* directed by Peter Greenaway, has even earned praise from new-video pioneer Hank Corwin: "Intellectually challenging and shockingly beautiful."[1]

Much of the action in Shakespeare's play is credited to Prospero's magic, and the acknowledged source of that magic is the exiled duke's library. Greenaway, unlike Shakespeare, names the volumes, shows them to us and seems to draw some of his scenes out of them. Most of these potent books, as the film presents them, teem with images and actions not normally found on pages. Indeed, one volume is called the Book of Motion. It bounces around on the shelf and, when opened, begins to come alive. We see, in about twenty seconds of film, multiple diagrams drawing themselves, then multiple human bodies contorting, straining and cavorting on the page.

Greenaway has taken us back to the days when wisdom was equated with magic, but he has also taken us forward to a time when gray, lifeless pages will be replaced, as if by magic, by enchanted processions of moving images—a time that is rapidly arriving.

The extent to which *Prospero's Books* succeeds as a film or as an example of the new video is debatable. (Greenaway's next film, *The Pillow Book,* released in 1996, extended his use of these techniques further.) But the Book of Motion makes an intriguing metaphor for the new video, which has the potential to be as "shockingly beautiful" and "intellectually challenging" as anything humankind has yet seen. And we have just begun to open it. This is the programming, the content, that will distinguish our new computer-accessed video systems. "I think we're stepping up here onto something really new, almost perhaps not to be called even cinema," Greenaway suggested. "This vast new revolution is about to explode."[2]

                &   &   &

Bertolt Brecht also had revolutionary ambitions for his medium, Shakespeare's medium: theater. He believed his plays might provide opportunities for "complex seeing."[3] Brecht, an acquaintance of Renoir and Eisenstein, also considered himself a supporter of film, but he saw it as something less than a magical Book of Motion. The medium was complex; the art it was capable of producing was not. Brecht viewed film, in its early years at least, as a naif with "no responsibilities," able, as in the work of Charlie Chaplin, to remain "simple."* "When a man bends a saw between his knees, you don't expect a fugue," Brecht wrote.[4] This is the sort of condescension that has been directed at moving images throughout their history.

No one has contributed as much to the development of television journalism as Don Hewitt, first associate director and then producer-director of the initial version of CBS television's evening news, and founding executive producer of *60 Minutes*. Yet Hewitt too believes there are types of music his instrument just cannot play. "We don't deal with issues very well," he told a group of journalism students in 1995. "We deal with the people who make the issues."[5] I heard a similar admission from a respected ABC News producer some months later: "The medium I work in does not tell complex stories well."†[6]

In a sense this is true and will remain true as long as video is shackled to standards imported from print. Don Hewitt is a hero of the old television, an old hero, I admit, of mine. But along with many of his fellows in the business, he is an obstacle to the arrival of the new video. "I've been in television forty-seven years," Hewitt told those students, "and I've never seen a picture that excited me as much as a well-turned phrase.... You don't always need pictures. Get out of that picture, picture, picture thing." Instead, Hewitt advised the students to remember "four key words: *Tell me a story.*"[7] If video is restricted to presenting printlike narratives, if images are deemphasized, then obviously it is not going to be able to play fugues.

The new video is that "picture, picture, picture thing"—intensified. It has the potential not only to "deal with issues" and "tell complex stories" but to fulfill, at a level unimaginable for theater, Brecht's goal of "complex seeing." Such a revolutionary accomplishment is well within the capabilities of this jittery, unruly Book of Motion. This chapter discusses steps that are beginning to be taken and might soon be taken to make use of those capabilities.

Picture one: bombs exploding. Picture two: a boy playing a video game. More pictures: the video-game screen, the boy again, two more explosions. Pictures seven and eight: Persian Gulf War commander

* In 1942, while working in Hollywood, Brecht wrote in his journal: "I never cease to marvel at how primitive the structure of films is." But by this point he was placing a significant portion of the blame on those who produced them.

† In his book *The Death of Literature,* Alvin Kernan observed that "those who work in TV are quite aware that their medium does not favor complex meanings."

General Norman Schwarzkopf in a close-up, then in an even tighter close-up. More pictures: planes drop bombs, that kid again, the screen, the kid, three more shots of exploding bombs.

These are the images Mark Pellington compressed into eight seconds of a music video made in 1991 for the song "Television," by a group called the Disposable Heroes of Hiphoprisy. These pictures demonstrate that most of the limitations Alan Kay and Umberto Eco saw in images have in the new video been overcome.

Pellington was able to make us watch the boy, the video game, the bombs and the general in exactly the order he intended. This sequence, consequently, is "sorted." And the ambiguities are reduced further through the use of words: The lyrics of the song speak of "armchair generals" and "the excitement of video warfare," and Pellington introduced the whole sequence by flashing the word *imitate* on-screen.

Of course, not all the excesses of meaning to which images are prone are eliminated here; viewers always have the opportunity to find significances in pictures others miss. But the sequence, the words and the short period of time each image is on-screen allow distracting or discordant meanings to be reasonably tightly controlled. Puzzlement on the part of "end users" no longer seems a great concern. When directors set their minds to the task, the new video, using fast-cut moving images and words, can communicate thoughts just about as directly as can printed words alone. It is possible, as Pellington has done in a very small way in these eight seconds, to plan and construct an argument.

But the new video can also do much more. The fifteen images in this short segment of Pellington's music video retain most of the advantages over written words that Thomas Aquinas and others credited to still images. They are easily accessible.* No great command of written English is required to interpret them. At eight seconds, this sequence of images is certainly concise. Pellington's images also take good advantage of the ability of our eyes to spot connections: The relationship between General Schwarzkopf and the young video game player is emphasized by the similarity we see in their expressions and their position on-screen.

In addition, such images— explosion, kid, general, more explosions—have the potential, as Aquinas put it, to "excite the emotions." This attribute of moving images, whether they are cut slow or fast, requires additional discussion, since, oddly, it is more likely to be cited by critics of this form of communication than by its supporters.

Roberta Goldberg, whose ninety-six seconds on religion opened this book, also produced the introduction to a 1995 ABC documentary on Bosnia. Its narration, read by Peter Jennings, speaks of the failure of the United Nations peacekeeping force. The images—skeleton-thin

* Schwarzkopf's was a well-known visage in 1991.

prisoners, men with blood oozing from their heads, crying women—
drive home, as televised images of sufferings in other far-off lands peri-
odically have, the cost of that failure. That moving images do this so
well has been the cause of much hand wringing.* "When you form
your ideas on the basis of words, you build on concepts," former secretary of state Henry Kissinger has contended. "When you form your
ideas on the basis of pictures, you form your views on the basis of
impressions and of moods." "A new style of politics," he asserted, is
consequently "emerging."8

Now, I have been arguing that moving pictures can assemble concepts too, although I will concede to Mr. Kissinger that they have to
date been a bit laggard in this area. I will not dispute the allegation
that moving pictures are proficient at forming impressions and moods
and that this has changed political equations (though the world, to my
eye, does not currently seem suffused with unprecedented amounts of
demagoguery or charitable impulses).9

The disruptive powers of the printing press were once feared, too.
It riled up and infuriated, and not only altered political equations but
lifted common denominators atop numerators. Eventually we accli-
mated ourselves to print and harnessed those powers. That is what we
are in the process of doing with moving images. We are learning not
to be swayed too much by haunting images—growing inured, I believe
it's called. However, while we are struggling to acclimate ourselves, let's
not forget that any medium that is skilled at placing impressions in
heads and forming moods is an effective medium indeed. What art
form would not want this listed among its attributes? In the end
video's emotional power, as long as it is supported by continued intellectual development, has to be considered a plus.

The power images possess seems particularly manifest in the lush,
sensual film *Prospero's Books*. Shakespeare writes of the spirit that had
been imprisoned in a "cloven pine." Greenaway pauses for a moment
to show that imprisonment in all its horror. He shows Prospero toying
with a ship. He shows us a young spirit urinating on that ship. He
shows us naked bodies drifting through water and then naked spirits
rescuing them. He brings on white horses to celebrate young lovers.
Greenaway, like Scher, does not seem much concerned with the problem of ambiguity (a possible criticism of his film). His arguments are
sketched more than constructed. But at times his pictures display an
intensity that stands up even to Shakespeare's words.

The new video, like those silent-film experiments in montage, also
has the ability to catch up with the pace of modern life and the pace
of human consciousness—another major advantage. It achieves the
"concentration of space and time" that Erich Auerbach believed to be

* The attack on
emotionalism
and pandering
in new forms of
communication
also has a long
history; Plato's
critique of new
techniques of
oratory in the
Gorgias is an
example.

beyond the capabilities of mere words—a concentration necessary if we are to analyze what we are seeing in our cities, on our roads, in our malls, on our screens, in our minds. Greenaway's central conceit (which owes much to Shakespeare) is that the whole play is an invention of Prospero's mind (which may equate with Shakespeare's mind). Images in *Prospero's Books,* consequently, flicker, mutate, rush against and overtake each other at something approaching the speed of thought.

What about montage's tendency, acknowledged by Eisenstein, to lose or befuddle audiences? Again *Prospero's Books,* with its weakness for evocative but hazy images, may be an exception. But obscurity does not seem a great problem for most examples of the new video, which have been speaking to mass audiences on large, commercially minded networks. With a liveliness, rhythm and compactness typical of this form, the video-game segment of Pellington's video manages to engage and engage again, even after repeated viewings. This is viewer-friendly montage.

Having overcome this problem too, might we begin to contemplate the realization of Eisenstein's grand hopes for montage? The Russian director wrote of the concepts that can arise from the *"collision"* between images. Isn't that what is happening when the picture of a kid playing video games is followed by a picture of General Schwarzkopf and some pictures of bombs exploding? A concept—maybe not the most profound of concepts—does arise.

In another Pellington video it is the song and the images that collide: The song here is "Beautiful Girl" by INXS from 1992. Among the dozens of images Pellington selected are a series of close-ups of women who are not obvious beauties, plus shots of fattening foods, scales, tape measures, silicon implants, surgical tools and a red-lipped woman with braces chomping on a large stick of celery. He also decorated the screen with dozens of words, including *model, mannequin, calories, binge* and *purge*—none of which appear in the lyrics. The song, which is wistful, even haunting, muses (with its own ironies) on the power of female beauty. The images, meanwhile, rip apart the notion of female beauty. This ability to sustain two or more contradictory thoughts simultaneously is one of the great strengths of the new video.

Much of the potential of the new video as an artistic and intellectual tool lies in these "collisions" or—to choose a less violent, less doctrinaire term—juxtapositions. And the ease and frequency with which they arrive in fast-cut moving images opens the possibility that more profound concepts might arise and longer arguments might be assembled. It opens the possibility, in Eisenstein's terms, of an "intellectual" video.

       &   &   &

Clearly, I want to argue that we are beginning to approach a solution to the problem of communicating issues, complex stories and even abstract thought through images. I want to argue that, as we begin to extricate ourselves from the first era of video, we can finally imagine a form of communication that is, to use Rabelais's words, better than print. But I'm aware that my argument has a serious weak point, one I've alluded to before: My examples are not that impressive.

Feminists, I realize, have been deconstructing beauty—in print— with varying degrees of power and efficiency for many decades now. The connection between video games and modern warfare has certainly been made before. And Greenaway, for all his inventiveness, can be said to have produced just another gloss on Shakespeare, another imitation. In fact, no ideas have surfaced on video yet that seem likely to reroute the course of human events, as ideas we owe to writing and print once did.

Some examples of the new video are quite lovely.* The beauty of *Prospero's Books* occasionally *is* shocking. But no fully realized work of art has surfaced here yet either: no *Madame Bovary* that is not like *Madame Bovary*, to recall earlier analogies; just Little Richard, not Bob Dylan or the Beatles; no fugues—yet.

> * My favorite remains Pellington's introduction to the 1996 PBS series *United States of Poetry.*

It takes time, to recall earlier arguments; it's still early; forms capable of taking advantage of new means of communication always develop more slowly than those living through that development expect. The tendency, in the meantime, is to dismiss those who dare experiment. Some are as eager to note that Oliver Stone is not Flaubert as our ancestors were to note that Defoe was not Virgil. Instead of acknowledging Peter Greenaway as a pathbreaker with aspirations, there is a temptation to dismiss him as an eccentric with pretensions. Some "vast new revolution"! We cut no slack. We persist in viewing the present without the benefit of the perspective that might be provided by the future—or at least the benefit of some historically based speculations on the future.

The development of the new video is being delayed by this shortsightedness, by the widespread belief that fast cutting is mindless and cheap, by the widespread belief that only imitative television is serious television. It is being delayed by the hold advertising agencies and music companies have maintained on these techniques. It is being delayed by the wait for computer-based editing equipment to become widely available.

As a result of all these factors, inventive artists and restless intellects—with few exceptions, some named in this book—have not been attracted to the new video. I guess the fact that the thoughts you are confronting right now are presented in a book and not a video might also be seen as evidence of the problem.

Walter Benjamin had just completed a game of chess with his friend Bertolt Brecht in 1934 when Brecht began complaining about chess. "The game does not develop," he asserted; "it stays the same too long." Brecht suggested that the rules of chess needed to be changed.[10] He was equally impatient, of course, with the rules of art.

In reporting on this scene, Benjamin did not record his own reaction to Brecht's proposal for updating chess. (Nor did he tell us who won their match.) However, Benjamin saw, probably more clearly than Brecht, the effect moving photographic images would have on the rules of art. Benjamin understood, as I noted in a previous chapter, that these "multiple fragments" lasting tenths of a second would have to be "assembled under a new law."

The early development of the moving image has proceeded slowly, almost as slowly as the early development of writing and print. The evidence remains incomplete; our examples, I acknowledge and acknowledge again, remain inadequate. Nonetheless, I believe we can now start to glimpse what might be the provisions of such a new law—provisions that would replace the mostly useless old rules film and television have recently been shedding.

Here, then, are some speculations on how the Book of Motion might be composed, how Benjamin's new law might read. Artistic principles, I'll call them. First a warning, however: These are not minor revisions in the old laws. Brecht wasn't talking about simply having pawns move two spaces forward anywhere on the chess board. He envisioned a game "where the function of the pieces changes if they have stood for a while on the same square."[11] Some of the changes under way in the rules of art may qualify as similarly profound.

I'll begin with the most obvious new artistic principle: *The new video will be extremely fast.* Annabel Jankel and Rocky Morton, who directed the original, experimental, partly computer-generated *Max Headroom* television program, have asserted that they often watch movies, French movies in particular, on fast forward.[12] Let's just say that for the new video this will not be necessary. How much faster can moving images go? "The shortest unit you can get on videotape is one-thirtieth of a second," answered advertising executive Jeffrey Goodby, whose agency, Goodby, Silverstein and Partners, produced some blistering ads for Sega video games. "And the eye can see that," he added portentously.[13]

Another way of looking at this question is that images now succeed each other in television commercials or music videos at almost the rate at which phrases succeed each other when we read. Might they be heading toward the rate at which we can read individual words?

Of course, the lamentations have already begun over this, over the loss of such mainstays of a creative and reflective life as pacing and slowness. But pacing is by definition relative, and slowness (which, I might note, was not always so prized) is to a large extent relative. All this speed will not necessarily deprive us of their pleasures. Consider the second half—the new-video half—of that 1993 Pepsi commercial that begins with an artichoke chef. Among its rush of images is the *de rigueur* woman-in-a-bathing-suit shot (in this case she is rotating a Hula Hoop). This shot seems to stay on-screen an awfully long time— "an eternity," BBDO's Don Schneider, who helped produce the ad, called it.[14] It is actually on for slightly less than a second. The commercial has altered our sense of time: In the land of half-second images, a second seems almost languid.

The new video will be densely packed. It will, to begin with, condense: A half second of the Capitol may be enough to indicate the federal government, a quick shot of a white-haired woman may represent age. The part, in other words, will be substituted for the whole so that in a given period of time it will be possible to consider a larger number of wholes.*

And the new video will have other means of achieving greater density. I'll choose a different kind of example here: Too much television news simply shows us some neatly coiffed person reading. In the early months of Rupert Murdoch's Fox News Channel, however, sentences were often flashed on the side of the screen next to that neatly coiffed person's head—sentences that did not simply repeat what was being said but added additional information. If the story was about a missing airplane, those words on-screen might provide background on the pilot. (The *Pop Up Video* show on the VH-1 network uses a similar technique. So do the various cable networks that regularly flash sports scores at the bottom of the screen and the Bloomberg computer terminals—with screens splattered with data and moving images—that now appear on desks at so many businesses. Other news channels also appear to have begun borrowing the idea from Fox.)

I don't know whether this experiment will help Fox News steal a sufficient number of viewers from CNN; it requires more effort to watch than viewers are used to expending. But it creates in yet another way a video in which there is *more,* not less, going on than we can easily follow. And this is a quality that video will have to have if we are to be challenged by it, if is to be studied as great books are studied. Video is going to have to be rich—with pictures (of more interesting things than news anchors' heads), narration, music and text.

* The rhetorical technique echoed here is *synecdoche*.

Vincent Canby in the *New York Times* called *Prospero's Books* "tumultuously overpacked."[15] My point is that most television and film has been boringly underpacked.

A basic unit of the new video will be the scene. A basic unit of our spoken and written languages is the word. The rules of grammar and syntax are designed to help us combine words into statements.

Filmed dramas are composed of shots—a shot of the woman slamming the door, then a shot of the man's stunned face. These shots are combined into scenes by following various cinematic guidelines.

The new video, however, will be composed in large part of quick, entire scenes, not shots within scenes. The scene will no longer be the larger entity. It will be an element, and we will be responsible for inventing new kinds of larger entities to contain these elements. Might there be a grammar or syntax that would facilitate the construction of something larger out of collections of scenes? Not clear. We are only just beginning to learn how to choreograph this fourth kind of cinematic motion.

One consequence of this new form of composition, however, is clear, and it is important. Writing objectified words, making it possible to look for logical connections between them, to rearrange them in lists, to fit them under new rubrics. The new video will make it possible to objectify scenes—not just to stage a few of them in sequence or to cut between a couple of them, but to shuffle, reorder and compare large numbers of scenes. It will make it possible to make lists out of them, to pull scenes out of their original contexts and look at them in new ways, to find new patterns and categories in them, to analyze scenes with the kind of detachment writing enabled us to bring to the study of words. The objectification of words changed thought. Can we expect anything less from the objectification of scenes?

The lexicon of images will be broad. When we speak or write, we are restricted, for the most part, to words that are already understood by those with whom we're trying to communicate. We try to form, in essence, new thoughts out of old words.

And, yes, in order to reduce ambiguity, many of the scenes out of which the new video is composed will want to be similarly familiar. Oftentimes the intellectual will be asked to pose in front of a bookcase; bombs will be used to say "violence"; white horses will be used to show "love"; and a second or two of Gene Kelly and his umbrella will be excerpted to elicit a hopeful smile.

Nevertheless, I don't see the new video having any great difficulty escaping banality. For there seems to be room, even in scenes lasting less than a second, for creative takes on the familiar. When that commercial for General Electric airplane engines needs to illustrate Tokyo, yes, it uses a sumo wrestler, but it shows him being held aloft by a group of very young sumo wrestlers.

And we have already seen entirely original images—a stick of celery surrounded by braces and lipsticked lips, a boy urinating on a ship—in versions of the new video. If the overall meaning of a sequence of scenes is clear, there seems little risk in including some surprising shots within it, just as a paragraph might want to include a few unexpected words or metaphors.

Still, much of the originality of the new video will come not from the scenes themselves but from the ways in which they are edited, from the ways these sequences are composed.

Forget the old symmetries. Consistency of tone? The new video seems to enjoy flipping from color to black and white, from one film stock to another, in and out of slow motion—as in Oliver Stone's *Natural Born Killers.* Stone's film even flips from one genre to another. To present the family circumstances that spawned the female half of its team of homicidal maniacs, for example, the film suddenly transforms itself into a macabre situation comedy complete with canned laughter and Rodney Dangerfield as a horridly abusive dad. "I decided to push the envelope in terms of technique," Stone explained.[16]

Unity of place is similarly violated as soon as we do what Stone's film does occasionally and other examples of the new video do incessantly: jump from scene to scene. Balance? Framing? They, too, are often honored, as I have noted, in the breach.

In other words, the disjunctions and asymmetries that have riled up twentieth-century art, music, architecture, literature and theater may finally find a home in the moving image.

What of our other long-revered rules of composition (rules that date back to classical times) and the deeper symmetries they embody? Can we expect videos that don't strain to sustain themes, that don't go out of their way to allude to their beginnings at their ends? This writer (who remains smitten with these rules) will admit (for once) that this is an answer he can't find in his crystal ball. But such rules of composition, already under assault in this century, will certainly face a stern new challenge, if not outright defeat, with this radical transformation in the methods and materials out of which we compose.

The new video won't completely forsake narrative. In one well-regarded commercial we see a man gleefully yelling into a cellular phone on the street, "You're fired!" Just then a truck bears down on him. Suddenly we are in a white world—"Welcome to eternity"—filled with giant cookies. "Heaven," the man chuckles. He opens a refrigerator. It is stocked with cartons of milk (the product, incidentally, for which this is an advertisement). But the cartons are all empty. "Where am I?" he wonders. Flames appear.

This half-minute commercial,* produced by Goodby, Silverstein and Partners in 1994, demonstrates that video, even fast-cut video, *can* tell stories when it makes the effort. In fact, when video is set to the task, it can tell stories with impressive effectiveness in remarkably short periods of time: While in Vietnam, a classic 1986 commercial informs us, Bill Demby dreamed of coming home and playing basketball, but he lost both of his legs to a Viet Cong rocket. With the help of the DuPont corporation, Demby gets artificial legs. We watch him on a neighborhood basketball court, where he shoots, falls, picks himself up and hits a couple of shots. All this in one minute.†

So Don Hewitt's four-word injunction won't be entirely ignored; at times the new video will work to *tell us a story*. However, these may not be traditional kinds of stories. The new video will often prove too energetic, capacious and resourceful to content itself with *just* telling a simple story. Its inclination will be to tell an excess of stories. (Situation comedies and television dramas, even without recourse to these advanced techniques for compression, now routinely sustain three or more crisscrossing narratives in a single episode.) And the new video, when it does deign to tell stories, will want to tell them from an excess of perspectives.

If a simple story can be told in a minute or a half minute (not the quarter hour or so *60 Minutes* and its competitors require), how many additional stories can be told, and how much complexity can be added to those stories, in a quarter hour? Once the new video escapes the limited form of the commercial or music video, there will be room for pictures of a dozen disabled veterans; room for the views of doctors, nurses, parents, siblings, coaches and women friends; room for cynicism, despondency, humor and bitterness, as well as inspiration. And the threat grows, all the while, that some of these other perspectives will controvert the message of the original narrative and that new messages will arise from their collision. Few narratives are deep enough to contain this superfluidity of perspectives. They will often overflow.

The new video will venture beyond narrative. Not only will it have difficulty sticking to printlike, isolated, one-point-after-another narratives, but by its nature the new video will tend to subvert or, often, ignore them. Stories will sometimes be told; yet this should be the least story-oriented form of communication humankind has come upon.

Scenes already succeed each other at such a rate in these productions that we are returned to the domain of the instant: An embrace is followed by a volleyball spike and then a race car crossing the finish line. Such collections of brazen, photolike moments can stymie even

---

* A one-minute version was also made.

† Print, as my summaries here may demonstrate, can also tell stories quickly, but not with the same detail, emotion and entertainment value.

the most creative tale spinner. It's not just that these moments are often too disparate to be contained in stories or that they tend to swamp stories; it's that they often seem proud of having escaped the mundane this-leads-to-that logic of stories. A three-quarter-second embrace acknowledges no courtship and no consequences. It announces itself instead as evidence of a new kind of logic—a logic of discontinuous peak moments. (For those of us who continue to respect causes and consequences, this seems a scary logic, but we might expect that new ethics and new responsibilities will confront us in the new kinds of relationships that are being created among these moments.)

This will hardly be humankind's first experiment with nonnarrative techniques. Print has not always contented itself with organizing its material into stories. Inverted-pyramid—most important facts first—newspaper articles are not constructed primarily around narratives, nor are gossip columns, nor are the short items scattered in the front of magazines, nor are some avant-garde novels, nor are many nonfiction books (including this one). But although these exceptions are growing more numerous (thanks, in part, to the influence of moving images), print still abandons narrative hesitantly and at some risk. To pull readers through lines of type without the aid of anecdotes and extended stories requires particularly compelling facts, juicy gossip or impressive analyses. This section of this book would probably be easier going were its list of the new video's attributes replaced by some tale from Don Hewitt's or Prospero's life. Video, despite Hewitt's injunction, needs narrative less.

Information can be scattered, stacked, swirled and layered in moving images without causing viewers to flee. We've seen this in commercials and music videos, where narratives remain relatively rare. We've seen it too in television newscasts, where, as Raymond Williams put it, "the elements of speed, variety and miscellaneity can be seen as organizing." We've even seen it in the disjointed progression of the television experience itself, where the programs "flow," to use Williams's term, into commercials and other programs—a flow made more complicated still by an impatient hand on a remote control.[17] What remains to be seen is what art and ideas can arise from such nonnarrative, nontraditional forms of organization.

Alternatives to narratives have also been explored for many decades now in rock songs, where storytelling remains the exception. They provide an important model for these experiments in video.

The new video will be structured more like music than like prose. The scenes and sounds come so fast in our music videos, commercials, highlights, trailers and intros that they trip over each other. Impressions and thoughts invariably overlap; sometimes, thanks to various forms of superimposition, images themselves overlap. Coordinating this mix, therefore, is something like coordinating the mix of instruments and voices that perform simultaneously in a band. Instead of guidelines that enable one thought to follow another, directors and producers are looking for guidelines that enable thoughts to be layered on top of one another.

Rhythm is the simplest of such organizing principles. That is why it is crucial to all these early forms of new video. The music is not there just for the youth market or for baby-boomers conditioned to respond to Motown; it is there to order and coordinate, to hold everything together. "The eye loves film cut to fast, heavy rock and roll," BBDO's Schneider observed.[18]

As the new video develops, more sophisticated organizing principles will likely be explored, including, perhaps, visual equivalents of harmony, counterpoint, variation and accent.

Of the many metaphors that have been applied to moving images in the attempt to figure out what to do with them, the music metaphor may prove the most helpful. Nevertheless, it too can lead us astray. Our ears are remarkably tolerant of repetition. We are content, even eager, to listen to choruses, riffs and whole songs over and over. Our eyes have rarely exhibited a similar patience. This is one place where the metaphor breaks down.

The first "video groups" are now beginning to surface. The model here is, of course, the rock band, so it is not surprising that their art leans heavily on the music metaphor. The Emergency Broadcast Network, for example, which describes itself as "an alternative video, music and performance production company," assembles clever melanges of "found" footage (of news anchors and national politicians, for example) to a hip-hop beat. Their videos, however, are occasionally annoying to watch: too repetitious. For example, when an EBN video entitled "Lawrence Welk Is Dead" has George Bush state, "This is a fact," more than a dozen times—as if the phrase were a guitar riff—the experience threatens to become the opposite of the opposite of dull. The imitation has, once again, gotten too close.

Music should prove a useful model, but ultimately moving images will be engaging in behaviors for which there are no models.

The new video will find a new role for words. Words will certainly survive in image communication. They will be read aloud or printed on the screen. But their role will change.

For most of history, if something clear and precise needed to be expressed, it was expressed in words. Images most often served to illuminate those words. But a reversal has been taking place. "The image no longer *illustrates* the words," wrote Roland Barthes, with characteristic prescience, in 1961; "it is now the words which, structurally, are parasitic on the image."[19] I would say, using a gentler metaphor, that narration and text now often serve as handmaidens to images. At times words are used to point out something in a series of fly-by images—to reduce their ambiguity. At other times words simply underline the thoughts expressed by such a montage.* "Increasingly," George Steiner wrote recently, "language is caption."[20]

> * The graphic arts have made similar use of words in recent decades.

With this new, reduced function, the way words relate to each other and the standards by which they are judged are also changing. Consider as an example what happens to sentences when sports broadcasts switch from radio to television. Without pictures, words must describe and explain. With pictures, they tend to devote themselves to more modest goals: "Yes!" "Boom!" "Look at him go!"

Words that serve images need not always be arrayed in complete sentences. Some of the wordings used in broadcast news—"More trouble for the White House"—already are not. Traditional rules of grammar and syntax may be routinely violated. The content and order of these words often matters less than their "feel." Instead of worrying whether a word is apt, the question may be whether it is sufficiently colorful, playful and concise.

These changes in the way we use words will not be confined to video; they will inevitably seep into our spoken and written languages. Indeed, that infiltration has already begun. For those of us who treasure carefully crafted sentences, this is proving among the hardest of the transformations wrought by the rise of the image to abide.

The new video will rely heavily on computer graphics. Graphs and charts produced by computer have remade newspaper pages in the past couple of decades. Computer graphics in television news have received less attention, but they are probably more important. On TV computers can produce graphs and designs that rise and fall, fold and unfold, collect or disperse themselves. They can demonstrate, not just portray. Using these moving graphics, colors can change on a map to point out the effects of various proposals; foods can hop in and out of shopping baskets to represent long-term variations in eating habits; dollar bills can fly into the wallets of the segments of society that have benefited from a recent tax cut.

"I always said the one thing television didn't report very well was lists and numbers," Bob Schieffer of CBS News explained. "Now we can give people lists and numbers in a way they can understand."[21] Martin Plissner, who is also at CBS News, concurred: "Most of the issues that are being fought over today are complicated. Computerized graphics make a huge contribution to clarifying them."[22]

These moving graphics are now also called upon to open television programs, present statistics in sports coverage and detail selling points in commercials. They work comfortably with text, giving words a rare opportunity to communicate by their behavior as well as their meaning. And moving graphics are getting easier and easier to produce. I have caught glimpses of my children using software purchased at Toys "Я" Us to create graphs and designs that perform reasonably impressive on-screen tricks. At their high end these tricks merge with animation, and computer-based editing devices should make them easy to mix with live action. They would seem to have the potential not only to explain complex issues but to explain complex ideas. (Perhaps the closest we've come is in the economic lessons imparted by clever moving graphics on *Adam Smith's Money World* on PBS.)

The new video will introduce symbols of its own. Writing won't be the only visual code that shows up on these screens. The new video will develop new forms of representation. These symbols—offspring of computer graphics—likely will be less abstract and more visual than the letters of our alphabet, more like earlier systems of writing, such as hieroglyphic. They won't be restricted to black on white, and they won't have to freeze in place in tight little lines.

Along with the computer screen, where the icons originally introduced by Alan Kay have continued to multiply, a good place to observe what such symbols can do is the television weather map. Clouds, sun and the various forms of precipitation have their representations, all of which are now capable of sashaying across the map or mutating before our eyes.

The old danger of ambiguity returns here, of course, but words are available, where necessary, to fend it off—the words of the weather person, for example. And we may be getting better at producing and interpreting these symbols. Some of us still might not be able to determine whether that European-made garment needs to be dry cleaned, but we have taught ourselves with little difficulty to recognize symbols for rain and symbols for thunderstorms as well as symbols for saving a computer file. Might we be able, in time, to develop similarly clever and intelligible symbols for such abstract notions as democracy, truth or irony?

The new video will not be after mere vérité. Television and film—in the name of truth, in accordance with Bazin's instructions—have plunked down attractive vistas and intriguing circumstances before us; we've looked, more or less at our leisure, and thought, "Hmm. Yeah. Nice. Okay." And maybe we noticed the light or the "verticals." Maybe we even got a chance to observe something true and profound about the flow of life. This is "far seeing." It's often interesting, sometimes stimulating, sometimes moving.

I want to give the more noble examples of this "far seeing" their due. Take, for example, Frederick Wiseman's 1975 film *Welfare,* which peeks in at the goings-on in a New York City welfare office. This film, broadcast on public television, represents the opposite of the new video. Scenes last fractions of an hour, not fractions of a second; they play out slowly—so slowly that we sometimes share the exasperation of the poor who are waiting for assistance or of the welfare workers who must listen to their occasional diatribes. In accordance with the rules of a Bazin-like cinema vérité, Wiseman forswears not only fancy cutting and graphics but also narration and any other cinematic devices that might obstruct our view of that welfare office.

What we see there is fascinating. In one eight-and-a-half-minute scene, for example, we observe a young man and woman straining to convince a case worker that they deserve public assistance; we can watch the tension build as these young people attempt to coordinate their stories; we can evaluate their situation and judge their veracity on our own by studying their voices, mannerisms, expressions. We have time to look as hard at them and their behaviors as we might at the frozen moment in a photograph or a painting.

Wiseman's film succeeds marvelously, in other words, in enabling us to see what we would have seen had we been well placed in that welfare office—an accomplishment of no small merit. Nonetheless, it never makes an effort to let us see more than we might have seen in that office. The new video is more ambitious. In its effort to communicate new understandings, it is prepared to rearrange the world.

Wiseman's approach does not allow him to recall or speculate; it limits his ability to characterize. He is in a poor position to do what those who work with words routinely do: help us see situations not only as they saw them but as they *thought* of them. This seems to be fine with Wiseman; he wants to leave much of the thinking to his audience. It is not good enough for an entire new form of communication—not if it aspires to say more about the world than, "Here's what at one time, in one place might have been seen," not if it hopes to "elevate" (Duhamel's term again) us. Wiseman, having chosen this style, left himself with little power to do what most artists and thinkers do: guide us not only with sufficient vision but with sufficient precision so that we might grasp what is on their minds and not just in front of their eyes. His style did not allow him to *edit* the visual world with sufficient thoroughness and fluidity.

This is what the new video makes possible. By chopping the world into fragments, by layering on words and graphics, by arranging those fragments in new and meaningful patterns, the new video gives us ways to see much more than is available at any one place or time to any one gaze. It enables us to see new patterns and connections, to reach new understandings. It enables artists to think new thoughts, and it enables us to see more clearly what they are thinking.

We didn't know what we were missing, of course. We never do. But what a remarkable power this is. "The task I'm trying to achieve is above all to make you see," D.W. Griffith stated in 1913.[23] Now we have the means to accomplish that.

However, we're not going to be seeing through the new video what we used to see. The world for a time will look different, unfamiliar. An oft-told anecdote about Picasso comes to mind. After someone complained that his portrait of Gertrude Stein did not look like her, the artist is said to have responded, "No matter; it will."[24]

The new video will tamper with photographs. The photo on the front page of *New York Newsday* one day in 1994 showed two well-known Olympic ice-skaters practicing together. However, Tonya Harding and the rival she had been accused of plotting to assault, Nancy Kerrigan, had not yet practiced together. The photo was a computer-generated composite. Some hackles were raised. "A composite photograph is not the truth," Stephen D. Isaacs, then acting dean of the Columbia University Graduate School of Journalism, thundered. "It is a lie and, therefore, a great danger to the standards and integrity of what we do."[25]

A lie? Perhaps. But what form of communication—fictional or true—has succeeded in wrestling with issues of significance without intentionally taking leave of the truth. The "raised hackles" metaphor is an example. I have no reason to believe the hairs on the back of Isaacs's neck were in fact standing up as he delivered this sermon to a reporter. Words "lie" in metaphors. Words take leave of the truth when they speculate on the future. If it was acceptable to place those two skaters in the same sentence—"Nancy Kerrigan and Tonya Harding will practice together"—why was it not acceptable to place them in the same photo, assuming the "tense" of the photograph was made clear in a label? (The Kerrigan-Harding photo *was* labeled as a "composite illustration"—"Tomorrow, they'll really take to the ice together"—though not in as large type as we journalism professors would have liked.)

Semiotics, Umberto Eco has explained, is "the study of whatever can be used to lie."[26] Thanks to the computer, photographs, including moving photographs, are now gaining the capacity to rework the truth almost as freely and easily as words do. As long as those who view them are aware that these photos have embarked on such flights of fancy—and initially, at least, that will require some sort of large-type disclaimer—this power can only make photographic images a richer, more powerful form of communication.

"Pictures," Sol Worth wrote dismissively in 1975, "cannot depict conditionals, counter-factuals, negatives or past future tenses."[27] Well, now they can. The new video will want to have all tenses open to it—including the subjunctive. It will want to be able to speculate, predict, hypothesize, compare and sometimes speak in the negative. It may choose to show, through deft computer manipulations, two competing candidates arm-wrestling. It will want to have access to all the powers of metaphor. It may want to show how the plane might have, should have and could have landed. It may expand, as writing has, our notions of truth and reality.

This will take some getting used to. We are in the habit of accepting photography as the "pencil of nature," not as just another pencil in the hands of sometimes fanciful artists. We'll have to wise up.

The new video will be casually surrealistic. Television commercials have already begun to exhibit some strange behaviors: Toes burst into flames. Faces become cubelike in shape or merge into one another. A man suffering in the heat opens a beer bottle, and it begins to snow. Chimps talk. Fred Astaire dances with a Dirt Devil vacuum cleaner. In the film *Trainspotting* a man enters a toilet bowl. In a music video Michael Jackson is transformed into a panther. CGI, for computer-generated imagery, is currently the acronym of choice for this capability.* CGI enables the new video to easily overcome such trivialities as physical laws: You don't have to convince people, as you would in a book, that there is a world where snow might suddenly fall on a hot day; you simply show it suddenly falling.

In a sense, video montage has returned to its origins in photomontage. However, the surrealism that shocked audiences in the first half of this century now appears every few minutes on American TV, and (as long as sacrosanct news pictures are not distorted) no one is shocked.[28] We are beginning to accept the idea that the world can be distorted, reimagined, that it can be made to collide with alternate versions of itself. (Our views of news will come around soon as well.)

The new video will create new worlds. This sort of thing happens sometimes in writing; that milk commercial hardly provided our first account of Hades, and we've certainly visited our share of other universes in science fiction. However, the vast majority of writers are too concerned with sustaining belief in their creations to stray too far from the known facts about this world.

Video is different. The authenticity of performances or scenery is sometimes questioned, but in general eyes are content to follow wherever the screen leads. A 1996 commercial for the U.S. Postal Service's Global Priority Mail can put the World Trade Center and the Eiffel Tower together in one landscape without worrying that the shot will be dismissed as unintelligible or absurd. That *is* most assuredly the

* As Jeff Scher has demonstrated, some similarly remarkable effects can also be "generated"—laboriously, it is true—by film techniques that have been around for two thirds of a century.

World Trade Center, that *is* the Eiffel Tower. The realness of the photographic image makes possible confident, extended excursions into
the unreal.

Greenaway has created a new world for his film version of *The
Tempest:* Crowds of naked humans parade through the ruins on this
almost deserted island. Who are these people? Spirits. Enchanted
beings. Occasionally they accompany or assist, but only one of them
has any impact on the plot: Ariel. And he often appears in triplicate—
played by three different actors at once, each a different age. It is difficult to imagine serious writers attempting such fancies. Who would
believe them? Shakespeare did not go quite this far. But in *Prospero's
Books* it is all in front of our eyes.

A video directed by J.B. Mondino for the 1988 Neneh Cherry song
"Manchild" gives another, less literary example of the sort of new
world that the new video might create. Gauzy curtains are pulled back
to reveal what looks almost like an overlit beach—except the sand is
covered with a layer of water. A girl on a swing drifts in and out of the
picture. The camera too swings back and forth, discovering various
backup singers, a tree branch, a woman hanging laundry and more
than one dancing, singing, splashing Neneh Cherry. A baby's bottle
floats through the air. Where are we? Nowhere we've ever been before;
nowhere we could be taken, without frustration and confusion, by
print. But this world—like Greenaway's creation—has an eerie beauty
and a kind of interest when watched, to a pleasing beat, on-screen.

Except for dreams and religious or scientific speculations, the
unreal has remained mostly unexplored territory. The new video,
thanks to the great flexibility computer-based editing is beginning to
provide, will go there easily and often. Artists and thinkers will be able
to present physical objects and physical laws to us in some of their
unlimited number of alternative configurations. We'll visit places
where gravity doesn't hold, where race and gender shift, where dogs
talk and humans hear each other's thoughts. We'll zoom video-game-
like through often abstract realms of extraordinary color—in the mode
of a Jackson Pollock or a Paul Klee. We'll visit territories filled with
extraordinary people and objects of extraordinary power. Indeed,
we've already visited early versions of most of these locales in music
videos and, especially, commercials.

More and more of our time is likely to be spent in such worlds, and
we will return from them to a world that increasingly embodies the possibility of such alternative realities and, alas, may seem to suffer by comparison with them. The experience might initially be disturbing, but it
will teach us in the same way the fantasy we have found in tales or in
print has taught us: by commenting—through analogy, exaggeration or

negation—on that which is not fanciful. It will teach us, too, by leaping barriers and opening possibilities. And as associated technologies continue to improve, some of those possibilities for life in "virtual" worlds may themselves cross the line from fantasy into reality. We may find *ourselves,* in some electronic way, doing laundry on a beach covered with water, where baby bottles sail through the air. We may find ourselves among spirits or in that nasty milk drinker's hell.

The new video will make many of its points through juxtaposition. It will find much of its meaning not from causes and effects within scenes but from analogies, contrasts and other relationships between scenes.*[29] The new video, in other words, will take great advantage of the ability to create meanings Lev Kuleshov noted in montage. One (possibly computer-altered) scene will be held up against another— and another and another. Repeatedly.

I'll resort to a hypothetical, fairly pedestrian example here. Picture one: President Clinton speaking. Picture two: former Republican presidential candidate Bob Dole speaking. A simple and mostly uninteresting juxtaposition. But say that after a couple of seconds of this, we throw onto the screen pictures of Abraham Lincoln and Stephen Douglas speaking—perhaps computer-altered so that they move like the two 1996 candidates. A new contrast has been created. Or what if, in another juxtaposition, Clinton was followed by John F. Kennedy and Dole by Richard Nixon or, alternatively, Clinton was followed by some glimpses of his aides testifying before various investigative committees, and then by Nixon; and Dole, in a World War II photo, was followed by a picture of Kennedy in uniform? New contrasts. New meanings. Dole might also be juxtaposed with Franklin Delano Roosevelt and George Wallace, to release different meanings; or Clinton, jogging, with similar pictures of George Bush and Jimmy Carter looking sweaty and exhausted.

There would be plenty of room in such videos for more traditional expositions too. I'm not saying we'll be reduced to explaining only by comparing. But such juxtapositions are an interesting and powerful mental tool, and video can spin them off in seconds.

The new video also makes possible—and this is crucial—the easy juxtaposition of juxtapositions: Various views of President Clinton, to pick up the example, might be compared: Clinton as Kennedy-like, Clinton as Nixon-like. Then—and this is where things begin to get more interesting—various standards for measuring a president might also be juxtaposed. Picture forty-six might be of James Polk, picture fifty-one of Thomas Jefferson, and so on.

Is this not a possible recipe for wisdom?

      &   &   &

* Roland Barthes, discussing sequences of still photographs, had a rather academic way of putting this: "The signifier of connotation is then no longer to be found at the level of any one of the fragments of the sequence but at that—what the linguists would call the suprasegmental level—of the concatenation." Exactly.

I don't mean to dismiss the efforts or the anxieties of television's producers, but it's about time we acknowledge something about the new
video's lethargic predecessor: It's easy. Aim a camera at a play, a news
event, a conversation or a comedian, and people—thousands, sometimes millions of us—will watch. And, oddly, the interest with which
we watch is not always dependent on the merit of that which is being
presented. We watch, sometimes, to appreciate the awkwardness, the
tackiness, the camp value. Johnny Carson, that master of the old television, understood early on that the largest laughs often come from
the jokes that fail.

Poorly chosen, poorly arranged words are unreadable. Poorly chosen, poorly arranged images retain a certain interest. The directors of
live TV—news, sports, talk—live in fear of the obvious error, but on the
rare occasions when such errors occur, they're generally viewed as part
of the fun. Carson, his predecessors and his successors understand this
too. Indeed, give us humans just about any collection of moving
images to stare at—preferably something a little strange—and likely as
not we'll watch it. Place a camera in front of a Gap store, call it the
Mall-Life Channel, and a lot of us—perhaps too few to please advertisers, perhaps not—would watch that too.

We have been settling, as I have argued, for bad imitations of other
media, for shrunken movies, flattened-out theater, diminished concerts and conversations in which we can't participate. We have been
settling, often, for shows that are dominated by words, even though,
since we hear slower than we read, programs that simply show people
talking are not particularly efficient conveyers of words. We have been
settling, often, for the opportunity to watch others living their lives,
thereby surrendering the thrills and torments that might arise were we
to devote that time to living our own lives. Sometimes we learn from
these shows; sometimes they are provocative, as *60 Minutes* so often is;
frequently we are left feeling enervated.

We have been settling, in part, because TV is also disturbingly easy
to watch. The images it presents—even when cut slow—are often
attractive, often interesting, but they don't have to be. We're capable
of watching attentively; we're capable of watching bemusedly; we're
also capable of watching half asleep. We come from a long line of
organisms who survived because they surveyed their environment,
because they stared at anything that moved in front of them. TV,
although it yields information of little apparent survival value, moves
in front of us. We watch.

Television will undoubtedly continue to present us with numerous
such occasions for lazy, mostly unrewarding "far seeing." In proclaiming
the arrival of the new video, I don't mean to suggest that it will evict the

old television from our screens. With the new "converged" technologies, people undoubtedly will order up at a time of their choosing most of the same talk shows, police dramas, soap operas, football games and *I Love Lucy* reruns they now switch to at a time of the broadcaster's choosing. I am prophesying a step forward in human communication, not a cultural utopia. Flaubert and Joyce, after all, did not push trashy romances off the shelves, and the *New York Times* continues to share newsstands with the *National Enquirer*. ("The proportion of trash in the total artistic output is greater now than at any other period," Aldous Huxley wrote— more than a decade *before* the arrival of commercial television.)[30] But I am arguing that something else is beginning to be added to the mix (to the "total artistic output"): dense, off-center, narrative-challenging, often surrealistic programming.

Some of the productions that honor these new artistic principles will be pointless; we've seen plenty of examples of that already on MTV. Some will be deceptive and manipulative; commercials have shown the way here. Some may be propagandistic. Some may be lewd or sensational. Some may be progressive, some conservative. In other words, this new form should be open to as wide a range of uses as any other form of communication. But some productions should turn these techniques to the task of communicating complex stories and issues. Some of them likely will do it with creativity and intelligence. And because the techniques will be new, some of the slants obtained on those stories and issues should also be new.

This new video—at its high end—should be difficult to produce. It may require, as *Madame Bovary* did, five years of work in a quiet room to get the images, sounds, words and graphics in one two-hour production right. It may require an artist who declares, paraphrasing Flaubert, "May I die like a dog rather than hurry by a single second a sequence that isn't ripe!"[31]

If I am correct, this new video should be judged by the strength and clarity of its perceptions, not by its faithfulness to earlier art forms. It will sometimes disappoint, as all forms sometimes do, but I believe it has the potential to amaze in the hands of substantial artists and thinkers.

This new video—the best new video—should also sometimes be difficult to watch. It can be expected to require and reward effort, not button pushing but a mental alertness. It should, to make use of a dichotomy discussed by Walter Benjamin, not just provide "distraction" but require "concentration."[32] It should indeed, to use Sontag's terms, "demand...full attention." It may not be the best thing to call up after a hard day. This new video will occasionally want to be rewound and watched again, and segments may have to be replayed to be fully understood. The Book of Motion, once we master the art of "writing" and "reading" it, may be more, not less, stimulating than print.

Is this possible? Could something really break through that heavy-lidded, blank-faced television stupor? (TV's detractors sometimes essay analogies to heroin.) There is some evidence that staring at a two-foot-wide screen five feet in front of us produces fewer of the brain waves associated with mental activity and attention than does scanning a book. The explanation is not that we're all reading Proust but watching *Married with Children;* it may have to do, television researchers Robert Kubey and Mihaly Csikszentmihalyi suggest, with how little our eyes move when focused on a TV set.*[33]

*Large screen TV may help.

Nonetheless, television has certainly demonstrated that it is capable of producing alertness, even agitation, upon occasion. We've all experienced it: when bombs are landing and reporters are talking through gas masks, when something large and full has crashed, when thirty seconds are left and one team is two points behind. It may take a little more to rouse us for moving images than for a book, but there's no doubt it can be done.

Might jumpy, fast-cut, sometimes surreal, sometimes abstract images, however, have the opposite effect and actually deepen the trance? Such a conclusion, raised with some frequency by opponents of these arguments, would have to be based on some sort of theory of television hypnosis—a theory I have not encountered in the literature. To the contrary, highly kinetic, unbalanced, unfamiliar, unexpected images, with some intelligence behind them, seem more likely to perk us up than pictures of Ted Koppel and a few other middle-aged men in suits talking. A video chockablock with energy and ideas should have no trouble getting the brain waves crackling.

The bulk of the population may well ignore the menus that offer such dense, concentration-dependent programming. The bulk of the population, after all, doesn't often pay much attention to the more challenging works of literature or modern thought. Nevertheless, this "picture, picture, picture thing" seems likely to present the occupants of our couches with an opportunity, should they choose to accept it, to "elevate" themselves. And while the audiences disposed to grappling with the more adventurous examples of the new video may be as small as those traditionally gathered by pathbreaking artists, the ideas experimented with in these videos should eventually diffuse out into the larger culture, as the ideas of pathbreaking artists generally, eventually do.

Ridley Scott, director of *Blade Runner* and *Thelma and Louise,* is one of the growing number of filmmakers who has admitted to being influenced by, if not yet adopting, some of the techniques summed up here under the term "new video." Indeed, he worked for a time directing television commercials. Scott is also one of those filmmakers who has tried to keep an eye on the future. He has seen how these methods could enable a full-length film to tell "an incredibly complex story," and he has considered what that might mean for human communication: "Film is twentieth-century theater, and it will become twenty-first-century writing," Scott proclaimed in 1992, adding another variation on a metaphor to this book's collection.[34]

There's one metaphor, however, that I've kept out of these final chapters. I've mentioned hieroglyphic. Usually that is a sign that bold talk about a language of images—in this case moving images—is about to follow. I'm not that bold. The use of the language metaphor, even when peering into the next century, strikes me as premature.

Clearly, something with profound consequences for human language is afoot. Our first communications revolution, the introduction of writing, was based on words. Our second communications revolution, the introduction of printing, was also based on words. Our third, in large part, is not. Nevertheless, we're still a long way from the development of a lexicon of moving images and a syntax for organizing moving images.[35] We're still a long way from creating a new language; at least, we're a long way from creating a new language with characteristics similar to our current languages.

Becoming "twenty-first-century writing," on the other hand, does seem a realizable goal for this Book of Motion (as long as we're not merely trying, as André Bazin put it, to write "in" moving images). The new video, with the assistance of computers, should become the means by which our more sophisticated information, ideas and experiences are recorded, shared, explored and analyzed. And as writing and print once did, the new video should begin to transform the nature of our information, ideas and experiences.

In explaining what he meant by "complex seeing," Brecht made use of an example with which many of us today have difficulty: "smoking and watching." Brecht wanted a theater that instead of merely carrying its audiences away, forced them to step back and see things in new ways, more complex ways: "This passion for propelling the spectator along a single track where he can look neither right nor left, up nor down, is something that the new school of playwriting must reject." Which is where smoking comes in: "It is hopeless to try to 'carry away' any man who is smoking and accordingly pretty well occupied with himself," the playwright stated.[36]

Brecht no doubt had the cultural and political situation in Germany in 1931 in mind as he argued for this more detached art. An uncontrolled emotionalism was, he believed, connected to fascism; new, more objective ways of seeing would, he believed, reveal the virtues of socialism. However, I do want to try, as delicately as I can, to lift Brecht's analysis out of this situation and to lay it atop our own. (In this I may have received some assistance from Brecht himself, whose pronouncements often were rather sweeping.)

Brecht said his goal was to encourage his audiences to "think above the stream" more than "in the stream," to produce "a theater full of experts, just as one has sporting arenas full of experts." He said he wanted audiences to be critical of what they are seeing and prepared to examine it from a variety of perspectives. This is a goal that might also be aspired to by artists from other times, with other cultural and political concerns.

It can be accomplished in two ways: One is by changing the audience's attitude. Brecht's not entirely serious strategy—making sure smoking is allowed in the theater—has lost much of its resonance. However, the case can be made that the attitude change Brecht wanted has quietly, subtly been taking place in the audience for images.

Susan Sontag saw a distancing effect, similar to that desired by Brecht, in photographs, with their ability to pull experiences out of time and "miniaturize" them.[37] Benjamin saw something like this in film, which by separating spectators and actors makes it easier for "the audience to take the position of a critic."[38] But if modern audiences have to some extent been transformed into more distant, more critical "experts," most of the credit must go to television—imitative, easy, mind-deadening, old television.

Were Brecht analyzing American television, he likely would have little patience for its insipidness and commercialism, and he wouldn't be able to ignore the medium's narcotic capabilities: Its users do often lack alertness. Yet Brecht would have to note that with dozens of channels spread out before them, TV audiences are increasingly, undeniably distant and critical. They might as well all be smoking while they watch. Moisture occasionally can be spotted forming in a couch potato's eye; they are not entirely immune to being carried away. But, given the amount of time the set is on, this is an infrequent occurrence. To watch TV—munchies at the ready, "zapper" in hand—is mostly to stand back and judge. That means we're muttering to ourselves: "Bo-o-o-ring!" or "Gosh, he's aged!" But also: "What lousy acting!" "Hey, this is kind of interesting." "Not that routine again!" "Why are they showing this?" A television viewer, to make the same point in another way, is more likely to conclude, "Hey, that's funny," than to laugh.

We're all—tobacco users or not—experts when on our own couches. Television viewers are justly accused of lethargy and cynicism, but gullibility and naiveté are less and less frequently included among the charges.* In fact, although this is the most massive of mass audiences, its members are probably less reverential and sentimental than their fellows in the theater or a movie house, or even in an armchair with a book. (Prophets of doom take note: Television seems to have left us grumbling and joking about our leaders, not falling into lockstep behind them.) What thinking couch potatoes do they tend to do "above," not "in," the stream. This is a start.

A second strategy for creating Brecht's audience "full of experts" is to fashion the performance itself so that it embodies another, self-critical level of understanding. Brecht called for a self-consciousness in acting: the musicians visible during the songs, singers stepping back from their parts to display "a stubborn, incorruptible sobriety." He also arranged for the titles of his scenes to be projected onto screens onstage—a "primitive attempt," he admitted, to make his audiences less lost in and more expert on the progress of his plays.

Precisely because it is moving away from the "complete imitation of nature" called for by Bazin, precisely because it does not limit itself to presenting what *is,* the new video is developing more varied and more sophisticated tools with which to accomplish this. Its performances—with their hordes of objectified scenes, illuminated by words, graphics and symbols—provide endless opportunities for commentary upon themselves. Pellington's video about beauty, for example, does little else. Titles, much more capable than those with which Brecht experimented, routinely appear on-screen. All these elements make it difficult not to view situations from many levels at once.

In addition, the speed, the asymmetry, the nonnarrative techniques, the surrealism and the juxtapositions of the new video so thoroughly stir, muddy and divert the "stream" of these performances that even viewers inclined to sentimentality are forced to climb up on the bank and occasionally mull things over. The new video encourages a certain untelevisionlike alertness. But the larger point is that it has the potential to help us see, in Brecht's terms, with a formidable and unprecedented level of complexity.

Brecht's theory, extracted from its cultural time and political purposes, has it limitations. This is hardly the only valid kind of art. But it is the art we seem about to get, and, I will argue, the art we now need.

* Yes, we put up with a lot of commercials, but even the most effective ads persuade only a tiny percentage of viewers.

13 thinking

IBM
APTIVA
"TOTAL IMAGE" NON-TAG
TV 30 IMPC 6855

MUSIC THROUGHOUT

COMPUTER
FILMORE

2./3.
a stream of
memories and
projections:
two images from Mark
Pellington's 1993 film
Father's Daze—
one from a family visit to the
beach, one more recent, both
showing the director and his
father, Bill Pellington,
who suffered from
Alzheimer's disease.

4.   Stepping back:
a "story sheet" showing some of the images in a 1995
commercial made by Ogilvie & Mather for IBM's Aptiva
computers.

"above the stream":

new philosophies

1. **Avant-garde energies:** one of the barbers in the 1996 public-service film edited by Hank Corwin and directed by Samuel Bayer for Boston's Jimmy Fund charity.

Why do you
want to pull
me in every
direction, ye
unread?
—Heraclitus

n *The Tempest,* the "savage" Caliban has this advice for his drunken coconspirators in the attempt to take control of the island from Prospero: "Remember, first to possess his books; for without them he's but a sot, as I am."[1] All stages of this clumsy revolt fail, of course. But we now live in an age when it appears as if we *are* surrendering possession of our books. They are disappearing from our homes. Their place in front of our eyes is being usurped by the moving image.

Shakespeare's last play can be read as a disquisition on the power not of the Book of Motion, the magic of our time, but of the book, the magic of his. "My library was dukedom large enough," declares Prospero when recounting his exile. The "art" he finds in one of the books he was able to take with him to the island enables Prospero to conjure up the tempest itself; that's how he "put the wild waters in this roar." "I love my books," he says.[2]

We—maybe not you (If you've read this far, you might consider phoning Michael Kinsley), maybe not I, but we as a society—are losing the love of books, and therefore we risk losing a formidable source of magic, of power. It's not over yet, of course. Indeed, periods of transition from one form of communication to another, like ours, sometimes prove fertile even for old forms. Socrates, for example, perfected a method of developing ideas in spoken words in an Athens energized by written words. Shakespeare wrote for the stage in an England that, as this play indicates, was beginning to sense the power of works written for the printed page.[3] It is conceivable that someone in our time could channel the energy unleashed by the moving image into another transcendent novel. Perhaps James Joyce did. Perhaps some future author will. Still, it would likely be a last hurrah.

America is "on the eve of...becoming a literature-free zone," Philip Roth has lamented.[4] He was exaggerating. "To speak today of a famous novelist is like speaking of a famous cabinet maker or speedboat designer," the well-known novelist Gore Vidal has declared. "Adjective is inappropriate to noun. How can a novelist be famous, no matter how well known he may be personally to the press, when the novel itself is of no consequence to the civilized, much less the generality?"[5] Vidal too was exaggerating. Still, the truth is that literature in America and elsewhere continues to lose consequence, and it continues to lose the segment of the generality that controls the future: the young.

Our descendants undoubtedly will still learn to read and write, but they undoubtedly will read and write less often and, therefore, less well. (The tumble in verbal skills as measured by the SATs has abated for the moment. But since these are skills tested exclusively through reading, it would be surprising if they did not begin to decline once again with continued improvement in the selection of moving images available to distract children from reading.) And the language our descendants write and speak will increasingly be a less precise, less subtle language—one designed for use with images.

The end of the printed word—offscreen—won't come tomorrow; it may not come within the next century. Perhaps there won't be a clear, clean end, just continued slippage. Perhaps books, like legitimate theater today, will maintain a small, elite audience. Besides, the schools can always be counted upon to preserve a fading form of communication; look how long they insisted upon rhetoric, recitation, memorization and even the Socratic method. I'm not suggesting that those who work for publishers or newspapers seek new work. My wife edits magazines. I write books. But I would not advise our children to enter these fields.* All of them already read less than their father does and did, anyway.[6]

USA Today—that extremely rare phenomenon, a successful new newspaper—recently published an examination of twenty-four hours of American popular culture. In it television was mentioned twenty-three times, film and popular music six times each, radio three times and fiction once (*The Bridges of Madison County*).†[7] No one who has wandered beyond the graduate schools or Manhattan's Upper West Side should find these numbers surprising.

Every few months or so someone tries to explain in print why the novel, say, is not quite as feeble as measures like this indicate; why, as a *New York Times* editorial in 1994 put it, "Rumors about the death of the book are greatly exaggerated."[8] Usually there is talk of imagination and individualism, of souls and slowness. But I hear mostly nostalgia. I hear, too, echoes of a similar sanguineness expressed by Trithemius of Sponheim, the abbot, bibliographer and fancier of handwritten manuscripts, in 1492: "Yes, many books are now available in print," he wrote early in the previous communications revolution, "but no matter how many books will be printed, there will always be some left unprinted and worth copying."[9] I sense, in other words, that wishes are commandeering thinking.

We wish, of course, because we fear: Without our books, won't we

* The *New York Times* recently ran an article noting difficulties in finding "extra content for multichannel broadcasting" under a lengthy feature on the problems "midlist" authors are having getting their books published. The career advice lurking there for creative types went unremarked upon.

† Jonathan Franzen did the counting.

be nothing but "sots"—drunk on images, fooled by appearances, bereft of our intellectual powers? I take this fear very seriously. I have tried not to underplay the disruptions and losses already experienced and likely to be experienced in this transitional period. Yet the message of this chapter, the message of this book, is that in the long term the moving image is likely to make our thoughts not more feeble but more robust, that it is likely to lead us to stronger understandings.

Perhaps this book lover's most treasonable thought about print's fall is that it is time. Humankind has a talent for coming up with the new technologies it requires at about the time, give or take a couple of centuries, it requires them—or at least it looks that way in retrospect.[10] I suspect that, in retrospect, we will conclude that sometime in the twentieth century the print method of analyzing the world began to exhaust itself, that its magic began to run out.

"We are threatened by a new and peculiarly American menace," Daniel Boorstin wrote in his prophetic book *The Image,* published in 1962. "It is not the menace of class war, of ideology, of poverty, of disease, of illiteracy, of demagoguery, or of tyranny, though these now plague most of the world. It is the menace of unreality."[11]

This threat has only grown worse in the intervening third of a century, and it has spread to much of the rest of the world. Something, we seem to sense, has been leaking out of our lives: values, perhaps, or meaning, or a kind of surety. Many of us, if I can presume to speak for many of us, upon occasion feel weightless, directionless, uncertain; reality seems to lack realness.* That's why we produce so many tributes—in advertising, song, even politics—to "real clothes," "real love," "real experiences," "real events," "real people," "real issues" and, more generally, "making it real."

The villain for Boorstin and the multitudes of professional and amateur cultural observers who have followed is clear: the image. "In our world we sleep and eat the image and pray to it and wear it too," Don DeLillo wrote in *Mao II.*[12] Images are winning—materialistic, entertainment-besotting, civic-life-depleting images; vain, phony, surface-loving, fantasy-promoting, reality-murdering images. I've quibbled with one or two of the particulars in this long indictment; nevertheless Boorstin et al. have a point: Television *has* played a major role in creating what Bill McKibben called "the current emptiness."[13] But so have printed words.

Print's linear, one-word-follows-another, one-thing-at-a-time logic is perhaps its greatest strength. Expanding on the work begun by writing in the time of the pre-Socratic philosopher Heraclitus, print has pulled us in an exceedingly profitable direction. We owe it much:

* The *Utne Reader* went so far as to wonder in its July-August 1997 issue: "Is Real Life Possible Anymore?"

Modern science, modern medicine, modern democracy, our reformations and enlightenments—all were advanced by the printed word. But with the alchemists debunked, the leeches removed and the kings decapitated, it sometimes seems as if print has been reduced to chasing its own long, straight tail.

Print eventually turned the same unyielding logic that had helped overturn superstitions, monarchies and social hierarchies upon words and logic themselves. Some of the writers who trekked most intrepidly up lines of type—Kafka, Beckett, Camus—found the meanings getting thinner as they ascended. "Nothing, nothing mattered" is the wisdom impending execution brings to Albert Camus's protagonist in *The Stranger*. Philosophers and literary theorists undertook similar journeys. Indeed, close readers, many of them French, discovered that when carefully examined, metaphors conflict, arguments undercut themselves, precepts seem suspended in air. Such print-guided excursions into the absurd or the postmodern, such exercises in existentialism, poststructuralism or deconstruction, left language, meaning and reason looking like more "false fronts."[14] No solid ground upon which to construct a secure sense of the real here.

"You taught me language," Caliban fumes at Prospero's daughter, "and my profit on't is, I know how to curse."[15] We have been taught print. We might say, were we to succumb to a similar bitterness, that our "profit on't" is that we now know how to deconstruct.

It is time to repeat a caveat from an early chapter: I don't mean to discount the contributions made to the uneasinesses of our time by shifts in politics, economics, religion or others of the many social and cultural forces that are not the subject of this book. Still, I believe it is fair to conclude that printed words, like images, have played *a* major role in leading us to this crisis. And I believe it is important to note that printed words may not have the range to help lead us out.

Lines of type seem to have bent themselves into logical circles: trying to find the matter in the fact that nothing matters. In the twentieth century the limits of writing may have been written. "Philosophy is a battle against the bewitchment of our intelligence by means of language," proposed Ludwig Wittgenstein, writing in 1945.[16] That is not a battle easily won by means of language. Perhaps print has taken us as far as it can.

As a writer I feel as if I can describe anything, so I will attempt to describe this: It is a short 1996 public-service film edited by Hank Corwin and directed by Samuel Bayer for Boston's Jimmy Fund charity, and in there somewhere is a boy whose hair is growing back after treatment for cancer. The film, shot in black and white, is occupied mostly with jaggedly cut images of a number of strange-looking barbers. We see them discussing their work, wielding their combs and brushes, snipping their scissors, smiling sometimes almost "demonically" (Corwin's word).[17] I should also mention the odd angles and glaring lighting. In a spot ostensibly about the joy of returning to the world, Corwin and Bayer have confronted, through these echoes of childhood (and maybe biblical or historical) barber nightmares, some of the terrors of that world.

It is odd. It is disturbing. Within the limits of the form, a public-service announcement, it looks to me to be art. And whether or not I've had any success describing this film in print, it is difficult to imagine *experiencing* what this film communicates through print.

Print took the world apart and reassembled it in straight, regularly shaped, black-and-white lines. The problem is that not everything can be made to fit.

"What reading does, ultimately," concludes the essayist Sven Birkerts, one of its champions, "is keep alive the dangerous and exhilarating idea that a life is not a sequence of lived moments, but a destiny, that, God or no God, life has a unitary pattern inscribed within it."[18] I would not go that far. Twentieth-century print has certainly not been limited to proselytizing for destiny and unitary patterns. Indeed, I am sympathetic with Milan Kundera's statement that "the novelist teaches the reader to comprehend the world as a question."[19] However, I believe print tends to raise its questions in a way that allows for a limited set of possible answers: a cause-and-effect destiny, for example, an underlying pattern, or its absurd absence ("Nothing, nothing mattered"). Even to think of life as "a sequence of lived moments"—the prosaic view Birkerts sees reading as moving us beyond—is to surrender to prose, to the biases of the sequential line of type.

We have learned from print to squeeze even death into the sequences. Here is Flaubert:

> A spasm flung her down on the mattress. Everyone drew close. She had ceased to exist.[20]

Here is the *New York Times*:

> CHARLESTOWN STATE PRISON, Mass., Tuesday, Aug. 23 — Nicola Sacco and Bartolomeo Vanzetti died in the electric chair early this morning, carrying out the sentence imposed on them for the South Braintree murders of April 15, 1920.
>
> Sacco marched to the death chair at 12:11 and was pronounced lifeless at 12:19.

Vanzetti entered the execution room at 12:20 and was declared dead at 12:26.

To the last they protested their innocence, and the efforts of many who believed them guiltless proved futile, although they fought a legal and extra legal battle unprecedented in the history of American jurisprudence.

Events—even events at their most terrible, sensational, unfathomable, tempestuous—tend to display a certain calm, ordered clarity when portrayed in print. (I know it is possible to think of exceptions; perhaps it is time to notice the rule.) Louis Stark, who wrote this story on the execution of Sacco and Vanzetti for the *New York Times* in 1927, later recalled the scene at the prison that night to be one of "the utmost confusion." That confusion does not come through in the procession of isolated facts that form his story.[21]

Shakespeare shows us how the magic contained in books can make and unmake a tempest. A ship is wrecked. "We split, we split, we split!" cries one of those on board.[22] Feelings of recrimination, romance and reconciliation are set loose. A plot is moved forward. Otherwise all the storm's effects, once they have served their narrative purposes, are simply undone: ship restored, victims reunited, their clothes unsullied.

This is a formidable magic. But let's take a closer look at the tempest it has produced. The tempest divides, for a time, daughter from father, prince from king. It erases, in time, confusion between the legitimate and the illegitimate. It splits. It reconciles. It does not muddle, overwhelm or, in the end, even destroy.

Prospero—who deserves the byline on this tempest—ultimately rejects the book he has used to create it. We are presumably to see in this an artist renouncing his art in favor of life. We might also see a conjurer frustrated with the limitations of the book's magic, as conjurers before him must have grown frustrated with the limitations of the spoken word. "Deeper than ever did plummet sound," Prospero vows, "I'll drown my book."[23] It has, after all, been a rather anemic storm.

It would be hypocritical for me to insist too strenuously on the limitations of words while enlisting the services of ninety-some-odd thousand of them. When challenged, print has demonstrated a remarkable ability to expand. That is why I write. As I set sentences after images and ask them to tiptoe into the future, I worry a great deal about my abilities, not much about theirs. However, my ideas—historically based, ultimately rather dualistic—probably don't represent that great a test for this medium.* Others have posed sterner tests.

In the twentieth century, some of the best of them that write this

* Some of the philosophic ▫

noodlings in this chapter may be exceptions.

*Poetry—an oral form, never entirely comfortable in print—has long been engaged in that effort.

writing, to paraphrase Shakespeare once again, have struggled to do our tempests more justice.[24] They have strained to escape the thinness of the line, the flatness of the page.* These writers have been trying to say in print what print is not comfortable saying: that the world can't always be split into categories, that our thoughts are often scattered, that contradictions aren't always clarified, that our experiences are determined in part by contingency, that reality sometimes reduces itself to indeterminate clouds, that life resists encapsulation in narratives or processions of facts, that our existences, our cultures, are full of confusions. However, enabling readers to *experience* this has required surrendering some of the strategies that have traditionally made print effective. Avant-garde writers in this century have engaged in sometimes reader-unfriendly subtractions of clarity, message, coherence or entertainment value. (In the *New York Times Magazine,* the impeccably cultured James Atlas recently went so far as to admit that much of the "great literature" of the twentieth century "bores" him.)[25]

Hank Corwin and Samuel Bayer were working in the new video, a much less mature form; they were making a public-service announcement only a couple of minutes long; yet Corwin and Bayer were able to present one or two similarly challenging notions with much less sacrifice, much less strain. The avant-garde energies released by photography and film are finally beginning to settle where they belong: in the successor to photography and film, in the new video.

Corwin and Bayer's messages and the messages of these adventurous novelists and theorists seem dangerous; they have helped raise the specter of unreality. But would they scare us so if our culture did not remain, for the most part, trapped in print's narrow logic? Scattered thoughts, unclarified contradictions, contingency and indeterminacy are direct threats to *print's* reality. The new video, however, is much more comfortable with them. Mark Pellington had no difficulty presenting a few entirely different perspectives on beauty *simultaneously* in a music video. Corwin and Bayer were willing to intermingle joy and nightmare in a disjointed, stream-of-consciousness montage. They pull us, to use Heraclitus's words, in more than one direction at once.†[26] In the new video the confusions, the tempests, fit.

† Raymond Williams: "The flow of hurried items establishes a sense of the world: of surprising and miscellaneous events coming in, tumbling over each other, from all sides." And he was just talking

In its early centuries print helped spread an older set of frightening messages: that the earth might not be at the center of the universe, that kings might not rule by divine right. It was print itself that eventually helped supply the wisdom the populace needed to survive those shocks. Now, in the midst of a new communications revolution, we face a new set of shocks attributable in part to the exhaustion of print and the arrival of video. Video may be able to help us survive them. It may help reassure us that scattered thoughts, unclarified contradictions, contingency and indeterminacy are not necessarily threats to *our* reality.

about early 1970s newscasts.

Boorstin insisted that we are foolish to think moving images will ever succeed in giving us "the nub of the matter."[27] Perhaps moving images won't. Perhaps moving images can't. But they may give us other perspectives on reality—less constricted perspectives.

One way of viewing Corwin and Bayer's little film is that it presents barbers and their implements as they might appear to that young cancer patient. We don't see what is going on in that child's head, but this mix of uplifting and nightmarish views gives us an idea of how the world outside might look from in there. This from-the-inside-*out* perspective is more or less the one to which most of us head-bearing creatures are accustomed. It is not, however, the angle of vision that has become characteristic of print.

Print, as I have noted, wants to look from the outside *in.* Its narrow searchlight is well suited to the dark recesses it finds there. Print must strain mightily to present the visible with anything near the richness or completeness we can get from our own eyes, but in presenting the invisible—in the "attempt to interpret...state of mind and inner life," to borrow a phrase from Fyodor Dostoevsky—the printed word has no competition. The novel, back as far as *Don Quixote,* justified its existence by introducing us to the world with*in.* Here, from *Crime and Punishment,* is one of the countless scenes Dostoevsky observed there:

> The hopeless misery and anxiety of all that time, especially of the last hours, had weighed so heavily upon him that he positively clutched at the chance of this new unmixed, complete sensation. It came over him like a fit; it was like a single spark kindled in his soul and spreading fire through him. Everything in him softened at once.[28]

"Novelists," Jonathan Franzen wrote recently in a meditation on the continued relevance of his craft, "are preserving...a habit of looking past surfaces into interiors."[29] Humans searching for understanding did not always turn this way. First, we can suppose, they had looked with the aid of spoken language mostly *out,* toward the edges of their worlds, for signs of the useful or the dangerous. The *Iliad,* the *Odyssey* and the Bible do communicate the urgings of "the heart inside," but often their search for understanding causes eyes to turn *up*—to Olympus, to the heavens.[30] However, the four centuries that are now ending have been dominated by this compulsion to stare not *out* or *up* but *in.*

It is here, under our skins, that our psyches, subconsciouses, "true selves" and souls were found. Descartes, Rousseau, Flaubert, Dostoevsky, Freud, Woolf, Proust—these were explorers of the inner world, of our hidden thoughts, inner selves, hidden natures, inner states and hidden feelings.[31] With their help, we clutched at sensations and kindled sparks in our souls. With their help, we constructed mythologies of the psyche, complete with warring powers and walled-off territories. With their help, we developed a whole profession devoted to guiding people, pilgrims in search of *in*sight, around these hidden inner lands. (Kundera satirized our obsession by having a pretentious professor assert, "Homer's odyssey has been taken inside. It has been interiorized. The islands, the seas, the sirens seducing us, Ithaca summoning us—nowadays they are only the voices of our interior being.")[32]

Although it is about hopes and fears, Corwin and Bayer's film is not a psychological study. Few examples of the new video are. They frequently take their shape, as this film seems to, from the flow of impressions through a single consciousness. However, what we see is not some imagining of the nature of that consciousness but those particular, telling impressions. Such videos show us psyches in action; they do not attempt to conjure up psyches themselves.

There is a reason for this: Video is a bright floodlight. It has its way with the visible and with perspectives on the visible, but has little facility for presenting the buried, the invisible. Our churning ids, deepest selves or immortal souls are even more difficult to capture in a photographic image than hearts, hopes, virtue, integrity or character. Video, consequently, tends not to look in that direction.*[33]

To those of us still conditioned to the idea that truth is to be found only through such inner vision, video's perspective seems more than just superficial; it seems a blindness, a stupidity. This is one of the largest of the mistakes that has been made about the rise of the image.

For when we speak of our inner natures, it must be remembered, we are speaking metaphorically. Exactly where our own unvoiced thoughts might be located on some topology of consciousness is unclear. But certainly whatever we know of the "inner lives" of others we know not from X rays of their hearts or examinations of their entrails but from surface manifestations. Surgeons have happened upon no Oedipal yearnings, kernels of identity, souls or spirits beneath our skins. After centuries of print's fascinating imaginings, this is easy to forget.

That this metaphor has been hugely productive no one can deny, but it has its limitations. And those limitations have, over time, formed ruts and barriers.

* Bertolt Brecht, writing about film, put it bluntly (too bluntly): "Character is never used as a source of motivation; the inner life of the persons never supplies the principal cause of the plot and seldom is its main result."

[handwritten margin note:] Print can spend quite a bit of time on developing characters & making them more 3D, image is more constrained by time & must work to tell the story more because we already see the characters as 3D. Print isn't so constrained by time or length. (EX LOTR movie underdevelopment of characters)

By the middle years of this century we had explored our insides to the point of self-obsession, to the point of solipsism. We had looked into this metaphorical inner world so long and so intently that we sometimes seemed oblivious to what was taking place in that other, more tangible world. We learned, "against the stomach of [our] sense," to borrow another wording from *The Tempest,* to place more stock in the unseen than the seen.[34] We cupped our ears not to the importunings of our fellows but to inner voices. We judged our mental health not by our social circumstances but by unconscious urges. We began to imagine ourselves not so much as actors in the world but as stages for private dramas, as atomistic units—as if we were not so hopelessly dependent on a borrowed language, on borrowed perspectives, so thoroughly covered by the fingerprints of others, that it is almost absurd to speak of us having independent beings.* The more we looked inward, into individuals, the less we saw of the connections between individuals.[35]

However, since the advent of TV, we have lost the sense of neighborhood & community ... why is that?

Why do we assume there is more truth inside us than out? Why is there not as much to be learned by picking apart, rethinking, reimaging our surfaces—from a *superficial* analysis—as there is from an analysis of those mythical insides? Perhaps we have gained what we can gain from this metaphor. Perhaps it is time for it to be dropped, time for our gaze—with all the powers of the new video—to return to what can actually be seen.

"If serious reading dwindles to near nothingness," DeLillo has suggested, "it will probably mean that the thing we're talking about when we use the word 'identity' has reached an end."[36] He may be right. Perhaps we will have to learn to talk of new things.[37]

"The world is all outside," developments in nineteenth-century molecular theory inspired Emerson to conclude; "it has no inside."[38] It could be said, similarly, that human beings are all outside. Our natures—like the atoms of a molecule—are not inside us; they make up us. Oscar Wilde was always sensitive to this point. "It is only shallow people who do not judge by appearances," he remarked in a letter. "The mystery of the world is the visible, not the invisible."[39] Now, for the first time in human history, we have a means of communication, an art form, strong enough to grapple with the all-encompassing outside, with the visible.

* Joseph Brodsky described the book as encouraging a "flight in the direction of...autonomy, in the direction of privacy."

In 1993 Mark Pellington took a camera along on a visit to his parents' home, edited in some old 8mm movie footage and other images of memorable family moments, and produced a thirty-minute film. His motivations, sadly, had little to do with those behind the typical home video. The director's father, Bill Pellington, once a star linebacker for the Baltimore Colts, was suffering from Alzheimer's disease.

Pellington's film, *Father's Daze,* was broadcast on PBS and screened at a number of film festivals. Nevertheless, this film might be taken as a model of the future home video and of the future world as seen through the new video.

Father's Daze is resolutely, unflaggingly nonnarrative. Words on screen at the beginning inform us of the situation of Pellington's father. But no story of decline is told. No chronology is presented. Various scenes from the father's past—a celebration at the stadium of his career, an afternoon at the beach with his young family, his wedding—are mixed in with various glimpses of him today: an uncomprehending interaction with his son, being fed by a nurse, shuffling in front of the house. Micki Pellington—Bill's wife, Mark's mother—voices her frustration and sadness. Leafless trees are shown against a gray sky. Steep highs and deep lows, to revisit one of McKibben's critiques, are indeed presented. Feeling and emotion flow freely, but they are not channeled into stories. No one explains how long this has been going on. No one remembers him when. No one uses the word *tragedy.*

Can't we do the same w/ photos then, if we use juxtaposition correctly?

Moments are pulled out of time in Pellington's film as they are in photographs: the imposing bulk of the aged father immobile on the edge of his bed, the vitality of the young father swinging his son high over the sand. Sometimes all we see is a pajama-covered hip; sometimes the film speeds up to show repetitive routine; sometimes images and sounds are repeated. The film places these moments before us— ungraceful, neither virtuous nor unvirtuous, unburdened by explanatory system.

The subtractions caused by the abandonment of traditional kinds of meaning are as evident in Pellington's film as they are in empty-headed thrillers like *Mission: Impossible.* However, here we can also begin to glimpse—at a very early stage—some of the kinds of meaning this new form might add.

Pellington is forcing us, in part, to examine social behaviors and interactions: son tries to convince father to sit down, football star is interviewed on television, wife places food in husband's mouth. I don't know if Pellington believes there to be a swirling mass of psychological motivations buried beneath these behaviors and interactions, but I know his film doesn't think there is. The new video has neither the talent nor the inclination for such psychological excavations.

What we see here is how his father's situation appeared to Pellington, but the filmmaker did that not by looking from the world into himself but by looking from himself *at* the world. Eisenstein was probably right: "*The true material of the sound-film is...the monologue.*"[40] Pellington didn't share the thoughts that might have made this more clearly an "inner monologue" (though he might have). Still, his film can be understood as a representation of the stream of memories and impressions in his head. He presented no models or metaphors for the stream itself; he made no attempt to describe it or his own psychology. All he showed us is the world as seen by his mind's eye. We are not, therefore, on print's centuries-long quest for the essence of a person. Rather, we are on a quest (new and not so new) for an understanding of the perspectives of people: how and what they see.

We are on a quest too—here in the world of the visible—for an understanding of the performances of people, for glimpses of the dexterity and comfort with which they play their roles as, in this case, father, wife, son, athlete, caregiver, patient, filmmaker. The new video observes a ballet of behaviors. It sees not consciences and unconsciousnesses squaring off in private chambers within, but connections and the absence of connections overlapping in society without.

The new video also has the power to see the shadows cast on individuals by larger forces: politics, economics, illness, forms of communication, language. Pellington allowed us to listen in on some phrases: "Let go of his fingers," his mother tells his father. But the director was eavesdropping not so much because, as Renoir maintained, the voice is "the best means of conveying the personality of a human being"; instead Pellington seemed interested in letting us hear what language can and cannot say.*

In his film Pellington unabashedly relied on surface images: father and son dive into the ocean together, father sits dumbly in a chair, father makes a dramatic tackle. Again, I don't know whether Pellington thinks there is a hidden, more real world behind these images, but I know that the new video is unable to think that way. It is forced to confront the images—including images of filial love, poignant infirmity, football glory. It can't leave surfaces behind in search of *deeper* truths. Instead, it finds many of its truths through the deft juxtaposition of carefully selected aspects of surfaces: The chair moment was pulled out of time, objectified and held up against the ocean moment and the football moment. All these moments were shaken and transformed in the process. Truths arise that are no less subtle and meaningful for not being "deep." Maybe the new video will help us understand more fully the consequences of the fact that even cores themselves turn out, when exposed, to have surfaces.†

In looking *at*, rather than *out* or *up* or *in*, Pellington's film is not simply staring. He is not often asking us to lose ourselves in the intricacies of a scene, as a painting, photo or piece of cinema vérité might. This is instead a jumpy, fragmented, rapidly moving, directed, *analytic* kind of examination. Pellington mixed an array of isolated glimpses

* A similar preoccupation with the strengths and limitations of language has evidenced itself in more traditional television, particularly in such situation comedies as *Friends* and *Seinfeld*.

† One of the final sentences in Susan Sontag's book *On Photography* is, "Images are more real than anyone could have supposed."

from past and present, from here and there—instants, facets, slants: a cloudy eye, a father swinging his son in the air, large, folded, purposeless hands. Deep contemplation of a single scene is not often possible in the new video, but a guided dissection of the visible world becomes possible. (Jeff Scher's *Milk of Amnesia* also points to this possibility.)

"Behavior items shown in a movie can be analyzed much more precisely and from more points of view than those presented on paintings or on the stage," Walter Benjamin noted.[41] The new video is even more precise and capable of deploying even more points of view. It has the potential to take the surfaces of behaviors, of scenes, and make of them the stuff of a new art. It opens the possibility that we may learn to analyze such surfaces as thoroughly as adept print diagnosticians have analyzed our insides. These surfaces—rippled by the winds of fashion, conformism, rebellion, pretense, longing—are, I contend, the next frontier. There are unexplored territories here, discoveries to be made.

The events Pellington showed us repeatedly fail to arrange themselves in an easily comprehensible order. Again, I don't know if he himself thinks that larger patterns were discernible behind the unhappy present moments and happy past moments that intermingle in his film. I don't know if he believes his father has a core identity or shoulders a destiny. But I do know that his film neither tells such stories nor concerns itself with the absence of such stories. The new video is after different kinds of meanings. As we begin to edit our own home videos, as we are presented with more examples of the new video, we might expect the world to fill with these different kinds of meanings.

One of the key words in the scene from Plato's *Phaedrus* in which the Egyptian god Thoth tries to make the case for writing can be translated in another way. The word is *pharmakon*—usually represented here by "recipe": Thoth's "invention is a recipe for both memory and wisdom." But *pharmakon,* as Jacques Derrida has pointed out, is also the Greek word for "drug," and this translation opens up an interesting new reading.[42]

All technologies can be looked upon as drugs. They have disturbing side effects: The automobile, for example, has puffed poisons into our air, evacuated our downtowns and enfeebled our legs. (Emerson noted a similar effect in 1839: "The civilized man has built a coach, but has lost the use of his feet.")*[43] And technologies have medicinal powers: The automobile (like the coach) has relieved much physical isolation.

Such drugs are ingested with excitement and anxiety. We spend a great deal of time obsessing about how the warning label should have read. In writing about television, I have acknowledged that it can

* This entire passage in "Self-Reliance" discusses the debilitations of technologies, from watches to notebooks.

addict and debilitate, but my main goal has been to raise the possibility that the moving image—particularly in its most concentrated form, the new video—can alleviate, if not cure, certain turn-of-the-millennium maladies.

This particular psychoactive medicine works in two ways. The first is a product primarily of the fourth kind of motion—hopping from scene to scene—which the new video has helped introduce into the world. This new motion enables us to head in a marvelously therapeutic direction: *back,* not in time but in mental space, back to where we can gain perspective.

A 1995 commercial for IBM's Aptiva computers turned out to be a demonstration (probably unintentional) of the new video's proficiency in taking us there. We see, as the ad begins, a computer screen with a small video playing in one corner. The video shows a Native American standing upon a spectacular southwestern rock formation (of the sort normally reserved in advertisements for something with four-wheel drive). Suddenly the entire screen fills with that video. The commercial, by Ogilvy and Mather, has thus made its main point (which has nothing to do, of course, with native Americans or precipitous rocks): Aptiva computers offer full-screen video. Now the commercial begins to make my point.

The camera—again suddenly—pulls back, and we learn, to our surprise, that the video we have been watching is only the content of the screen of a computer onstage with a jazz band. Silly us! But then, while we're still coming to grips with our shortsightedness, the camera lurches back once again, and this shot of the jazz band is revealed to be on another computer monitor floating in space next to an astronaut. More shocks follow: Another jump back and we see that our astronaut and his weightless computer are in a video playing on a monitor held by a cross-legged mime. This time the camera, disdaining cuts, retreats in one (relatively) lengthy tracking shot: Said mime is sitting in an exotic glass bubble; then the camera reveals that this bubble is one of many in a surreal carny scene populated by musicians on stilts; then we see the native American and the astronaut together in another bubble; then a cameraman and director appear in front of the scene. Yet another sudden and surprising break awaits us. The whole carny scene, it turns out, is on a computer screen in a boy's room, complete with fish tank. Thirty seconds have almost passed; an announcer intones the name of the product; the commercial is clearly ending. Is this as far back as we'll go? Maybe not. Just then, in the corner of the screen, a large fish begins to float by, and it appears as if, were there time, our perspective would shift once again.

In the end this commercial, whose purpose is probably just to give a vaguely avant-garde feel to the product being sold, doesn't have all that much on its mind. I don't pretend it extends the breadth of human knowledge; however, the vertiginous cutting of which it makes such a show just might. Words too can "yank" us—to use George Kennan's word—from a particular situation back into a larger context, but words can't do it again and again with such ease, rapidity and verisimilitude. The new video, thanks to its ability to make objects out of scenes, has the power to shift our focus—artistic and intellectual— from changes in particular scenes or situations to changes in the contexts of scenes, and changes in the contexts of contexts. Is this, as Kennan charged, "a massive abuse of the capacity for concentrated thought"? I think not. It is instead a demand for a new kind of concentration. But it is true that such shifts aren't healthy for matters we once concentrated upon, matters such as simple beliefs or basic values. These shifts have philosophic consequences.

Back is, of course, the direction of irony: A dog is attempting some odd feat. Cut back. The grin on the face of the talk-show host reminds us that it is only a "stupid pet trick," to be enjoyed for its absurdity as much as its accomplishment. Back, in this sense, is located "above the stream"—a vantage point from which our flounderings, foolishnesses, inconsistencies and hypocrisies become apparent, the object of talk-show chuckles.

Ironies obviously predate moving images by many millennia. Authors have certainly proven themselves capable of standing back from their modest proposals as they are making them. It is possible to write a line and then, in the next line, comment upon, even contradict what has been written. It is even possible to lift above lines as they are written through sarcasm or satire (as might be accomplished by italicizing the word *possible* in this sentence).

But video appears to have made a special contribution to irony. Even without fast cutting and the rapid shifts back it facilitates, even in the first era of video, these electronically distributed moving images have encouraged a detached, lighthearted point of view—a David Letterman point of view. A world parades before us on television— small, slight, without consequence for our lives or purchase on our emotions. Relieved of responsibility for caring a whole lot about that world, we settle into the role of detatched observers. We examine, in our usual half-alert fashion, whatever is on-screen. Is it pretentious? Is it hypocritical? Is it wearing some silly Spanish-cowgirl outfit? We're the experts. We hold the "zapper." Inevitably we smirk.

"Television was practically *made* for irony," the young novelist David Foster Wallace has concluded.[44] Pretty soon we lost whatever ability we may have had to watch the McGuire Sisters without seeing them as camp. Pretty soon that which was on-screen began to defend itself against our smirks by smirking along with us, by including ironic comments on its own conventions: Talk-show hosts seemed to wink at the audience as they held up a sponsor's product; commercials mocked commercials; sportscasters camped their way through the prohibition against rebroadcast of their events. Actions, gestures, behaviors were increasingly presented as if in quotations marks.

And that was *before* the new video, which dramatically accelerates the ironic distancing. Each element in these rapid flows of images and words is in a position to smirk at the one that proceeded it. The new video is continually stepping back from what it has just shown. My favorite example is the last of a series of slogans flashed on the screen in a 1993 Planet Reebok commercial: "No Slogans." The new video lifts us higher and higher "above the stream."

I am aware that, at century's end, many have come to conclude that this is not a good thing. All this smirking has come to seem unattractive. Our indifference about that which is on television seems to have metastasized into an indifference about much of life. "The 'girl-who's-dancing-with-you-but-would-obviously-rather-be-dancing-with-somebody-else' expression," Wallace reported, "has become my generation's version of cool."[45] From these cold altitudes that old, lazy stream has come to look rather warm and comfortable; our position up on the bluffs has come to seem rather sad. We yearn, even the undeniably with-it Wallace yearns, for an escape from this incessant irony, for reimmersion in a world of caring, commitment and concern. We yearn for sincerity.

Fortunately, our position above the stream does not prevent us from sometimes taking a dip. Eventually, whatever our expression, we find ourselves dancing with someone we deeply desire. Caring, commitment and concern continue to retain a place in the lives of most of us. Still, enlarging that place—restoring what has been eroded by irony—seems a swell idea, the obvious solution to our irony problem. But how exactly might that be accomplished? Are we capable, as Wallace imagined, of shrinking "away from ironic watching," of returning to "single-entendre principles"? Are we capable once again of rhyming *June* and *moon*, of selfless devotion to a political party, of saying "I truly love you" without stepping back and noting that we have arrived at a moment when we are saying "I truly love you"?

This solution to the drawbacks of irony seems similar to the monarchist's solution to the drawbacks of democracy: If only we could believe once again in divine right. If only we could believe once again in simple virtue or in the unclouded wisdom of giving to each according to need or in endless, unquestioned love. If only we could, without giggling, stick a carnation in our lapel, don a red beret or dress up like Spanish cowgirls. I don't think we can—most of us. I don't think we can even say "without the express consent of the National Football League" anymore without the hint of a smile. I think those forms of sincerity are gone—gone, for most of us, like omens and kings.

However, there is another possible response to the pull of irony. We might, instead, go with it; we might choose to see what tricks this great, ghostly genie might perform for us.

The new video cuts with such ease to ironic distances that it has no difficulty stacking them on top of each other. It gives us an opportunity to be not only ironic about irony (which Wallace is) or ironic about irony about irony (my goal?) but to jitterbug among these various ironies. We have a chance to do this repeatedly and engagingly. We have a chance to become adept at juxtaposing and negotiating the various levels of irony. We have a chance to become reconciled to their existence, to grow comfortable with them, to understand them. The new video, to pick up Wallace's wording, was *made* for mastering irony. Perhaps we will learn better how to replace some of our smirks with knowing but affectionate smiles. Perhaps we will learn better how to increase the space for caring, commitment and concern between the quotation marks. Or perhaps we will learn something else entirely.

Two paths, it might be said, lead away from the joke-fest with David Letterman in which we now seem to find ourselves: One would return to old certainties, to a bygone seriousness. It calls to us; I know that. However, I think this other path—while certainly unfamiliar, even frightening—is more promising.

Irony travels with an even less reputable companion, of course: cynicism. There's no doubt that the new video's propensity for stepping back also encourages a kind of cynicism. The president delivers a speech. Cut to the handlers behind him, feeding lines and dispensing spin. Silly us! It is as foolish to accept that speech as a sincere expression of the president's own thoughts as it is to believe that Aptiva commercial will stick with the Native American. We are being taught by the moving image in general, and by this new kind of motion in particular, that there is always a broader perspective to be had. We are learning to view art, politics and life as scenes from which it is always possible to move back.

This seems, initially, rather dispiriting. Hence the disturbing nihilism that seems as common in the young as acne. Hence all the critical, cynical earfuls we've been getting from our pundits lately about how critical and cynical we've all become. But perhaps we might be a little cynical about this cynicism about cynicism. Yes, there are higher states, but does the path to them pass through gullibility?

Might not a clear view of the imperfections of the world and of ourselves be a prerequisite to changing or accepting them? Might these
additional steps back be useful in finally getting a handle on spins and
those who dispense them?

Back is the direction of self-consciousness, too: A comment is
made at a party. Cut. Cut. Cut. We see three other people making the
same comment. A simple unselfconscious self-consciousness can para-
lyze. But there is a freedom in a self-consciousness that is aware of itself
and of its own limits, that can accept the extent to which party chat-
ter is predictable. A Nike commercial from 1993 starring Michael
Jordan and Bugs Bunny steps back for an instant to place a sign reading, "Product Shot," next to a picture of the sneakers it is hawking. In
that too there is a freedom, though I realize applying this word to a
Nike commercial is at the very least problematic.

The rise of moving images has certainly been associated with the
rise of a commercial, product-oriented culture, with the rise, for
instance, of corporations like Nike. There's no getting around the
extent to which television and the techniques I celebrate in particular
have been put to the task of selling.* And we have bought a lot—too
much, many would say—of what they have sold: The Nike logo is now
proudly displayed on our hats, our socks, our shorts and our shirts, as
well as on sneakers probably made in whatever country currently has
the lowest-paid workers. Some might tattoo that logo on their fore-
heads if they thought it would increase the chance of their being perceived to be like Michael Jordan.

> * Newspapers and magazines sell too, but the spiels somehow haven't seemed as loud or unavoidable in print.

The new video, with its heavy debt to television commercials, can
hardly separate itself from this commercial culture. But I note that as
we become more ironic, cynical and self-aware, as we become alert to
how and why product shots are inserted, we become somewhat more
difficult to sell to, harder marks. Irony, cynicism and self-consciousness may have helped undercut the alternatives to acquisitiveness—
thrift, selflessness, spiritual values; but they may also begin to call into
question our compulsion to acquire. It is hard to see uses of the new
video beyond Nike commercials because there have been, to date, so
few of them and so many Nike commercials. However, the new
video—with its irony, cynicism and self-consciousness—may ultimately be more at home presenting, as Mark Pellington did in a video for
Information Society's song "Peace and Love, Inc.," a sneaker displaying the logo "ENVY."

A Josie & the Pussycats / social commentary on this...

I won't underestimate the resourcefulness of advertisers armed
with these techniques in anticipating and responding to our changing
attitudes, in following us back. But I do suspect we may visit places
they may not want us to reach. A Sprite commercial from 1996 that

makes use of the slogan "Image Is Nothing/Thirst Is Everything" is a good example of the chase on which advertisers now find themselves. Sprite is clearly after what philosopher Jacques Derrida has called "the image of the nonimage."[46] But this is a tougher image to sell than older, pre-selfconscious images of virility, beauty, athleticism, femininity, suavity. It is too wispy, too amorphous, too negative, and it gives away too much of the image/product-shot/slogan game. These ads are making us into experts.

A series of Miller Lite commercials in 1997, the source of considerable controversy within the advertising industry, illustrates part of the problem: In a burst of ironic pseudo-selfconsciousness, the commercials, produced by Fallon McElligott, credit themselves to a young "creative superstar" named Dick, and then proceed to present such unattractive images as a bunch of aged, bedraggled singing cowboys walking off into a men's room.[47] Perhaps a rare satiric sensibility is on display here; perhaps not. Still, it must have been easier to sell beer when audiences were content with chummy old football stars on-screen and advertisers could stay hidden away in their plush offices.

Following us further in this backward spiral away from obvious enticements—to the image of the non-nonimage, for example, the "shot of product shot" shot, the "no slogan about no slogans" slogan—may create even more problems. This is a chase advertisers—early experts in the new video—may prove good at (though not as good as some twenty-seven-year-old singer-songwriters), and no doubt it will get some of their creative juices flowing. However, we shouldn't therefore conclude that this is a chase advertisers want to be on. It will force them to surrender more and more of their tools for selling, and it will increasingly enable us to watch ourselves being sold to. The freedom of that Nike commercial's self-consciousness may ultimately be our freedom.

And as the scenes shift and recede, we can be taken back further still: We might, for instance, be given an opportunity to watch ourselves watching ourselves watching. The new video allows us, in Roland Barthes's phrase, to "take off the brake" on this kind of reflective awareness.[48] Is there not a chance that a new wisdom might manifest itself amongst all these mirrors?

For back is, most crucially, the direction of perspective. "There is only a perspective seeing, only a perspective 'knowing,'" maintained Friedrich Nietzsche (producing, not for the first time, an archetypal twentieth-century thought in the nineteenth century). He then concluded: "The more eyes, different eyes, we can use to observe, the more complete our vision will be."[49] The new video, thanks to its ability to dance from perspective to perspective, gives us more eyes.

Were I to produce a video version of this book, it would necessarily rest on my ideas a bit less firmly. It would want to include other perspectives: questioning voices (asking whether changes in communications really are that important), cynical voices (pouncing on the inanity of some current exercises in fast cutting), ironic and self-conscious voices (proclaiming, perhaps in words printed on-screen, that all this irony and self-consciousness is *well* beyond the capabilities of mere print).

I have tried to hone the words in this book into an argument. That argument would wend its way through the video version too—well served by pictures, film clips, video clips, words on-screen, graphics and narration. But there would be many more opportunities to step back from it. Moving images are not easily honed; they tend to swell and engulf.

A more substantial example, if only hypothetical, would seem to be in order. The following brief script—really a mind experiment—was conceived some years ago.*

The subject of this hypothetical script was a very serious one: At the time the Serbs were brutalizing sections of Bosnia. Say we edited together a second or two from a shot of a Serb-run prison camp with a shot of a Nazi concentration camp and a shot of the Clinton White House, whose responses to the Serbian outrages struck many at the time as insufficient. A simple (then rather familiar) point would have been made. A different point, reflecting another school of thought at the time, might have been made by editing together quick shots of similarly armed and aggressive-looking Croats, Bosnian Muslims and Serbs, with the words *Croats, Muslims* and *Serbs* on-screen below their pictures. But what point would be made were these two little montages edited together, with some music and a couple of phrases from statements by politicians tacked on? That would be a fair amount of complexity for perhaps twenty seconds.

Then we might have edited in some similarly contradictory sequences from Somalia and Azerbaijan—two other places where outrages were then being committed against innocents. And that half minute on the world's moral tangles could have been used as an element in a larger juxtaposition on the difficulties of action, mixing in sections on, for example, inner-city poverty. That could then have been a piece in a production evaluating possible strategies for living a life: moral action, hedonistic pursuits, material acquisitions, etc. Finally, the issue of whether such life strategies have any meaning might have been raised through further juxtapositions involving representative instants selected from a wide variety of lives.

Back and back and back. The "stream" is still there—in front of us

* Speaking of ironies: I am aware that the better the job I do of describing here, the worse it is for my case. However, I ask the skeptical reader to focus on the extent to which the sentences that follow outline rather than present.

in photographic moving images—but we are also making ourselves at home above the "stream." The new video allows our thoughts to explore places that before they had only visited.

The second strength of the new video as a philosophical pharmaceutical is a product of its speed and our growing ability to grasp things that move at such speeds. So much is happening in such short segments of time that those segments seem to expand before a fast and alert consciousness. Half a minute, when filled with a few dozen images, gains depth and breadth. New artistic and philosophical spaces are opened up in time. Words, of course, create some substantial spaces of their own. They can grow scenes in our thoughts, but the new video, because it tends to swarm rather than queue up, can fill our thoughts with flurries of such scenes.

According to the laws that govern the world of the moving image, I'm asserting, speed generates space. It gives the new video an unprecedented capaciousness. Some of those who work in this form have indeed felt themselves to be exploring new realms: "I'm playing this four-dimensional chess in my head," Hank Corwin reported.[50]

There is room in the dimensions opened by these flocks of pictures, graphics and words for numerous, overlapping trains of thought; for digressions, exceptions and contradictions; for indeterminacy and even confusion; for ideas too oddly shaped or freighted with paradox to settle comfortably between the covers of a book. Multiple levels of understanding can exist simultaneously here.*[51] The new video, because it moves so quickly among these levels, has room for thoughts that protrude onto more than one, such as the views of normal life expressed in Corwin and Bayer's public-service announcement.

Consider, for a larger example, a particular philosophic dance, stomped out in one version or another by a number of twentieth-century philosophers.† It involves rejecting the possibility of various forms of beliefs/truths/meanings while at the same time rejecting the possibility of making it through the day without various forms of beliefs/truths/meanings. (Other variants of this dance have appeared in this chapter: climbing up above the stream, then taking a dip in the stream, for example.) The leaps and turns this dance demands have made for some strained sentences and convoluted paragraphs. (Not here, of course; in other books.) These are moves that don't *print* well. However, it is possible to imagine such a dance captured in a video of no great length or loftiness, in which scenes from a life of engagement might simply be mated with a narration summing up a seminar's worth of philosophic doubts.

This is the sort of double-jointed dance the new video enjoys and

* T. W. Adorno, writing in 1954, also spoke of television being "multilayered," but he saw those layers as mostly hidden. Now they are often overt, sometimes even celebrated.

† "Continental" philosophers, for the most part; analytic philosophers tend not to be as light on their feet.

is capable of helping its audiences enjoy. Indeed, when transferred to the screen, our grand philosophic enigma might appear perhaps not so confounding after all; it might appear rather obvious, as the beginning and not the end of the discussion. The new video, in the hands of an inventive editor, seems able to manage more complex steps. It seems able to help *us* manage more complex steps. And we have an obligation to wonder whether our puzzlement about such existential questions may someday appear as quaint as that of those preliterate Soviet peasants when Alexander Luria confronted them with the syllogism about white bears.

Italo Calvino's name belongs on a list I have alluded to but not presented: that of twentieth-century authors whose words seem to strain against the narrowness and regularity of print's long word queue. Calvino's name also belongs on a second list, one I have not before discussed but have kept in my head: that of subjects mentioned at the beginning of this book to which a lingering fidelity to aged rules of composition compels me to return. The words of this Italian novelist, who died in 1985 at the age of sixty-one, introduced the book's introduction; now we are within hailing distance of the conclusion of its conclusion.

Calvino's novel *If on a Winter's Night a Traveler...*, first published in 1979, experiments with a number of the ways of thought that will, I argue, be facilitated by the new video. It refuses, to begin with, to restrict itself to a simple narrative. Calvino certainly did not forgo narrative entirely, as Mark Pellington did in *Father's Daze*. But his stories in this book come and go—a superabundance of them. Just when readers have lost themselves in one, it disappears. A character in the novel talks of "producing too many stories at once because what I want is for you to feel, around the story, a saturation of other stories that I could tell and maybe will tell." Calvino's narratives are not as condensed as they are in some videos; most are a dozen or so pages long. Nevertheless, we begin to feel that saturation.

This novel is also compulsively self-conscious. The reader is even made a character in it: "You are about to begin reading. Best to close the door; the TV is always on in the next room." And the pleasures and frustrations of reading this procession of incomplete tales are formed into a story of their own. We are asked to climb to some airy vantage points here: asked to examine the nature of narrative and the process of reading.

My kind of stuff, right? It's true; I much admire Calvino's novel. However, I must admit I had a difficult time pulling myself through it. The problem was that each time one of the stories in the book ended,

*[handwritten margin note: * Compare Calvino to Vonnegut who liked to cut from thought to thought to tell his story by both narrative and juxtaposition]*

I had to force myself, with phone calls to make and a book of my own to write, to pick the novel up once again and begin a new one.

I don't think this would happen in "the next room," the room where the videos are playing. For video not only can execute with more speed and dexterity the sorts of jumps and twists in which Calvino delighted, it can make them considerably more entertaining.

Our Platos and King Thamuses have managed, typically, to portray video's remarkable ability to captivate as a failing, a cheap trick. (The novel, of course, was subject to similar criticism.) Recall Susan Sontag's distress at the thought that fast-cut images might be "attention grabbing." Yet it is precisely this facility for grabbing attention, for entertaining, that makes it possible to surrender many of the devices, the crutches, of traditional storytelling. With video we might head out in Calvino-like directions, in Joyce-like directions and still remain confident that audiences—maybe not huge audiences, but certainly audiences as large as those interested in authors such as Calvino—will be able to follow, that they won't (like James Atlas) grow bored.

And video might give us the reserves of entertainment value needed to venture beyond Calvino, beyond Joyce: We might be able to disdain narrative entirely or overwhelm with dozens of almost simultaneous narratives; we might layer on multiple levels of selfconsciousness; we might hop and skip stream-of-consciousness-like not only through this world but through various possible worlds. This new medium should allow our scouts, our explorers, once they get their hands on it, to take many new risks. Let me propose a rule: The more entertaining the medium, the more artistically and intellectually adventurous it has the potential to become.

As our transition from print to moving images proceeds, most of us spend more and more of our time in Calvino's "next room." It is my purpose to suggest that we may find there a better form for saying the sorts of things Calvino was straining to say. It is my purpose to raise the possibility that the video you are about to begin watching—perhaps next year, perhaps in the next decade, perhaps decades from now—may make possible some grand adventures.

A frequently asked question: Can we entrust video with the education of our young? I've tried to suggest how ideas might find their way into this medium as it matures. But can ideas formulated under the influence of such a *pharmakon*, such a drug, be trusted? Can such a melange of juxtapositions, ironic perspectives, oddly shaped notions and philosophic high stepping "mold a brain," as the author and "techno-skeptic" David Shenk has put it, "into a disciplined thinking organ"?[52]

The answer, I believe, is yes, though I add my usual qualification:

in time. New ways of thinking generally seem unruly at first; their initial *raison d'être,* after all, is often to loosen the grip of the old rules. However, these new cognitive tools are not trotted out in high-school or college classes with any great haste. First they must be corralled and saddled—categorized, interpreted, tested, made accessible. In the process various kinds of intellectual discipline—some familiar, some not—are located in them. New orthodoxies form.

We will have to learn how to undertake this process in video, just as our ancestors (worrying all the while about the education of their young)* had to learn how to undertake it in writing and then again in print. We will have to develop kinds of digitally accessed video textbooks and journals. We might even expect, as the decades pass, the accumulation of a "canon" of *old* new videos. In time some sufficiently sturdy molds should be at the disposal of young brains.

> * In 1756, when print was the upstart, Thomas Sheridan traced an increase in "Immorality, Ignorance and false Taste" to a decline in the study of "the Art of Speaking" in the schools.

A question of my own: Don't we have a responsibility to these same young to find fresh approaches to the conundrums that seem to have left a residue of nihilism in much of their music and in many of their minds? Two other related (and similarly rhetorical) questions present themselves: Can we continue to submit our responses to Nirvana songs and Nike commercials only in print? As equipment for shooting and editing plummets in price, are we to continue to leave video, with all its power, to rock stars and advertising agencies?

When the strains inherent in a revolution like this become evident, retreat seems an increasingly attractive alternative: Publish some more celebrations of reading. Grumble about "the menace of unreality." Suggest to some green-haired, body-pierced, fast-eyed, image-bedazzled young persons that all their answers await them in books. I don't think this is, in the end, an acceptable alternative. I think we must push on. I think we must learn some new steps.

New philosophies made possible by moving images might begin to fill the current emptiness. A medicine of such power might begin to cure our children's reality sickness and our own. Put some ideas on video and call me in a millennium.

All this will not happen, if it happens, without pain. "Poison" is another meaning that lurks in the Greek word *pharmakon.* Indeed, it may come closest to what Plato was getting at when he applied the term to the invention of writing.[53] New intellectual tools do not merely polish old ways of thinking or fill gaps in them; they tear some of them down.

The mind-set that preceded the arrival of writing was poisoned. The mind-set that preceded our communications revolution is being poisoned. "I can no longer think what I want to think," lamented the

French novelist Georges Duhamel in 1930. "My thoughts have been replaced by moving images."[54]

This new form of communication, wherever it is leading us, is probably not going to restore our old ways of looking at the world. Fondly remembered certitudes about reality are unlikely to return. Truths revealed on brightly lit surfaces are unlikely to resemble truths uncovered in dark spaces within. The place beyond irony and cynicism, if there is such a place, is unlikely to look like sincerity. We are going to have to deal with new, unfamiliar and often discomfiting notions. Many of us will find that we "can no longer think what [we] want to think." Indeed, many of us already have.

What might be our reward for going through this transition? The arts may regain their steam. Political thought may awake from its slumber. But life won't seem significantly easier or become significantly fairer. We likely will find our way around our current philosophic crisis, but new crises inevitably will arise. I doubt the effort will make us much happier. I foresee no "brave new world"—no Huxleyan nightmare of cheerfully drugged video watchers, but no utopia similar to that one of the characters in *The Tempest* proclaims when Shakespeare introduces this phrase, either.[55]

Nevertheless, I can't look at the history of human communication without concluding—unfashionable as such a conclusion may currently be in the historical community—that a kind of progress has been made. Yes, we've lost some wisdom along the way, but I believe we've gained more. And I can't look at the magical devices we are coming up with for capturing, editing and making available moving images without concluding that they will help us make additional progress.

I know this is hard to accept. Believe me, on an evening when each of my children lies prone before a different TV carrying a different vapid program, it is hard to write. The fall of the printed word—the loss of our beloved books—is a large loss. Nevertheless, the rise of the moving image, as we perfect new, nonvapid uses of video, should prove an even larger gain.

All our enlightenments are not behind us. We are beginning again, and in this new beginning is the moving image.

acknowledgments

Much of my work on this book was completed at the Freedom Forum
Media Studies Center in the midst of an extended, often-heated
debate. At issue: Whether things are getting worse or better. On one
side, muttering and frowning, stood the "declinists." I, of course, lined
up with the "neo-Pollyannas."

Such ideological battles have grown uncommon enough to seem
precious. I am grateful for the stimulation, suggestions and challenges
of my fellow fellows at the Center: Asa Briggs, Veronica Chambers,
Edna Einsiedal, Marjorie Ferguson, Bill Fox, Al Gollin, Hank Klibanoff,
Michael Janeway, Orville Schell, David Shenk, Jeffrey Toobin and
Margaret Usdansky. The book also was improved by the support and
advice there of Ev Dennis, Nancy Maynard, Larry McGill, Adam
Powell, Robert Snyder, András Szántó, Nancy Woodhull and Charles
Overby. Dirk Standen and Julie Beglin, two unusually capable graduate
students working at the Center, pitched in on the research and read
through an early draft; their contributions were substantial.

I benefitted from the suggestions of many other thoughtful, some-
times critical readers of various ideological persuasions. They included
Jim Hauser, Arthur Engoron, Larry Madison, David Shenk, David
Mindich, Thomas Keenan, Gerald Lanson, András Szántó, Debra
Goldman, Jay Rosen, Nancy Maynard, David Bornstein, Lillian
Stephens and Esther Davidowitz. Thanks too to my agent, Joe Spieler;
to Adam Bohannon for the energy and creativity he put into the
book's design; to my editors, Susan Chang and Kim Torre-Tasso; to
Elizabeth Eisenstein, Mark Pellington and Liss Jeffrey; and to the scores
of students at New York University (including a group of particularly
sharp freshmen) who helped me clarify these thoughts.

I owe a deep debt to Esther Davidowitz with whom I built and
have shared a house—filled with children, books and TVs—in which it
has been possible to contemplate the future with something of a smile.

photo credits

Chapter One: JFK on TV (Photo No. ST-C276-7-63 in the John F. Kennedy Library); Family watching TV (Archive Photos/Lambert); Madonna head; People with hands raised; Three candles (Courtesy of ABC News); Commuters reading newspapers (Popperfoto/Archive Photos).

Chapter Two: Thoth (Corbis-Bettmann); Polar Bears (John Hatlem/Archive Photos); Babylonian cylinders (New York Public Library Rare Books and Manuscripts Division); Papyrus fragment (The Fales Library, New York University).

Chapter Three: Gutenberg Bible (New York Public Library Rare Books and Manuscripts Division); Pencil with eraser (Sanford Corporation); *Natural Born Killers* (Trimark Pictures).

Chapter Four: Handwritten book; Printed book by Aquinas (The Fales Library, New York University); Pope bust (Yale Center for British Art, gift of Paul Mellon in memory of the British art historian Basil Taylor [1922-1975]); *Studio One* (Corbis-Bettmann).

Chapter Five: Danger symbol (Photo by Mitchell Stephens); Apple file-folder icon (Courtesy of Apple Computer Inc.); Sistine ceiling (Corbis-Bettmann); NASA plaque (NASA).

Chapter Six: Muybridge horse, four feet off the ground; Muybridge horse, awkward legs (Eadweard Muybridge Collection, Kingston Museum); *Buzz* (Courtesy of Mark Pellington); Trainspotting (Miramax Films).

Chapter Seven: Early motion-picture projector; Waltzing couple, man faces camera; Waltzing couple, in profile (Courtesy of the Franklin Institute; photo by Charles Musser); Greaser's Gauntlet, bar scene; Greaser's Gauntlet, long shot of hanging tree; Greaser's Gauntlet, cut-in to couple (Photograph by Catherine Holter, New York University); United States of Poetry, map in front of road; United States of Poetry, "poetry"; United States of Poetry, title (Courtesy of Number Seventeen); McGuire Sisters (Courtesy of the McGuire Sisters and the Coca-Cola Company).

Chapter Eight: Covered bridge (Courtesy of the Coca-Cola Company); *Potemkin,* soldiers; *Potemkin,* baby carriage; *Potemkin,* shattered glasses; *October,* beaked god; *October,* round-faced god; *October,* open-mouthed god (The Museum of Modern Art/Film Stills Archive).

Chapter Nine: Jackie Gleason (Archive Photos); Madame Bovary, window scene (Alexander Sesonske); French café (AFP/Archive Photos).

Chapter Ten: *A Movie,* periscope; *A Movie,* atomic bomb (Robert A. Haller, Anthology Film Archives); *American Time Capsule,* Wright Bros. (Pyramid Films); *Mission: Impossible* (Paramount Pictures).

Chapter Eleven: *Milk of Amnesia,* Kiki (Courtesy of Jeff Scher); Ampex recorder (Courtesy of Ampex Corporation); American Dreamers (Courtesy of Number Seventeen).

Chapter Twelve: Prospero's Books (Eve Ramboz/Courtesy Peter Greenaway); INXS, teeth with celery (Courtesy of Mark Pellington); Fox News (Courtesy of Fox News Channel); U.S. Postal Service (U.S. Postal Service).

Chapter Thirteen: Jimmy Fund, barber (Agency: Hill, Holliday; editor: Hank Corwin; director: Samuel Bayer); *Father's Daze,* Pellington and his aged father; *Father's Daze,* Pellington as a child with his father (Courtesy of Mark Pellington); IBM Aptiva, story sheet (Courtesy of Ogilvy & Mather and IBM).

Preface
1   Rabelais 189 ("Letter to Pantagruel," bk. 2, chapt. 7).

Introduction
1   Calvino 3.
2   David Firestone, "Quayle's No TV Plan Turns Off Ga. Kids," *Newsday,* September 2, 1992.
3   Gomery.
4   Statistics from John Carey, based on information from the Electronic Industries Association and the U. S. Department of Commerce; John Carey. See also Putnam, "Tuning In, Tuning Out," 667. Barnouw 92. Carey chooses 1947 as the first full year of the introduction of full-scale commercial television.
5   Kubey and Csikszentmihalyi xi. Four hours and fifty minutes a day, according to a Nielsen survey in January 1997.
6   National Assessment of Educational Progress, 1992.
7   Fisher and Fisher, 43-45, 121, 151.
8   The international figures are from a study coordinated by Roper Starch Worldwide, cosponsored by the Discovery Channel, in 1995. Kubey and Csikszentmihalyi xi.
9   Gary Wolf, "Steve Jobs: The Next Insanely Great Thing," *Wired,* February 1996.
10   Interview with Roberta Goldberg, New York, November 5, 1995.
11   Much of the information and many of the quotations in this section are from Mitchell Stephens, "The Death of Reading," *Los Angeles Times Magazine,* September 22, 1991.
12   Esther B. Fein, "Philip Roth Sees Double and Maybe Triple, Too," *New York Times,* March 9, 1993.
13   Barr 518.
14   Barr 518; D.T. Max, "The End of the Book?" *Atlantic Monthly,* August 1994, 61-71.
15   Michael Kinsley, "TRB: The Myth of Books," *New Republic,* June 17, 1985.
16   Cited, Wilson.
17   John P. Robinson, "About Time: Thanks for Reading This," *American Demographics,* May 1990.
18   "Perot Stresses Hominess, but Image Is No Accident," *New York Times,* May 26, 1992.
19   *The Media and Campaign 96 Briefing,* by the Freedom Forum Media Studies Center, April 1996.
20   Dickinson 53-54 (poem XCIX).
21   Chartier 91.
22   John J. O'Connor, "Avedon, From Paris Fashion to Haiku," *New York Times,* January 24, 1996.

Chapter 2
1   See Koch 135, 220; Lieberman 2; Brogyanyi 48; Martin 2; Eco 23-24.

2   See Stephen Jay Gould, "This View of Life," "Evolution by Walking," *Natural History,* March 1995. For the Dogon, see Calame-Griaule 640-41.
3   See Berger 9; Worth.
4   Martin 3. Dating of the earliest art to seventy-five thousand years ago is based on the report in 1996 of the discovery of Australian dotlike carvings; John Noble Wilford, "Art, but for Whose Sake," *New York Times,* September 29, 1996.
5   Birkerts 6.
6   Martin 16; Driver (1944) 133-34.
7   This brief history of writing is drawn from Jack Goody, "Alphabets and Writing," in Raymond Williams, *Contact*; Gelb; Martin.
8   Cited, Gelb 13.
9   Havelock, *The Literate Revolution,* 6.
10   Havelock, *The Literate Revolution,* 59, 82, 185, 187. Martin, 33, credits some of this to early consonantal systems.
11   Armour 154-60; Derrida 86-89; Shafer 20, 37.
12   Plato, *Phaedrus,* 67-71.
13   Plato, *Phaedrus,* 67-71
14   See Havelock, *The Literate Revolution,* 4, 42.
15   Luria 54, 108-15; Ong 52-53. See Carothers for another early (1959) approach to these issues.
16   Luria v-vii, xi-xvi; Ong 49-51, 56.
17   Ong 49-57; Goody 44, 109-11.
18   Luria 32-33.
19   See Goody 12-13, 115; Ong 55.
20   Luria 60, 75; Ong 51-52.
21   Goody 44; see Lévi-Strauss 13-15.
22   Goody 11, 70.
23   See Raymond Williams, *Television,* 6-8.
24   See Goody 51, 93, 100-2.
25   Havelock, *The Literate Revolution,* 89-93, 166-67; Raymond Williams, *Contact,* 114-15. For the argument that the Greek alphabet may have arrived early enough to contribute to the composition of these poems, see Goody in Raymond Williams, *Contact,* 121.
26   Ong 34-35, 39-41, 58, 69-71; Parry 51.
27   Finley.
28   Derrida 76, 87; Armour 155.
29   Plato, *Phaedrus,* 67-71.
30   Cited, Robert D. Richardson Jr. 333.

Chapter 3
1   Cited, MZTV exhibit, Royal Ontario Museum, Toronto, December 1995; see also Boorstin 258.
2   Adorno 479; cited, Rosenthal 266-67; cited, Briggs, *Competition,* 147.
3   Kennan 173; "Turn Off Tube, Pope Warns," *New York Newsday,* January 25, 1994; Marchand 101.
4   Postman, *Amusing Ourselves,* 159.
5   "Despite Awareness of the Risk, More in U.S. Are Getting Fat," *New York Times,* July 17, 1994. Reading too is an awfully sedentary activity, however.
6   Charles McGrath, "The Triumph of the Prime-Time Novel," *New York Times Magazine,* October 22, 1995.
7   At the Freedom Forum Media Studies Center at Columbia University in 1991.
8   Parkinson and Quirke 65-70; Howatson 91-93.
9   T.F. Carter, "Paper and Block Printing—From China to Europe," in Crowley and Heyer, 83-94.
10   Chappell 12-13; Febvre and Martin 18, 30-31, 45.
11   T.F. Carter, "Paper and Block Printing—From China to Europe," in Crowley and Heyer, 83-94.
12   Henri-Jean Martin, "Printing," in Raymond Williams, *Contact,* 128.
13   Cited, Elizabeth Eisenstein, "Printing as a Divine Art."
14   Chappell 38-57; Williams, *Contact,* 131.

15 Williams, *Contact*, 132; Stephens, *A History of News*, 76.

16 Febvre and Martin 248; Alexander 163.

17 Francis Bacon, *Philosophical Works*, 300.

18 The list of print's contributions in this and the following paragraphs is based on Elizabeth Eisenstein, *The Printing Press*, 53, 72, 89, 105, 121, 303-10; Williams, *Contact*, 133; Ong 117-18, 124, 125; Watt 13-15; Febvre and Martin 261, 321-28; Dantzig 33; Postman, *Technopoly*, 62; Stephens, *A History of News*, 75-76, 160-63. I have also noted Saenger's important reservations about the extent of these contributions.

19 Cited, Eisenstein, *The Printing Press*, 306.

20 Carlyle 26.

21 Cited, Eisenstein, "Printing as a Divine Art."

22 Febvre and Martin 30-31; see Trithemius 63.

23 Dantzig 33.

24 Aubrey Williams 123-24; Pope 492-93.

25 Cited, Robert D. Richardson Jr. 42.

26 Thoreau 66-67.

27 Cited, Marvin 68, 87.

28 *Nation*, April 27, 1893.

29 Irwin 252; see Jackaway for a discussion of attacks on radio.

30 Petroski 178-79; *New York Times*, August 22, 1938; Robert D. Richardson Jr. 210, 548.

31 "The Forbidden Books of Youth," *New York Times Book Review*, June 6, 1993.

32 Maureen Dowd, "The Cult of Lee Atwater," *New York Times Magazine*, November 21, 1993.

33 Plato, *Phaedrus*, 67-71; Derrida 148-49.

34 Aquinas, *Summa Theologica*, 2: 2249 (question 42, article 4, part III).

35 Trithemius 65.

36 Vespasiano 104; Alexander, 19; Eisenstein, *The Printing Press*, 48-49.

37 Eisenstein, "Printing as a Divine Art."

38 Káldy-Nagy 201-3, 210.

39 Mott, *American Journalism*, 6

40 Cited, McLuhan, *Gutenberg Galaxy*, 254.

41 Cited, Mack 457.

42 Pope 439.

43 Audrey Williams 9-12, 109n; Mack 479-88.

44 Cited, Aubrey Williams 109n. For satiric treatment of the "Moderns," see Pope 375-77.

45 *Spectator*, 582, August 18, 1714.

46 Emerson 67; Robert D. Richardson Jr. 417.

47 Cited, Wilson.

48 Cervantes 24-25.

49 Watt 14-16

50 Cited, Ioan Williams 304, 306.

51 Ioan Williams 13; George Colman, *Polly Honeycombe, A Dramatick Novel of One Act*, London, 1760.

52 Stephens, *A History of News*, 286.

53 *Dearborn Independent*, June 13, 1925; cited, Covert and Stevens 208.

54 *Spectator*, 3202, November 9, 1889.

55 Judith Crist, "Horror in the Nursery," *Collier's*, March 27, 1948.

56 "Newspaperism," *Lippincott's Monthly Magazine*, 38, November 1886.

57 Cited, Boorstin 258.

58 Reiser 34-35.

59 Interview with Oliver Stone, Santa Monica, March 15, 1996.

60 Carlyle 27.

Chapter 4

1 Fisher and Fisher 151-52, 158. See also Hofer; Ritchie 11-12.

2 Jenkins 12.

3 Fisher and Fisher 163; Ritchie 12.

4   Driver (1976) 2-3; Raymond Williams, *Contact,* 112-13; Manguel 179.
5   Winston 25, 67, 162, 208.
6   Mitchell Stephens, "Radio: From Dots and Dashes to Rock and Larry King," *New York Times,* November 20, 1995.
7   Brecht, *Brecht on Theatre,* 51-52.
8   Armour 156-59; Shafer 113.
9   Elizabeth Eisenstein, "Encounter with the Printed Text."
10   Greene 42.
11   Saenger; Chartier 90-91; Howatson 91-93.
12   Cited, Ioan Williams 306; Ioan Williams 13.
13   Birkerts 121.
14   Dunlap 1; see also Hubbell.
15   Fisher and Fisher 45, 278-80; Ritchie 26.
16   Waldemar Kaempffeert in Porterfield and Reynolds 23.
17   Newhall, *Photography,* 9; Tom Wolfe, "Miss America by Astral Projection," in Rabb 509; Whelan 157-58; Longwell 16-19; Kracauer 6.
18   Cited, Whelan 158.
19   See Forster 213.
20   Moholy-Nagy 27.
21   Much of the information on early printing in this section is from Febvre and Martin 57, 77-88, 97, 249-64; see Beaulieux 53.
22   Alexander 36, 78.
23   Elizabeth Eisenstein, *The Printing Press,* 106n; Alexander 78. See Landau and Parshall, 33-38.
24   See also Goldschmidt 23.
25   McIntyre 21-22.
26   See Eastman. Stephens, *A History of News,* 135.
27   Cited, Levine 14.
28   Mack 458, 563-65, 590, 622, 680, 682, 686, 688, 695.
29   Pope 449-50.
30   Mack 571.
31   See Brecht, *Brecht on Theatre,* 51-52, on the "first phase" of radio; Raymond Williams, *Television,* 82.
32   Porterfield and Reynolds 277; see Winston 6-7.
33   Cited, Wilk 4.
34   De Forest 353; *All Things Considered,* February 8, 1996.
35   Cited, Boddy 87.
36   Mellencamp 108; see Sturcken 46-93.
37   Mellencamp 108.
38   Cited, Mellencamp 108.
39   Grossman 168.
40   Postman, *Amusing Ourselves,* 91.
41   Elizabeth Eisenstein, "Printing as a Divine Art"; Elizabeth Eisenstein, "Encounter with the Printed Text."
42   See Berman 78.
43   Cited, Richard Foster Jones 42.
44   Gary Wolf, "Steve Jobs: The Next Insanely Great Thing," *Wired,* February 1996.
45   Welles and Bogdanovich 217.

Chapter 5
1   Cited, John Hartl, "Fractured Reality—Oliver Stone's Latest Manic Movie Mixes Fiction with Today's Headlines," *Seattle Times,* August 21, 1994.
2   Mitchell Stephens, "The New TV," *Washington Post,* April 25, 1993.
3   Norman Mailer, "Like a Lady (Madonna)," *Esquire,* August 1994.
4   Smith and Alexander 231, 235; Kay 193, 201, 202.
5   Levy 69-70, 77-79, 98, 278-79.
6   Arthur Smith 113-14, 121.
7   Book X; Plato, *The Great Dialogues,* 464. Papadopoulo 49.
8   Book X; Plato, *The Great Dialogues,* 463-4. This echoes Plato's attack on orators in the *Gorgias.*

    9 Baudrillard 255-56.
   10 Boorstin 26-29, 204; see also Mourier 310.
   11 Cited, Briggs, *Competition*, 147n.
   12 For an investigation of this apparent irony, see Gombrich 154-60.
   13 Cited, Freedberg 162-64. For a discussion of the philosophic underpin-
nings of Aquinas's thoughts on images, see Copleston 47-48, 167-68, 181-83.
   14 See Samuel Y. Edgerton Jr. 124-42; Bazin 11; Hogben 186-88; Berger 16.
   15 Cited, Crowley and Heyer 195.
   16 Cited, Freedberg 162.
   17 Gelb 29.
   18 Cited, Freedberg 162.
   19 Cited, Freedberg 451n.
   20 Hogben 188-89.
   21 Stephen Jay Gould, "Evolution by Walking," *Natural History*, March
1995.
   22 McKibben 147, 189, 190, 197, 198, 211-12.
   23 Robert Wright, "Washington Diarist: Channeling," *New Republic*, June
15, 1992.
   24 See Aristotle 40 (*De Interpretatione*, 1).
   25 McKibben 192.
   26 Lanham 9.
   27 Cited, Freedberg 50.
   28 Kay 196, 202.
   29 Plotinus 427.
   30 Cited, Eco 166; see also Martin 19.
   31 See Gombrich 148-49.
   32 Eco 144-76.
   33 Eco 144-76.
   34 Kay 202.
   35 Cited, Eco 173-74.
   36 French historian Roger Chartier talked about how images "mirrored"
writing; Chartier 19.
   37 See Worth.
   38 See Gombrich 21 for the importance of genre.
   39 William E. Wallace 260-61. For another discussion of possible interpretations of the Sistine ceiling, see Richmond 63-68.
   40 Godard 123; translated by Dirk Standen.
   41 Eco 174; see also Martin 6.
   42 Cited, Gombrich 14.
   43 Barthes 201-2.
   44 Cited, Alden Whitman, "Picasso: Protean and Prodigious," *New York
Times*, April 8, 1973.
   45 Kay 202.
   46 Eco 174.
   47 Eco 175-77.

Chapter 6

    1 The comments by Pellington here are from an interview in New York on
November 5, 1995. Pellington's account of his MTV promo was confirmed by
Judy McGrath, April 2, 1997.
    2 See Nash.
    3 Nash uses this term.
    4 Davenport 4-5.
    5 Oliver Wendell Holmes, "The Stereoscope and the Stereograph," in
Newhall, *Photography* 54.
    6 Gernsheim 24-38; Davenport 6-7; Hogben 241.
    7 Gernsheim 39-43; Davenport 7-9; Hogben 241.
    8 Cited, Sontag, *On Photography*, 188.
    9 Talbot.
   10 See Starkie 334-35.
   11 Cited, Crowley and Heyer 215; cited, Sontag, *On Photography*, 184.

12   Oliver Wendell Holmes, "The Stereoscope and the Sterograph"; Newhall, *Photography,* 61.

13   Charles Baudelaire, "Photography," in Newhall, *Photography,* 112. See Berman 139-41.

14   Cited, Sontag, *On Photography,* 87.

15   Weston, II, 230.

16   Flaubert, *Madame Bovary,* 36.

17   Cited, Troyat 116.

18   Flaubert, *Madame Bovary,* 41, 95, 171, 174.

19   Flaubert, *Madame Bovary,* 42, 112, 132.

20   MacDonnell 14-15; Musser 48.

21   MacDonnell 15-25; Musser 48-49.

22   Cited, Freedberg 50.

23   *Philadelphia Photographer,* August 1878; cited, MacDonnell 24.

24   *San Francisco Evening Post,* in MacDonnell 22.

25   July 9, 1878; cited, Musser 49. See Sklar 7.

26   Flaubert, *Madame Bovary,* 70-71.

27   Flaubert, *Madame Bovary,* 179.

28   Flaubert, *Madame Bovary,* 147, 157, 279.

29   Cited, Newhall, *Photography,* 13.

30   Oliver Wendell Holmes, "The Stereoscope and the Stereograph," in Newhall, *Photography,* 60.

31   Janouch 143-44.

32   See Calvino 36.

33   Sontag, *On Photography,* 52.

34   Flaubert, *Madame Bovary,* 155.

35   Cited, Musser 53.

36   Cited, MacDonnell 23.

37   Flaubert, *Correspondence,* letter 413 (August 14, 1853), 295.

38   Woolf 181.

39   Cited, Sontag, *On Photography*, 124.

40   Welsh 131.

Chapter 7

1   The early history of "screen practice" and motion pictures in this and the following paragraphs is from Musser 17-54; also Hogben 247-57.

2   MacDonnell 26-27.

3   Cited, Musser 50.

4   Cited, Musser 50.

5   Birkerts 214.

6   Mast 24-25; MacDonnell 28; Baldwin 208-12.

7   This account of Edison's work is based primarily on Musser 55-91 and Baldwin 208-12.

8   Cited, Musser 68.

9   Cited, Shipman 18.

10   Renoir 11, 16-18.

11   Musser 135-41; Mast 29-37.

12   Seton 66-67.

13   Musser 83-86, 118, 208-18, 349-55.

14   Gary R. Edgerton 137-38.

15   Gabler 28-38.

16   Musser 119.

17   Musser 194-200, 325-27, 355; Cook 27.

18   Musser 58-59.

19   This analysis of Griffith's film and its significance in the history of film is based on Gunning 75-81; I have not summarized the plot in its entirety.

20   See Bowser 56-62.

21   See Bowser 93-102.

22   Gunning 43-44; Cook 74.

23   Cited, Bowser 94, 97.

24   Münsterberg 37-38; Renoir 45-46.

25 Jesionowski 63.
26 Benjamin, *Illuminations,* 228.
27 Malraux 122-24.
28 Cited, Bowser 57.
29 Gunning 195-205.
30 Benjamin, *Illuminations,* 236.
31 Gunning 240-48.
32 Cook 87-93.
33 Cited, Berger 17.
34 Cook 94.

Chapter 8

1 Seton 99-100; Mast 204-5; Cook 173-74.
2 Sergei Eisenstein, *Selected Works,* vol. I, 194.
3 Sergei Eisenstein, *Selected Works,* vol. I, 193-94.
4 Telephone interview with Debra Goldman, November 1995.
5 See Raymond Williams, *Contact,* 112; Martin 31-32; Driver (1976) 2-3; Havelock, *The Literate Revolution,* 187.
6 Barry 24; Leyda 142-43; Cook 136.
7 Seton 82.
8 Lavin 9, 29, 47; Seton 62, 82; Hight 106.
9 Cited, Cook 137.
10 Cited, Cook 140.
11 Leyda 234; Seton 92; Sergei Eisenstein, *Film Form,* 36 40, Cook 145.
12 This description is based on that in Cook, 153-66.
13 Sergei Eisenstein, *Selected Works,* vol. II, 129-30.
14 Cited, Cook 65.
15 Sergei Eisenstein, *Film Sense,* 25-31, 46-65.
16 "Dickens, Griffith and the Film Today," in Sergei Eisenstein, *Film Form,* 195-255. The citations of Dickens that follow are from this essay as well as from Dickens 202-3.
17 Boorstin 149.
18 Cervantes 74; see Cervantes x.
19 Dickens 152.
20 Eisenstein, *Film Form,* 95-96; Seton 165-77.
21 Auerbach 546.
22 Cited, Eisenstein, *Film Form,* 217.
23 See Raymond Williams, *Television,* 51.
24 Eisenstein, *Film Form,* 104-7.
25 Cited, Seton 100.
26 Sergei Eisenstein, *Selected Works,* vol. I, 105; see also Leyda and Voynow 35.
27 Cited, Cook 177.
28 Mast 204-5; Eisenstein, *Film Form,* 62.
29 Seton 101-3; Cook 176.
30 Alexander Bakshy, "Moving Pictures: The Language of Images," *Nation,* December 26, 1928.
31 Sesonske 7-18; Leyda 117; Renoir 57.
32 Eisenstein, *Film Form,* 259.
33 Benjamin, *Illuminations,* 234.
34 Benjamin, *Illuminations,* 236.

Chapter 9

1 Mellencamp 88.
2 "Inside McCall's," *McCall's,* May 1954.
3 *Hamlet,* act 3, scene 1, 55-90.
4 Cited, Sally Bedell Smith 186; Lee 87.
5 Thomas Pynchon, "Nearer, My Couch, to Thee," *New York Times Book Review,* June 6, 1993.
6 Cook 243-50; Mast 228-29.
7 Cited, Cook 265.

8   Cited, Cook 244.
9   Renoir 103.
10   Bergan 130-31.
11   This "Statement," believed to have been written by Eisenstein, was also signed by V.I. Pudovkin and G.V. Alexandrov; Eisenstein, *Film Form,* 257-60.
12   I rely on Alexander Sesonske's counts of the close-ups and parallel edits; Sesonske 142-64; Bergan 130-35.
13   Cook 260-65. Larry Madison contributed to my understanding of these points.
14   Eisenstein, *Film Form,* 111.
15   Bazin 38.
16   Bazin 39.
17   Balio 13, 28-29; Mast 272-74; Koszarski 27.
18   Balio 190-92.
19   Duhamel 64; translation by Dirk Standen.
20   Mast 274-75.
21   Mast does the math and spells out the analogy; Mast 274-75.
22   Seneca (letter VII) 41.
23   Cited, Wilk 1-3. Wilk does not provide the name of the writer who made this comment.
24   Raymond Williams, *Television,* 53-54.
25   Pascal (205) 86. Pascal, however, remained concerned about these flights into diversion; see Mendelsohn 22-23.
26   Kubey and Csikszentmihalyi 138-39.
27   This description is based on that in Sesonske 157.
28   Sesonske 156-58.
29   Cook 388.
30   Renoir 57.
31   Bazin vi, 20-22.
32   Bazin 27, 28, 32, 33, 36.
33   He is citing, with approval, Villiers de l'Isle-Adam here; Bazin 21, 33-37.
34   Auerbach 545-46.
35   Sergei Eisenstein, *Film Form,* 104-6; Seton 149; cited, Leyda and Voynow 35.
36   Joyce, *Ulysses,* 164.
37   Eisenstein, *Film Form,* 104-6; Seton 149.
38   Eisenstein, *Film Form,* 103-6.
39   Eisenstein, *Film Form,* 104-6; Seton 149.
40   Brecht, *Brecht on Theatre,* 48.
41   Baudrillard 273. See also Mourier 323.
42   Cook 255, 462; Fisher and Fisher 328-29.
43   Cited, Robert D. Richardson Jr. 267.
44   Leopold vii.
45   Boorstin 250.
46   Gance 87. Translation by Dirk Standen.
47   White 3.
48   "Mass Observation Report on Television, July 1949"; cited, Briggs, *Sound and Vision,* 260.
49   Putnam, "The Strange Disappearance of Civic America."
50   Putnam, "Tuning In, Tuning Out: The Strange Disappearance of Social Capital in America."
51   Cited, MZTV exhibit, Royal Ontario Museum, Toronto, December 1995.
52   Tony Horwitz, "Local Pubs Are a Thing of the Past for Many in England," *Wall Street Journal,* March 2, 1993; Marlise Simons, "Paris Journal: Starved for Customers, the Bistros Die in Droves," *New York Times,* December 22, 1994.
53   David Foster Wallace 44.
54   Vivian Gornick, "Letters Are Acts of Faith; Telephone Calls Are a Reflex," *New York Times Book Review,* July 31, 1994.
55   Renoir 57.
56   Welles and Bogdanovich 318.

Chapter 10
1 Schatz 21-22; Cook 532-36, 921-23. Robert Haller also contributed to my understanding of this point.
2 Telephone interview with Philip Dusenberry, November 1, 1995.
3 Chuck Braverman's comments in this and the following paragraphs are from an interview in Santa Monica, March 14, 1996.
4 Telephone interview with Philip Dusenberry, November 1, 1995.
5 Interview with Hank Corwin, New York, April 5, 1996.
6 Cited, Kristine McKenna, "Bruce Conner in the Cultural Breach," *Los Angeles Times,* "Calendar," June 10, 1990.
7 Greil Marcus, "Days Between Stations: Some Islands of Music-Video Art in the Big, Wide Sea of MTV," *Interview,* November 1993.
8 Cited, Wees 82-85.
9 Telephone interview with Bruce Conner, November 3, 1995.
10 Cook 337; Pat Kirkham, "Saul Bass and Billy Wilder in Conversation," *Sight and Sound,* June 1995; Truffaut, 422, 427-29.
11 Lupton 39-47.
12 Wees 85.
13 See Williams, *Television* 98-112; Elizabeth Eisenstein, "The End of The Book?"; Stephens, *A History of News,* 137-43.
14 See Wees.
15 Telephone interview with Bruce Conner, November 3, 1995.
16 Telephone interview with Bruce Conner, November 3, 1995.
17 Calvin Tomkins, "Profiles: Video Visionary (Nam June Paik)," *New Yorker,* May 5, 1975.
18 Cited, Calvin Tomkins, "Profiles: Video Visionary (Nam June Paik)," *New Yorker,* May 5, 1975.
19 Telephone interview with Beth O'Connell, July 17, 1996.
20 McKibben 77-78.
21 Susan Sontag, "The Decay of Cinema," *New York Times Magazine,* February 25, 1996.
22 Kennan 169.
23 Stephen Jay Gould, "Say It Ain't So, 'Babe': Myth Confronts Reality," *New York Times,* April 26, 1992.
24 See also B. Drummond Ayres Jr., "Campaign Trail: The Eyes of the Clinton Strategists Are on Texas," *New York Times,* September 15, 1992.
25 *NewsHour with Jim Lehrer,* July 16, 1996.
26 Stephen Jay Gould, "Say It Ain't So, 'Babe': Myth Confronts Reality," *New York Times,* April 26, 1992.
27 Cited, Diane Holloway, "Will Prime-Time Democracy Make Us Better Citizens?" *Austin American-Statesman,* June 23, 1996.
28 Telephone interview with Bob Schieffer, July 18, 1996.
29 Cited, Richard L. Berke, "CBS's Sound Bite Ban Catches Pols Breathless," *International Herald Tribune,* July 4, 1992; telephone interview with Erik Sorenson, July 16, 1996.
30 Richard L. Berke, "CBS's Sound Bite Ban Catches Pols Breathless," *International Herald-Tribune,* July 4, 1992.
31 Telephone interview with Bob Schieffer, July 18, 1996.
32 Martin Plissner, "Inkbites," *Washington Post,* March 20, 1989.
33 See *"The MacNeil/Lehrer NewsHour* in the Context of Other Media," Freedom Forum Media Studies Center, September 1995.
34 See Stephens, *A History of News,* 102-7, 281-85.
35 See Stephens, *Broadcast News,* third edition, 202-5, 362-65.
36 Telephone interview with Martin Plissner, July 18, 1996.
37 Mitchell Stephens, "On Shrinking Soundbites," *Columbia Journalism Review,* September/October 1996.
38 B. Drummond Ayres Jr., "Campaign Trail: The Eyes of the Clinton Strategists Are on Texas," *New York Times,* September 15, 1992.
39 Telephone interview with Susan Zirinsky, July 15, 1996.
40 Telephone interview with Erik Sorenson, July 16, 1996.
41 Telephone interview with Martin Plissner, July 18, 1996.

42   Stephens, *Broadcast News,* first edition, 244-59.
43   Interview with Hank Corwin, New York, April 5, 1996.
44   Stephens, *Broadcast News,* second edition, 257-58.
45   Stephens, *Broadcast News,* first edition, 259.
46   Cited, Newcomb and Alley 62-63.
47   Interview with Hank Corwin, New York, April 5, 1996.
48   Kael 206, 221.
49   Kael 221.
50   Interview with Chuck Braverman, Santa Monica, March 14, 1996.
51   Michiko Kakutani, "Culture Zone: Stop Making Sense," *New York Times Magazine,* June 30, 1996.
52   Stephen Holden, "Mission Accepted: Tom Cruise as Superhero," *New York Times,* May 22, 1996.
53   Cited, Joyce Carol Oates, "Back to School," *New York Times Book Review,* September 1, 1996.
54   Boorstin 144.
55   Wees 78.
56   Godard 34; translation by Dirk Standen.
57   Interview with Hank Corwin, New York, April 5, 1996.
58   Mitchell Stephens, "The New TV," *Washington Post,* April 25, 1993.
59   Telephone interview with Philip Dusenberry, November 1, 1995.
60   Telephone interview with John Bergin, November 8, 1995.
61   Telephone interview with Bob Schieffer, July 18, 1996.

Chapter 11
1   The quotes here are from an interview with Jeff Scher, New York, March 29, 1997.
2   Sloan Commission 23-24.
3   Sloan Commission 24-25.
4   Sloan Commission 27.
5   Hiebert 374; Foster 176-79.
6   Thomas Pynchon, "Nearer, My Couch, to Thee," *New York Times Book Review,* June 6, 1993.
7   Rene Stutzman, "Happy 40th, Dear Remote Control," *Seattle Times,* June 8, 1996.
8   See the speech by Howard Stringer, of CBS, to the CBS Affiliates Meeting, May 26, 1993.
9   Talk by Michael Bloomberg, New York University Department of Journalism and Mass Communication, November 20, 1996.
10   Bogart 322.
11   Interview with Moses Znaimer, CITY-TV, Toronto, December 15, 1995.
12   Pool 242.
13   Nicholas Negroponte, "homeless@info.hwy.net," *New York Times,* February 11, 1995.
14   Cited, Laurie Flynn, "The Executive Computer: Intel Looks Beyond the Pentium," *New York Times,* February 26, 1995.
15   Cited, Daniel Burstein and David Kline, "In the Square-off Between TV and Computer, the Smart Money Might Be on the Boob Tube," *Los Angeles Times Magazine,* October 29, 1995.
16   Nicholas Negroponte, "homeless@info.hwy.net," *New York Times,* February 11, 1995.
17   See Havelock, *The Literate Revolution,* 328.
18   Kay 193.
19   Stewart Wolpin, "The Race to Video," *Invention and Technology,* Fall 1994; Charles P. Ginsburg, "The Ampex Videotape Recorder: An Evolution," a talk at the convention of the Society of Motion Picture and Television Engineers, October 5, 1957; Jim Bettinger, "Videorecording," *West,* November 6, 1994.
20   Telephone interview with Peter Hammar, founder and curator of the now defunct Ampex Museum of Magnetic Recording, April 4, 1997. Other prices have been given for this machine; see Foster 32; Barnouw 212; Fiona Matthias, "Origin of the Species," *TV Producer,* January 1992. Hammar's is based

on discussions with some of those involved in the project.
  21   Interview with Bonnie Siegler, New York, March 19, 1997.
  22   Interview with Jeff Scher, New York, March 29, 1997.
  23   DeLillo 32-34.
  24   Eco 175-76.
  25   Thomas Pynchon, "Nearer, My Couch, to Thee," *New York Times Book Review,* June 6, 1993.
  26   Brecht, *Brecht on Theatre,* 51-52.
  27   Barnouw 497-500; Foster 49, 181-82.
  28   See Worth; Raymond Williams, *Television,* xvii.
  29   Cited in the speech by Howard Stringer, of CBS, to the CBS Affiliates Meeting, June 3, 1994.
  30   Edmund L. Andrews, "Time Warner's Ordinary People Plug Interactive TV," *New York Times,* December 18, 1994.
  31   For a history and analysis of interactive television, see John Carey.
  32   Gilder 40-41, 50-51.
  33   Marchand 101.
  34   Brecht, *Brecht on Theatre,* 47-49.

Chapter 12

  1   Interview with Hank Corwin, New York, April 5, 1996.
  2   Cited, Frank DeCaro, "The Puzzling, Perplexing Peter Greenaway," *Newsday,* November 13, 1991.
  3   Brecht, *Brecht on Theatre,* 44.
  4   Brecht, *Brecht on Theatre* 51; Brecht, *Journals 1934-1955,* 254.
  5   New York University Department of Journalism, February 1995.
  6   Kernan 150-51.
  7   New York University Department of Journalism, February 1995.
  8   From the CBC television program *TVTV,* by Moses Znaimer, April 9, 1995.
  9   See Walter Goodman, "Horror vs. Hindsight: A War of TV Images," *New York Times,* December 4, 1995; and Saussez 27.
  10   Benjamin, *Reflections,* 206.
  11   Benjamin, *Reflections,* 206.
  12   Cited, Mellencamp 146.
  13   Cited, Mitchell Stephens, "The New TV," *Washington Post,* April 25, 1993.
  14   Mitchell Stephens, "The New TV," *Washington Post,* April 25, 1993.
  15   Vincent Canby, "Reams on Renaissance Fill 'Prospero's Books,'" *New York Times,* September 28, 1991.
  16   Interview with Oliver Stone, Santa Monica, March 15, 1996.
  17   Raymond Williams, *Television,* 89, 98-112.
  18   Cited, Mitchell Stephens, "The New TV," *Washington Post,* April 25, 1993.
  19   Barthes, *A Barthes Reader,* 204.
  20   See Lupton; George Steiner, "*Ex Libris,*" *New Yorker,* March 17, 1997.
  21   Telephone interview with Bob Schieffer, July 18, 1996.
  22   Telephone interview with Martin Plissner, July 18, 1996.
  23   Cited, Kracauer 41.
  24   Cited, Goodman 33.
  25   This discussion is based upon my articles "Let Pictures Speculate, Just Like Words," *New York Newsday,* February 24, 1994; and "Manipulating Photographs," *Media Studies Journal,* Spring 1997.
  26   Cited, Raymond Williams, *Contact,* 28.
  27   Worth.
  28   See Benjamin, *Illuminations,* 235.
  29   Barthes, *A Barthes Reader,* 203-4.
  30   Huxley, *Beyond the Mexique Bay,* 255.
  31   "May I die like a dog rather than hurry by a single second a sentence that isn't ripe"; cited, Troyat 121.
  32   Benjamin, *Illuminations,* 239.

33   Kubey and Csikszentmihalyi 135-37.
34   Cited, Jack Mathews, "High Stylist," *New York Newsday,* October 6, 1992.
35   See Worth; Barthes, *A Barthes Reader,* 202; Eco 175-76.
36   Most of the citations in this section are from Brecht, *Brecht on Theatre,* 43-45, 145, 227.
37   Sontag, *On Photography,* 108-9.
38   Benjamin, *Illuminations,* 228.

Chapter 13

1   *The Tempest,* act 3, scene 2, 93-95.
2   *The Tempest,* act 1, scene 2, 1-2; 109-10; 166.
3   Harold Innis makes a similar point; Innis 148.
4   In a blurb for Alfred Kazin's *A Lifetime Burning in Every Moment.*
5   Vidal 3.
6   Doren Carvajal, "Middling (and Unloved) in Publishing Land," and Joel Brinkley, "A Gulf Develops Among Broadcasters on Programming Pledge," *New York Times,* August 18, 1997.
7   Andy Seiler, "How Bad Is the Message: Audience's Options Run the Gamut," *USA Today,* June 6, 1995. Jonathan Franzen, "Perchance to Dream," *Harper's Magazine,* April 1996.
8   "Don't Believe the Cyberhype," *New York Times,* August 21, 1994.
9   Trithemius 65.
10   See Raymond Williams, *Television,* 13; on print, Febvre and Martin 28.
11   Boorstin 240.
12   DeLillo 37.
13   "The current emptiness is not television's fault," he said, surprisingly, "but television has made it visible"; McKibben 134.
14   For my take on these subjects, see my articles: "The Theologian of Talk: Jurgen Habermas," *Los Angeles Times Magazine,* October 23, 1994; "Jacques Derrida," *New York Times Magazine,* January 23, 1994; "The Professor of Disenchantment (Stephen Greenblatt and the New Historicism)," *West, San Jose Mercury,* March 1, 1992; "Deconstruction and the Get-Real Press," *Columbia Journalism Review,* September/October 1991; "Deconstructing Jacques Derrida," *Los Angeles Times Magazine,* July 21, 1991; "Deconstruction Crew," *Tikkun,* September-October 1990.
15   *The Tempest,* act 1, scene 2, 364-65.
16   Wittgenstein 47.
17   Interview with Hank Corwin, New York, April 5, 1996.
18   Birkerts 85.
19   Cited, Cervantes xvi.
20   Flaubert, *Madame Bovary,* 370.
21   Stephens, *A History of News,* 246-48.
22   *The Tempest,* act 1, scene 1, 61.
23   *The Tempest,* act 5, scene 1, 56-57.
24   *The Tempest,* act 1, scene 2, 434.
25   James Atlas, "Literature Bores Me," *New York Times Magazine,* March 16, 1997.
26   Williams, *Television,* 110.
27   Boorstin 148.
28   Dostoevsky 452-53, 464.
29   Jonathan Franzen, "Perchance to Dream," *Harper's Magazine,* April 1996.
30   Homer 231.
31   See Watt 18, 205-6.
32   Kundera 125.
33   Brecht, *Brecht on Theatre,* 48; cited, Benjamin, *Illuminations,* 246n (I rely on the translation in Benjamin).
34   *The Tempest,* act 2, scene 1, 109.
35   Joseph Brodsky, "The Nobel Lecture: Uncommon Visage," *New Republic,* January 4 and 11, 1988. For a different interpretation of the same symptoms, see Sass.
36   In a letter to Jonathan Franzen; cited, Jonathan Franzen, "Perchance to

Dream," *Harper's Magazine,* April 1996.
37 For alternative theories of identity, see Gergen; also Mitchell Stephens, "To Thine Own Selves Be True (Postmodern Psychology)," *Los Angeles Times Magazine,* August 23, 1992.
38 Cited, Robert D. Richardson Jr. 382.
39 Cited, Sontag, *Against Interpretation,* 3.
40 Sergei Eisenstein, *Film Form,* 103-6.
41 Benjamin, *Illuminations,* 235-36.
42 See Derrida 70-77.
43 Emerson 165.
44 David Foster Wallace 35.
45 David Foster Wallace 64.
46 Cited, Mitchell Stephens, "Jacques Derrida," *New York Times Magazine,* January 23, 1994.
47 See Stuart Elliott, "Advertising: A Big Brouhaha Erupts When *Advertising Age* Takes a Few Shots at a Miller Lite Campaign," *New York Times,* February 24, 1997.
48 Barthes, *Roland Barthes,* 66.
49 Nietzsche, *Genealogy of Morals,* III, 12.
50 Interview with Hank Corwin, New York, April 5, 1996.
51 Adorno 478-82.
52 See Shenk.
53 See Derrida 70-77.
54 Duhamel 52; I have used the translation in Benjamin, *Illuminations,* 238.
55 *The Tempest,* act 5, scene 1, 184.

bibliography

Adorno, T.W. "Television and the Patterns of Mass Culture," in *Mass Culture*. Edited by Bernard Rosenberg and David Manning White. London, 1994.

Aiton, E.J. *Leibniz: A Biography*. Boston, 1985.

Alexander, Jonathan J.G., ed. *The Painted Page: Italian Renaissance Book Illumination, 1450-1550*. New York, 1995.

Aquinas, Thomas. *Summa Theologica*. Translated by Fathers of the English Dominican Province. Three volumes. New York, 1948.

Aristotle. *The Basic Works of Aristotle*. Edited by Richard McKeon. New York, 1968.

Armour, Robert A. *Gods and Myths of Ancient Egypt*. Cairo, 1986.

Auden, W.H. *The Dyer's Hand and Other Essays*. New York, 1968.

Auerbach, Erich. *Mimesis: The Representation of Reality in Western Literature*. Translated by Willard R. Trask. Princeton, 1968.

Bacon, Francis. *The Advancement of Learning*. Edited by William Aldis Wright. Oxford, 1963.

———. *The Philosophical Works of Francis Bacon*. Edited by John M. Robertson. Freeport, N.Y., 1970.

Baker, Ernest A. *The History of the English Novel*. New York, 1967.

Baldwin, Neil. *Edison: Inventing the Century*. New York, 1995.

Balio, Tino. *Grand Design: Hollywood as a Modern Business Enterprise, 1930-1939*. Vol. V, *The History of the American Cinema*. Berkeley, 1995.

Barnouw, Erik. *Tube of Plenty: The Evolution of American Television*. New York, 1990.

Barr, Catherine, ed. *The Bowker Annual: Library and Book Trade Almanac*. 40th edition. New Providence, N.J., 1995.

Barry, Iris. *D.W. Griffith: American Film Master*. New York, 1940.

Barthes, Roland. *A Barthes Reader*. Edited by Susan Sontag. New York, 1987.

———. *Roland Barthes*. Translated by Richard Howard. New York, 1988.

Baudrillard, Jean. "The Precession of Simulacra," in *Art After Modernism: Rethinking Representation*. Edited by B. Wallis. New York, 1984.

Bazin, André, *What Is Cinéma?* Translated by Hugh Gray. Berkeley, 1971.

Beaulieux, Charles. "Manuscrits et imprimés en France, XVV-XVIV siecle," in *Mélanges Offerts à Émile Chatelain*. Paris, 1910.

Benjamin, Walter. *Reflections*. Edited by Peter Demetz. Translated by Edmund Jephcott. New York, 1986.

———. *Illuminations*. Edited by Hannah Arendt. Translated by Harry Zohn. New York, 1988.

Bergan, Ronald. *Jean Renoir: Projections of Paradise*. Woodstock, N.Y., 1995.

Berger, John. *Ways of Seeing*. London, 1977.

Berman, Marshall. *All That Is Solid Melts Into Air*. New York. 1988.

Birkerts, Sven. *The Gutenberg Elegies*. New York, 1995.

Boddy, William. *Fifties Television: The Industry and Its Critics*. Urbana, Ill., 1993.

Bogart, Leo. *The Age of Television*. Second edition. New York, 1958.

Boorstin, Daniel J. *The Image*. New York, 1962.

Bowser, Eileen. The Transformation of Cinema, 1907-1915. Vol. II, *The History of the American Cinema*. Berkeley, 1994.

Brakhage, Stan. *Film at Wit's End: Eight Avant-Garde Filmmakers*. Kingston, N.Y., 1989.

Brecht, Bertolt. *Journals 1934-1955*. Translated by Hugh Rorrison. New York, 1993.

———. *Brecht on Theatre: The Development of an Aesthetic*. Translated by John Willet. New York, 1994.

Brewer, John. *Party Ideology and Popular Politics at the Accession of George III*. Cambridge, 1976.

Briggs, Asa. *The History of Broadcasting in the United Kingdom*. Vol. IV, *Sound and Vision*. Oxford, 1979.

———. *The History of Broadcasting in the United Kingdom*. Vol. V, *Competition*. Oxford, 1995.

Brogyanyi, Bela, ed. *Prehistory, History and Historiography of Language, Speech and Linguistic Theory*. Amsterdam, 1992.

Burnett, Ron. *Cultures of Vision: Images, Media and the Imaginary*. Bloomington, Ind., 1995.

Calame-Griaule, Geneviève. *Words and the Dogon World*. Translated by Deirdre LaPin. Philadelphia, 1986.

Calvino, Italo. *If on a Winter's Night a Traveler...* Translated by William Weaver. San Diego, 1981.

Carlyle, Thomas. *Sartor Resartus*. London, 1831.

Carothers, J.C. "Culture, Psychiatry, and the Written Word," *Psychiatry*, November 1959.

Carey, James W. "The Language of Technology: Talk, Text, and Template as Metaphors for Communication," in *Communication and the Language of Technology*. Edited by Martin Midhurst et al. Pullman, Wash., 1990.

Carey, John. "The Interactive Television Puzzle," Technology Paper, Freedom Forum Media Studies Center, 1994.

Cervantes, Miguel de. *Don Quixote*. Translated by Charles Jarvis. Edited with an introduction by E.C. Riley. Oxford, 1992.

Chappell, Warren. *A Short History of the Printed Word*. Boston, 1980.

Chartier, Roger. *The Order of Books: Readers, Authors, and Libraries in Europe Between the Fourteenth and Eighteenth Centuries*. Translated by Lydia G. Cochrane. Stanford, Calif., 1994.

Clifford, James L., and Louis A. Landa, eds. *Pope and His Contemporaries*. Oxford, 1949.

Coleman, Dorothy Gabe. *Rabelais: A Critical Study in Prose Fiction*. Cambridge, 1971.

Cook, David A. *A History of Narrative Film*. Third edition. New York, 1996.

Copleston, F.C. *Aquinas*. New York, 1986.

Crowley, David, and Paul Heyer, eds. *Communication in History*. New York, 1991.

Covert, Catherine L., and John D. Stevens. *Mass Media Between the Wars*. Syracuse, N.Y., 1984.

Czitrom, Daniel J. *Media and the American Mind: From Morse to McLuhan*. Chapel Hill, N.C., 1982.

Dantzig, Tobias. *Number: The Language of Science*. Fourth edition. New York, 1954.

Darnton, Robert. *The Kiss of Lamourette: Reflections in Cultural History*. New York, 1990.

Davenport, Alma. *The History of Photography*. Boston, 1991.

De Forest, Lee. *Television: Today and Tomorrow*. New York, 1942.

DeLillo, Don. *Mao II*. New York, 1992.

Denby, David, ed. *Awake in the Dark: Anthology of American Film Criticism*. New York, 1977.

Derrida, Jacques. *Dissemination*. Translated by Barbara Johnson. Chicago, 1981.

Desmond, Kevin. *Inventions, Innovations, Discoveries*. London, 1987.

Dewey, John. *The Middle Works, 1899-1924*. Vol. 9: 1916. Edited by Jo Ann Boydston. Carbondale, Ill., 1980.

Dickens, Charles. *Oliver Twist*. London, 1985.

Dickinson, Emily. *The Complete Works of Emily Dickinson*. New York, 1924.

Dostoevsky, Fyodor. *Crime and Punishment.* Translated by Constance Garnett. New York, 1987.

Driver, G.R. *Semitic Writing: From Pictograph to Alphabet.* London, 1944. Revised edition. 1976.

Duhamel, Georges. *Scènes de la vie future.* Paris, 1930.

Dunlap, Orrin E., Jr. *The Future of Television.* New York, 1947.

Eastman, Richard M. *A Guide to the Novel.* San Francisco, 1965.

Eco, Umberto. *The Search for the Perfect Language.* Translated by James Fentress. Oxford, 1995.

Eddy, William C. *Television: The Eyes of Tomorrow.* New York, 1945.

Edgerton, Gary R., ed. *Film and the Arts in Symbiosis.* New York, 1988.

Edgerton, Samuel Y., Jr. *The Renaissance Rediscovery of Linear Perspective.* New York, 1976.

Eisenstein, Elizabeth L. *The Printing Press as an Agent of Change.* 2 vols. Cambridge, 1982.

———. "Printing as a Divine Art," Oberlin Library Lecture, November 4, 1995.

———. "The End of the Book?" *The American Scholar,* Autumn 1995.

———. "Encounter with the Printed Text in the Age of Incunabula." Lecture at the City University of New York Graduate Center, April 19, 1996.

Eisenstein, Sergei. *The Film Sense.* Translated and edited by Jay Leyda. San Diego, 1975.

———. *Film Form.* Translated and edited by Jay Leyda. San Diego, 1977.

———. *Selected Works.* Vol. I, *Writings 1922-34.* Translated and edited by Richard Taylor. London, 1988.

———. *Selected Works.* Vol. II, *Towards a Theory of Montage.* Translated by Michael Glenny. Edited by Michael Glenny and Richard Taylor. London, 1991.

Emerson, Ralph Waldo. *Selections from Ralph Waldo Emerson.* Edited by Stephen E. Whicher. Boston, 1960.

Ewen, Stuart. *All Consuming Images.* New York, 1988.

Febvre, Lucien, and Henri-Jean Martin. *The Coming of the Book: The Impact of Printing, 1450-1800.* Translated by David Gerard. London, 1976.

Feuerbach, Ludwig. *The Essence of Christianity.* Translated by George Eliot. New York, 1957.

Finley, M.I. "Myth, Memory and History." *History and Theory,* IV, 3, 1965.

Fisher, David E., and Marshall Jon Fisher. *Tube: The Invention of Television.* Washington, D.C., 1996.

Fiske, John, and John Hartley. *Reading Television.* London, 1988.

Flaubert, Gustave. *Correspondance, troisième série, Oeuvres completes de Gustave Flaubert.* Paris, 1927.

———. *Madame Bovary.* Translated by Francis Steegmuller. New York, 1957.

Flink, James J. *The Automobile Age.* Cambridge, Mass., 1988.

Forster, E.M. *Aspects of the Novel.* New York, 1954.

Foster, Eugene S. *Understanding Broadcasting.* Second edition. Reading, Mass., 1982.

Freedberg, David. *The Power of Images: Studies in the History and Theory of Response.* Chicago, 1989.

Gabler, Neal. *An Empire of Their Own: How the Jews Invented Hollywood.* New York, 1989.

Gance, Abel. "Le Temps de l'image est venu!" in *L'Art Cinématographique.* New York, 1970.

Gelb, I.J. *A Study of Writing.* Chicago, 1963.

Gergen, Kenneth J. *The Saturated Self: Dilemmas of Identity in Contemporary Life.* New York, 1991.

Gernsheim, Helmut. *The Origins of Photography.* New York, 1981.

Gilder, George. *Life After Television.* New York, 1992.

Gillie, Christopher. *A Companion to British Literature.* Detroit, 1977.

Gitlin, Todd. *Inside Prime Time.* New York, 1983.

———, ed. *Watching Television.* New York, 1986.

Godard, Jean-Luc. *Introduction a une véritable histoire du cinéma.* Vol. I. Paris, 1980.

Goldschmidt, E.P. *Medieval Texts and Their First Appearance in Print.* London, 1943.

Gombrich, E.H. *Gombrich on the Renaissance. Vol. II, Symbolic Images.* London, 1972.

Gomery, Douglas. "As the Dial Turns," *Wilson Quarterly,* Autumn 1993.

Goodman, Nelson. *Languages of Art: An Approach to a Theory of Symbols.* Indianapolis, 1968.

Goodwin, Andrew. *Dancing in the Distraction Factory: Music Television and Popular Culture.* Minneapolis, 1992.

Goody, Jack. *The Domestication of the Savage Mind.* Cambridge, 1977.

Goody, Jack, and Ian Watt, "The Consequences of Literacy," *Comparative Studies in Society and History,* V, 3, April 1963, 304-45.

Grazia, Edward de, and Roger K. Newman. *Banned Films: Movies, Censors and the First Amendment.* New York, 1982.

Greene, William Chase. "The Spoken and the Written Word," *Harvard Studies in Classical Philology,* 60, 1951, 23-59.

Grossman, Lawrence K., *The Electronic Republic.* New York, 1995.

Gunning, Tom. *D. W. Griffith and the Origins of American Narrative Film.* Urbana, Ill., 1994.

Gutmann, Joseph. *No Graven Images.* New York, 1971.

Harris, Neil, ed. *The Land of Contrasts: 1880-1901.* New York, 1970.

Havelock, Eric A. *Preface to Plato.* Cambridge, Mass., 1963.

———. *The Literate Revolution in Greece and Its Cultural Consequences.* Princeton, 1982.

Hiebert, Ray Eldon, Donald F. Ungurait, and Thomas W. Bohn. *Mass Media III.* New York, 1982.

Hight, Eleanor M. *Moholy-Nagy: Photography and Fim in Weimar Germany.* Wellesley, Mass., 1985.

Hofer, Stephen F. "Philo Farnsworth: Television's Pioneer," *Journal of Broadcasting,* 23, 2, Spring 1979, 153-66.

Hogben, Lancelot. *From Cave Painting to Comic Strip.* New York, 1949.

Homer. *The Iliad.* Translated by Robert Fagles. New York, 1991.

Howatson, M.C., ed. *The Oxford Companion to Classical Literature.* Second edition. Oxford, 1991.

Hubbell, Richard W. *4000 Years of Television.* New York, 1942.

Hughes, Robert. *The Shock of the New.* New York, 1991.

Hutchinson, Thomas H. *Here Is Television: Your Window to the World.* New York, 1950.

Huxley, Aldous. *Beyond the Mexique Bay.* Westport, Conn., 1975.

———. *Brave New World.* New York, 1989.

Innis, Harold A. *Empire and Communications.* Toronto, 1980.

Irwin, Will. *Propaganda and the News.* New York, 1936.

Jackaway, Gwenyth L. *Media at War: Radio's Challenge to the Newspapers, 1924-1939.* Westport, Conn., 1995.

Jacobs, Lewis. *The Emergence of Film Art.* Second edition. New York, 1979.

Janouch, Gustav. *Conversations with Kafka.* Translated by Goronwy Ross. New York, 1971.

Jenkins, C. Francis. *Vision by Radio: Radio Photographs, Radio Photograms.* Washington, D.C., 1925.

Jesionowski, Joyce E. *Thinking in Pictures: Dramatic Structure in D.W. Griffith's Biograph Films.* Berkeley, 1987.

Jones, Richard Foster. *Ancients and Moderns: A Study of the Rise of the Scientific Movement in Seventeenth-Century England.* Second edition. St. Louis, 1961.

Joyce, James. *Ulysses.* New York, 1961.

———. *A Portrait of the Artist as a Young Man.* New York, 1968.

Juster, F. Thomas, and Frank P. Stafford, eds. *Time, Goods, and Well-Being.* Ann Arbor, 1985.

Kael, Pauline. *For Keeps.* New York, 1994.

Káldy-Nagy, Gyorgy, ed. *The Muslim East: Studies in Honour of Julius Germanus.* Budapest, 1974.

Kay, Alan, "User Interface: A Personal View," in *The Art of Human-Computer*

Interface Design. Edited by Brenda Laurel. Reading, Mass., 1991.

Kennan, George F. *Around the Cragged Hill: A Personal and Political Philosophy*. New York, 1993.

Kernan, Alvin. *The Death of Literature*. New Haven, 1990.

Koch, Walter A., ed. *Genesis of Language*. Bochum, 1990.

Koszarski, Richard. *An Evening's Entertainment: The Age of the Silent Feature Picture, 1915-1928*. Vol. III, *The History of the American Cinema*. Berkeley, 1994.

Kracauer, Siegfried. *Theory of Film: The Redemption of Physical Reality*. London, 1960.

Kubey, Robert, and Mihaly Csikszentmihalyi. *Television and the Quality of Life: How Viewing Shapes Everyday Experience*. Hillsdale, N.J., 1990.

Kundera, Milan. *The Book of Laughter and Forgetting*. Translated by Aaron Asher. New York, 1996.

Kunzle, David. *The Early Comic Strip*. Berkeley, 1974.

Landau, David, and Peter Parshall. *The Renaissance Print: 1470-1550*. New Haven, 1994.

Lanham, Richard A. *The Electronic Word*. Chicago, 1993.

Lavin, Maud. *Cut with the Kitchen Knife: The Weimar Photomontages of Hannah Höch*. New Haven, 1993.

Lee, Robert E. *Television: The Revolution*. New York, 1944.

Leopold, Aldo. *A Sand County Almanac*. London, 1976.

Levine, Joseph M. *The Battle of the Books: History and Literature in the Augustan Age*. Ithaca, N.Y., 1991.

Lévi-Strauss, Claude. *The Savage Mind*. Chicago, 1966.

Levy, Steven. *Insanely Great: The Life and Times of Macintosh*. New York, 1994.

Lévy-Bruhl, Lucien. *How Natives Think*. Translated by Lilian A. Clare. Salem, N.H., 1984.

Leyda, Jay. *Kino: A History of the Russian and Soviet Film*. New York, 1960.

Leyda, Jay, and Zina Voynow. *Eisenstein at Work*. New York, 1982.

Lieberman, Philip. *The Biology and Evolution of Language*. Cambridge, Mass., 1984.

Longwell, Dennis. *Steichen: The Master Prints, 1895-1914: The Symbolist Period*. New York, 1978.

Lubar, Steven. *InfoCulture: The Smithsonian Book of Information Age Inventions*. New York, 1993.

Lupton, Ellen. *Mixing Messages: Graphic Design in Contemporary Culture*. New York, 1996.

Luria, A.R. *Cognitive Development: Its Cultural and Social Foundations*. Translated by Martin Lopez-Morillas and Lynn Solotaroff. Foreword by Michael Cole. Cambridge, Mass., 1976.

Mack, Maynard. *Alexander Pope: A Life*. New York, 1988.

Malraux, André. *The Voices of Silence*. Translated by Stuart Gilbert. New York, 1953.

Manguel, Alberto. *A History of Reading*. New York, 1996.

Marchand, Philip. *Marshall McLuhan: The Medium and the Messenger*. New York, 1989.

Marling, Karal Ann. *As Seen on TV: The Visual Culture of Everyday Life in the 1950s*. Cambridge, Mass., 1994.

Martin, Henri-Jean. *The History and Power of Writing*. Translated by Lydia G. Cochrane. Chicago, 1994.

Marvin, Carolyn. *When Old Technologies Were New*. New York, 1988.

Mast, Gerald. *A Short History of the Movies*. Indianapolis, 1971.

Mast, Gerald, Marshall Cohen, and Leo Brady, eds. *Film Theory and Criticism*. Fourth edition. New York, 1992.

MacDonnell, Kevin. *Eadweard Muybridge: The Man Who Invented the Moving Picture*. Boston, 1972.

McIntyre, J. Lewis. *Giordano Bruno*. London, 1903.

McKibben, Bill. *The Age of Missing Information*. New York, 1993.

McLuhan, Marshall. *Understanding Media: The Extensions of Man*. New York, 1964.

————. *The Gutenberg Galaxy*. Toronto, 1992.
Mellencamp, Patricia, ed. *The Logics of Television*. Bloomington, Ind., 1990.
Mendelsohn, Harold. *Mass Entertainment*. New Haven, 1966.
Moholy-Nagy, László. *Painting, Photography, Film*. Translated by Janet Seligman. Cambridge, Mass., 1987.
Mott, Frank Luther. *A History of the American Magazine*. New York, 1930.
————. *American Journalism*. New York, 1941.
Mourier, Maurice, ed. *Comment vivre avec l'image*. Paris, 1989.
Mumford, Lewis. *Technics and Civilization*. New York, 1934.
Münsterberg, Hugo. *The Film: A Psychological Study*. New York, 1970.
Musser, Charles. *The Emergence of Cinema: The American Screen to 1907*. Vol. I, *The History of the American Cinema*. Berkeley, 1994.
Nash, Michael. "The End of Video Art (and Television)," *Film Forum*, 1994.
National Assessment of Educational Progress. "Reading Report Card for the Nation and the States," 1992, 1994. National Center for Educational Statistics, U.S. Department of Education.
Negroponte, Nicholas. *Being Digital*. New York, 1995.
Neuman, Johanna. *Lights, Camera, War: Is Media Technology Driving International Politics?* New York, 1996.
Newcomb, Horace, and Robert S. Alley. *The Producer's Medium: Conversations with Creators of American TV*. New York, 1983.
Newhall, Beaumont, ed. *On Photography: A Source Book of Photo History in Facsimile*. Watkins Glen, N.Y., 1956.
———— *Photography: Essays and Images*. New York, 1980.
Nietzsche, Friedrich. *Beyond Good and Evil: Prelude to a Philosophy of the Future*. Translated by Walter Kaufman. New York, 1966.
————. *Genealogy of Morals*. New York, 1968.
Nöth, Winfried. *Handbook of Semiotics*. Bloomington, Indiana, 1990.
Ong, Walter J. *Orality and Literacy*. London, 1982.
Papadopoulo, Alexandre. *Islam and Muslim Art*. Translated by Robert Erich Wolf. New York, 1979.
Parkinson, Richard, and Stephen Quirke. *Papyrus*. Austin, Tex., 1995.
Parry, Milman. *The Making of Homeric Verse. The Collected Papers of Milman Parry*. Edited by Adam Parry. Oxford, 1971.
Pascal, Blaise. *The Pensées*. Translated by J.M. Cohen. Baltimore, 1961.
Petroski, Henry. *The Pencil: A History of Design and Circumstance*. New York, 1990.
Plato. *Phaedrus*. Translated by W.C. Helmbold and W.G. Rabinowitz. Indianapolis, 1956.
————. *Great Dialogues of Plato*. Translated by W.H.D. Rouse. New York, 1961.
Plotinus. *The Enneads*. Translated by Stephen MacKenna. London, 1966.
Pool, Ithiel de Sola. *Technologies Without Boundaries*. Cambridge, Mass., 1990.
Pope, Alexander. *Selected Poetry and Prose*. Second edition. Edited by William K. Wimsatt. New York, 1972.
Porterfield, John, and Kay Reynolds, eds. *We Present Television*, New York, 1940.
Postman, Neil. *Amusing Ourselves to Death*. New York, 1986.
————. *Technopoly: The Surrender of Culture to Technology*. New York, 1993.
Putnam, Robert D. "Bowling Alone: America's Declining Social Capital," *Journal of Democracy*, 6, 1, January 1995.
————. "Tuning In, Tuning Out: The Strange Disappearance of Social Capital in America," in *PS: Political Science and Politics*, 28, 4, December 1995.
————. "The Strange Disappearance of Civic America," *American Prospect*, Winter 1996.
Rabb, Jane M., ed. *Literature and Photography Interactions, 1840-1990: A Critical Anthology*. Alburquerque, N.M., 1995.
Rabelais, Francis. *Five Books of the Lives, Heroic Deeds and Sayings of Gargantua and His Son Pantgruel*. Translated by Sir Thomas Urquhart. London, 1892.
Renoir, Jean. *My Life and My Films*. Translated by Norman Denny. New York, 1974.
Reiser, Stanley Joel. *Medicine and the Reign of Technology*. Cambridge, 1978.
Richardson, Robert. *Literature and Film*. Bloomington, Ind., 1969.

Richardson, Robert D., Jr. *Emerson: The Mind on Fire.* Berkeley, 1995.
Ritchie, Michael. *Please Stand By: A Prehistory of Television.* Woodstock, N.Y., 1994.
Richmond, Robin. *Michelangelo and the Creation of the Sistine Chapel.* Tokyo, 1992.
Ripa, Cesare. *Baroque and Rococo Pictorial Imagery: The 1758-60 Hertel Edition of Ripa's Iconologia.* Edited by Edward A. Maser. New York, 1971.
Robinson, David. *The History of World Cinema.* New York, 1973.
Rosenthal, Raymond, ed. *McLuhan Pro and Con.* Baltimore, 1972.
Rushkoff, Douglas. *Media Virus: Hidden Agendas in Popular Culture.* New York, 1994.
Saenger, Paul. "Silent Reading: Its Impact on Late Medieval Script and Society," in *Viator: Medieval and Renaissance Studies,* 13, 1982, 367-414.
Salomon, Gavriel. *Interaction of Media, Cognition and Learning.* San Francisco, 1979.
Sass, Louis A. "The Epic of Disbelief: The Postmodernist Turn in Contemporary Psychoanalysis," in *Psychology in a Postmodern Landscape.* Edited by S. Kvale. London, 1992.
Saussez, Thierry. *Nous sommes ici par la volonté des médias.* Paris, 1990.
Schatz, Thomas. *Old Hollywood/New Hollywood.* Ann Arbor, 1983.
Seldes, Gilbert. *The Great Audience.* New York, 1950.
Seneca. *Letters from a Stoic.* Translated by Robin Campbell. Harmondsworth, U.K., 1969.
Sesonske, Alexander. *Jean Renoir: The French Films, 1924-1939.* Cambridge, Mass., 1980.
Seton, Marie. *Sergei M. Eisenstein.* New York, 1960.
Shafer, Byron E., ed. *Religion in Ancient Egypt.* Ithaca, N.Y., 1991.
Shenk, David. *Data Smog.* San Francisco, 1997.
Shakespeare, William. *The Complete Works.* New York, 1980.
Sheridan, Thomas. *British Education: Or, The Source of the Disorders of Great Britain....* Dublin, 1756.
Shipman, David. *The Story of Cinema.* Vol. I. London, 1982.
Sklar, Robert. *Movie-Made America: A Cultural History of American Movies.* New York, 1994.
Sloan Commission on Cable Communication. *On the Cable: The Television of Abundance.* New York, 1971.
Smith, Arthur. *Planetary Exploration: Thirty Years of Unmanned Space Probes.* Wellington, Northamptonshire, 1988.
Smith, Douglas K., and Robert C. Alexander. *Fumbling the Future: How Xerox Invented, Then Ignored, the First Personal Computer.* New York, 1988.
Smith, Sally Bedell. *In All His Glory: The Life of William S. Paley.* New York, 1990.
Sontag, Susan. *On Photography.* New York, 1990.
————. *Against Interpretation and Other Essays.* New York, 1990.
Spengler, Oswald. *The Decline of the West.* Translated by Charles Francis Atkinson. London, 1971.
Starkie, Enid. *Flaubert: The Making of the Master.* New York, 1967.
Steegmuller, Francis. *Flaubert and Madame Bovary: A Double Portrait.* New York, 1966.
Stephens, Mitchell. *Broadcast News.* First edition. New York, 1980. Second edition. New York, 1986. Third edition. Fort Worth, Tex., 1993.
————. *A History of News.* Fort Worth, Tex., 1997.
Sturcken, Frank. *Live Television: The Golden Age of 1946-1958 in New York.* Jefferson, N.C., 1990.
Talbot, William Henry Fox. *The Pencil of Nature.* New York, 1969.
Thoreau, Henry David. *Walden.* New York, 1951.
Tolstoy, *War and Peace.* Translated by Ann Dunnigan. New York, 1968.
Trilling, Lionel. *The Liberal Imagination: Essays on Literature and Society.* New York, 1976.
Trithemius, Johannes. *In Praise of Scribes.* Edited by Klaus Arnold. Lawrence, Kan., 1974.
Troyat, Henri. *Flaubert.* Translated by Joan Pinkham. New York, 1992.

Truffaut, François. *Hitchcock*. Revised edition. London, 1986.

Udelson, Joseph H. *The Great Television Race: A History of the American Television Industry, 1925-1941*. Alabama, 1982.

Updike, Daniel Berkeley. *Printing Types: Their History, Forms, and Use*. New York, 1980.

Valéry, Paul. *Aesthetics*. Translated by Ralph Manheim. New York, 1964.

Vespasiano, *Renaissance Princes, Popes, and Prelates: The Vespasiano Memoirs*. Translated by William George and Emily Waters. New York, 1963.

Vidal, Gore. *Screening History*. Cambridge, Mass., 1992.

Wallace, David Foster. *A Supposedly Fun Thing I'll Never Do Again*. Boston, 1997.

Wallace, William E., ed. *The Sistine Chapel*. New York, 1995.

Watt, Ian. *The Rise of the Novel*. Berkeley, 1967.

Wees, William C. *Recyled Images*. New York, 1993.

Welles, Orson, and Peter Bogdanovich. *This Is Orson Welles*. New York, 1993.

Welsh, Irvine. *Trainspotting*. New York, 1996.

Weston, Edward. *The Daybooks of Edward Weston*. Edited by Nancy Newhall. New York, 1961.

Whelan, Richard. *Alfred Stieglitz: A Biography*. Boston, 1995.

White, E.B. *One Man's Meat*. New York, 1944.

Wilk, Max. *The Golden Age of Television: Notes from the Survivors*. New York, 1976.

Williams, Aubrey L. *Pope's Dunciad: A Study of Its Meaning*. Baton Rouge, La., 1955.

Williams, Ioan, ed. *Novel and Romance, 1700-1800: A Documentary Record*. London, 1970.

Williams, Raymond. *Television: Technology and Cultural Form*. Hanover, N. H., 1992.

———, ed. *Contact: Human Communication and Its History*. London, 1981.

Wilson, Douglas L. "What Jefferson and Lincoln Read," *Atlantic Monthly*, January 1991.

Winston, Brian. *Misunderstanding Media*. London, 1986.

Wittgenstein, Ludwig. *Philosophical Investigations*. Translated by G.E.M. Anscombe. New York, 1968.

Woolf, Virginia. *To the Lighthouse*. New York, 1955.

Worth, Sol. "Pictures Can't Say Ain't," *Versus*, 12, September–December, 1975.

index

A NOTE ON THE TYPE AND DESIGN

the rise of the image the fall of the word was set in Stone Serif and Stone Sans, part of a family designed by Sumner Stone in 1987. The font is a modern interpretation of the transitional style of face.

Designers for the chapter spreads as follows:
One: Stewart Cauley
Two: Jeff Hoffman
Three: David Thorne
Four: Charles B. Hames
Five: Stewart Cauley
Six: Ron Reeves
Seven: Jeff Hoffman
Eight: Adam B. Bohannon
Nine: Helen Mules
Ten: Charles B. Hames
Eleven: David Thorne
Twelve: Adam B. Bohannon
Thirteen: Thomas Zummer

Text design and composition by Adam B. Bohannon